FOR RICHER, FOR POORER

A LOVE AFFAIR WITH POKER

VICTORIA COREN

CANONGATE

Edinburgh · London · New York · Melbourne

Published by Canongate Books in 2009

2

Copyright © Victoria Coren, 2009

The moral right of the author has been asserted

First published in Great Britain in 2009 by Canongate Books Ltd,
14 High Street, Edinburgh EH1 1TE

www.meetatthegate.com

British Library Cataloguing-in-Publication Data
A catalogue record for this book is available on
request from the British Library

ISBN 978 1 84767 291 9
Export ISBN 978 1 84767 292 6

Typeset in Bembo by Palimpsest Book Production Ltd,
Grangemouth, Stirlingshire

Printed and bound in Great Britain by
CPI Mackays, Chatham ME5 8TD

There from the beginning;
with love, for Giles.

FROM BELSIZE PARK TO BOW

Today, I might win a quarter of a million dollars.

There are only eleven opponents to beat. Unfortunately, they are the eleven toughest poker players in the world. According to the title of this televised battle, we are *The Premier League*.

Phil 'The Brat' Hellmuth is playing: he's won eleven world titles. Dave 'Devilfish' Ulliott is there: the most feared and celebrated player in Britain. Marcel Lüske, 'The Flying Dutchman', is in the line-up: he's such a big star now, he is releasing albums of himself singing poker songs. Between them, my opponents have won fifty million dollars playing cards.

So I'm a little nervous. The minicab, sent by the production company, has been waiting outside for ten minutes while I hunt around my flat for keys, phones, lipstick, newspaper for the lunch-break, £5,000 packet in case of a cash game in the hotel afterwards, pen, tissues, apple. I run out of the house pretty flustered and we have been cruising down Haverstock Hill for some time before I notice that the eyes in the driving mirror have a familiar mournful crinkle.

I say, 'Ray? Is that you?'

I met Riverboat Ray at a cash game somewhere round the back of Islington in about 1999. He stuck in my mind after he told a miserable story about losing a poker hand five years before. He recounted every card and every bet on every street of the hand, as bitterly as if it had been five minutes ago. Later that evening, he mentioned that he had a new granddaughter. 'What's her name?' I asked. Ray frowned, thought for a while, then shook his head. 'Nope. It's gone.'

I haven't seen him for ages. Now, here he is at the wheel of my courtesy car. Ray tells me he's been banned from the casino in Luton for three years, after a fight with Frank Farnham. It was all to do with an Omaha Hi-Lo hand where Ray is heads-up with Frank Farnham's dad, and Frank Farnham's dad says that Ray has won the pot with three of a kind, but then Frank leans over his dad's shoulder and points out that he has a straight. Frank Farnham has no business doing this, especially in a significant £200 pot, and it all turns ugly, and the car park is mentioned, and now Riverboat Ray is writing letter after letter to the card room manager in Luton to try and get himself reinstated.

I think about that old Islington game, and how frightened I would have been to lose a £200 pot. There were no televised tournaments then, no celebrities, no courtesy cars. None of that stuff existed in poker when I first met Riverboat Ray and I never saw it coming. I didn't want it, either. Poker wasn't about fame, it was about hiding.

But now here I am, lounging about in the back of a complimentary taxi, swept through London to be made up and photographed and settled at a table to take my shot at a million-dollar prize pool with a bunch of famous faces, while Ray is writing letters to try and get himself reinstated at the £50 table in Luton.

Why me? Why me and not him? How come I get to be Queen Alice, gliding across the chessboard to be crowned, while Ray is still the White Knight sitting on a gate?

Waiting to take the left-hand filter at Kings Cross, graciously wishing me luck, Riverboat Ray is probably wondering the same thing.

But if you asked my mother, she would say the question was what was I doing in an illegal poker game round the back of Islington with men called Riverboat anyway. My parents tried their best. French lessons, ballet lessons, lots of books, careful elocution. Yet I seem to have grown up into Nicely Nicely Johnson.

'Are you not going to take Mile End Road?' I ask.

'Nah,' says Ray. 'Solid traffic. We'll go the back way.'

As he launches into another unlucky Omaha story, I drift away a little. I don't think Ray would mind. We tell these gloomy tales to exorcise them, not because we need them listened to. The rhythm of his words . . . up and down . . . with the flush draw . . . bet the pot . . . the turn comes over . . . is like a gentle piece of familiar background music.

If I were driving my own car, I'd be listening to my poker tape. The story of my life, the soundtrack of the imaginary film, which I have played from Liverpool to the Isle of Man, from London to Baden, from Nice to Monte Carlo, from Los Angeles to Vegas.

The Gambler is on there, of course, which I first heard twenty years ago when it was recommended by the boys in my brother's game. *Better Not Look Down* by B.B. King, which reminded me, before those first tournaments in the Stakis basement, to be brave. *Rescue Me* by Fontella Bass, which made me laugh en route to *Late Night Poker* when I had no idea what I was doing. *There Is Always One More Time* by Johnny Adams, from when I first met the Hendon Mob, saw the hope in their eyes and the visions they hatched, and learned from it. *Beyond The Blue Horizon,* because that could inspire anyone to feel hopeful.

Killing Me Softly, which was playing in the cab as we drove back to McCarran airport in the magical Moneymaker year. *Desperado* by The Eagles, which filled my head with the romantic glamour of flying solo through life, until I got my heart broken and it stopped being funny for a while.

Come And Get It from The Beatles' *Anthology 3*, which makes me thump the steering wheel and think positive, tell myself I'm a winner like a man would. *Take Another Little Piece Of My Heart* by Janis Joplin, because I came to understand that tournament poker is a bruising, crippling, endlessly disappointing and rejecting enterprise so you have to embrace the masochism, and I love the way she sounds like she is begging for the pain. Then *Raindrops Keep Falling On My Head* by B.J. Thomas, because it's only a game.

You Can Get It If You Really Want by Jimmy Cliff, because it turned out I can win just like anybody else can, everything can click and flow, cards can fall right, spells can be cast, fireworks can go off, and if your trophy isn't shining yet, then you have to keep believing.

Only New York Going On by Francis Dunnery, because everything happens at 4 a.m. All the winning, all the losing, all the adrenaline, all the pain, and all the staring out of windows in empty hotel rooms, with money or without.

And *Let The River Run* by Carly Simon, because that is what it's all about. The river runs its own course, at its own pace, according to its own will, and all you can do is learn how to raft without drowning.

Funny how so many of them are about being alone. All of them, really. And yet, poker is the most companionable thing I do. The Tuesday game is my only regular social fixture. The Vic is my home from home. So much laughter and friendship and adventure – and money. It hasn't been lonely, has it?

I started playing poker to make friends and meet boys. Now I'm turning up with £5,000 in my pocket, thinking I can beat the world champion. I don't know if something went very right, or very wrong.

'You've gone quiet,' says Riverboat Ray as we clunk through the iron gates of the studio.

'Well . . . it's been a long journey,' I reply. 'From there to here.'

Ray says, 'It would've been longer if I took Mile End Road.'

PART ONE

1
1988

The World Series of Poker might as well be the moon.

My brother's game is on the other side of that wall. It makes the whole house smell of smoke. It sounds like a murmur and a clatter at once. Clop-clop go the clay chips, like a sound effect for horses' hooves. Clink-burble go the ice cubes and the whisky in the glasses. The conversation is low, male, rumbly, burst sometimes by laughter or howls of injustice. It is a rebellious, beckoning sound. I want to be there.

We're doing *Twelfth Night* this term. I'm enjoying it. I like Illyria, the magical island of nowhere. I like Feste, who drifts in and out. Where does he come from? Where does he go? Nobody knows. I like the madness below stairs, the rebellion of the un-containable games, the playfulness and cruelty, disguises and secrecy, the whirligigs of time bringing in their revenges.

But right now, I can't read it. I've been staring at the same page for an hour. Don't want to study Shakespeare. Don't want to solve equations, don't want to write up the effects of iodine on saliva, don't want to learn the dates of Henry VIII or draw an oxbow lake. Don't want to go to bed. Clink-burble-clatter go the chips and the drinks in the other room. The smoke floats and the boys laugh. I want to be there.

♠

The boys speak a weird language of 'trips', 'bullets', 'cowboys' for kings and 'a nugget' for a pound. Matt wears a T-shirt which says

NOT ALL TRAPPERS WEAR FUR HATS. He is going out with Al Alvarez's daughter. That's why the boys play this funny game that nobody else does, because Alvarez led the way. Al Alvarez has climbed mountains and written poetry, and he's been to the World Series of Poker, which might as well be the moon, and he has written a book about it. Al Alvarez is God.

And God knows why they are suddenly letting me play. What do they think? Maybe it's funny. Giles's kid sister – short, chubby, bookish, growing up slowly – putting her pocket money on the table and trying to fit in with the boys. I don't want to flirt with them. I want to *be* them. Big, brash, confident, 18-year-old boys.

Other girls at school have boyfriends. They have properly *old* boyfriends, who wear belts and drive cars. Other girls at school are willowy and graceful, flirty and coquettish, flawlessly bred and perfectly dressed, confident like 35-year-old bankers' wives. I still like climbing trees and visiting my grandma.

They know I'm from different stock. My bus home goes north, through Kilburn and up towards Golders Green, instead of west to elegant Richmond and Putney. I'm not glamorous.

And I don't want a boyfriend. When we were eleven years old, we did an exchange programme with our 'brother school' and had mixed lessons for a week. It was brilliant. The boys mucked around in class, played practical jokes, spent break-time kicking footballs around instead of putting nail varnish on. It was the most fun I've ever had at school. Then the exchange programme finished and all the boys went away again. I miss them.

I did kiss a boy once. It was at a party in a park. I'd stolen some of my brother's dope to impress everybody. I'd never had it before. Somebody held my hair while I threw up. I was no fool; I knew for a fact they were plotting to kill me. Plus there were those deadly herons everywhere. A few hours later, after a snooze in a flower bed, I found myself kissing a boy called Brian, who wanted to be a pilot. It was awkward, embarrassing and uncomfortable. I won't be doing that again for a while. A long while.

♠

My brother's a poker player but he isn't a gambler, not really. That's no thanks to Grandpa Sam. When we were little, Sam gave us a comprehensive education in blackjack, which he called pontoon. Here was the lesson: he was always the dealer, and we always lost. Sometimes we lost enough to buy him a Fry's Peppermint Cream. If he was really in form, enough to buy him a packet of Park Lane. But at the first sound of our parents' key in the front door, he'd move like a panther. By the time my mother and father had walked the three steps to the kitchen, the money had vanished and he was sitting there in all innocence, 'showing us a card trick'.

My parents only gamble once a year; £5 each way on four horses in the Grand National. That's unless you count their bridge games with Roger and Fiona, every Friday or Sunday night, 10p a hundred. But I don't think that counts. At the end of every bridge night, they put the losers' £2 or £3 or £5 into a jar, and at the end of the year they all go out for a big dinner with the money. The losers don't have to have a worse meal than the winners or anything like that. So it's not gambling, really, it's more like saving.

My father loves watching sport. He gets very involved but he doesn't bet on it. When we were little, he always let Giles stay up late when there was cricket on the radio or an Olympics in the middle of the night, but he only got excited because he actually cares who wins. I remember him once yelling at Jimmy Connors when Wimbledon was on television, 'Forwards!', 'Smash it!', 'Get back to the baseline!', then slumping back on the sofa and sighing, 'God, I wish I was there to shout advice.'

But it was just because he liked Jimmy Connors.

My father is not going to get sick on the dogs and the football, go skint and lose everything, like his uncles did. My father is not like them. He is a self-made man. He went to university and learned to speak 'properly'. He became editor of *Punch* magazine. He sent his children to private school. He was invited for lunch with the Queen, spent all month reading the broadsheets and planning elegant *bons mots* for the palace table, then the Queen took one look at him and asked, 'Why don't workmen wear boots any more?' Canny woman, that Queen. She sniffed a rum bloodline, just like the girls at my school. Nevertheless, some say it's the best girls' school in the country. My father's damned if his children aren't going to benefit from his hard work. They're not going to be poor. They're not going to live and die in Southgate. And they're certainly not going to be crooks, or gamblers.

My father's parents socialized only with other members of the family. They were actually related to each other, distant cousins, even before they got married; they'd never have met otherwise. They went through a fashionable phase as newlyweds, going to horse races and spiritualist meetings in the 1930s, but always with a safe group of uncles and in-laws. My father, an only child, broke that tradition among many others and we don't see much of the extended Corens. But we hear tales of Uncle Sid who nicked the silver at Dunkirk, Great-Grandpa Dave who went away for GBH on his own son-in-law, Fat Sam's spat with Ginger Phil, the Wet Fish Corens of Southgate, and the ones who threw their lives away in betting shops. It's close enough for my father to be glad he has left it behind. But I'm not. Whenever we do see the relatives, gathered together for weddings or funerals, I love them all. And I always loved sitting at the kitchen table with Grandpa while he smoked and dealt and chuckled, 'It'd take a lot of this to kill ya.' I didn't care that I lost. I just liked playing.

The bridge comes from my mother's side. Grandma Isabel has a heavy accent, wears big earrings, bakes chocolate-walnut cakes, and bids very loudly because she is deaf. She plays bridge with fellow Hungarian émigrés from one end of St John's Wood to the other. But she has always been very patient about playing with me, even when I was so small that I could only hold eight cards at once and I had to keep putting them down to check things in my little yellow *Book Of Bridge Rules*. She may be a tiny, frail, foreign lady with a bad hip replacement and a faulty hearing aid, but my grandma sparkles like a chandelier. She's the life and soul of a room. If you make an encouraging bid she will immediately go for slam, shouting, 'Don't invite me to a party if you don't expect me to dance!' She can't walk but she always dances.

♠

I hate being at school and I love being at home. Especially when the house is full of Giles's friends. Boys show off and tell jokes, and shout when they're angry. They don't smile and ask personal questions, then bitch behind your back and share your secrets with the class. They don't write diaries, all sweetly floral and girlish on the outside, for you to be unable to resist flicking through at break-time, which say things like, 'I hope Vicky leaves school soon, we all hate her, the fat cow,' and then smile at you across the tuck shop and ask if you want a Highland Toffee.

Boys say what they think to your face. Bit harsh, sometimes, but straightforward. This room feels, for all its billowing smoke and whisky fumes, safe and healthy.

And they are playing this game . . . you get two cards face-down and one face-up, and you put chips in the pot if you like your cards, and more get dealt. Or sometimes you only have two cards, and three are dealt face-up in the middle, and you hope that the three in the middle will chime somehow with your secret two. But even if they don't, you can pretend that they do. And if you pretend right, you can double your pocket money.

It is a serious game. I don't know if they play well or not, since I barely understand the rules myself, but they play seriously. Lots of macho stuff and poker jargon, pocket rockets and big slick (or is it big stick? I'm not sure and don't want to ask) that Matt has picked up from books and his trip to Vegas. It's really cool. One time, we played all night and whoever won the most money took us all up to the Coffee Cup in Hampstead and bought us breakfast.

My entire poker strategy is based on one of Matt's phrases, 'Don't disgrace an ace.' I never pass any hand with an ace in it. I sit waiting for aces to come.

♠

I don't want to go back to school. It's the first day of term, dark as a maths book and cold as its owner's wit. The warmth and laughter of the holidays are already shrinking into a walnut of memory. Yesterday I was a happy, funny, bright kid, playing games and laughing with my family. Today I am fat, clumsy, uncool, living in the wrong part of town, wearing the wrong clothes. And I haven't even got on the bus yet.

My brother walks me up the hill and gives me a cigarette to stop me from crying, and promises that I won't be at school for ever.

♠

On the other side of the ocean, Johnny Chan is winning the 1988 World Series of Poker. Johnny Chan is nicknamed 'The Orient Express', for obvious reasons: he arrived in America before political correctness did.

He was born in the Guangzhou province of China, and in 1962 moved to Texas, where his family ran restaurants. What must they have thought, that good and hardworking Chinese family, when their number one son dropped out of the University of Houston to become a full-time gambler in Las Vegas? He had been majoring in hotel and restaurant management. He was going to be big in catering. And off he ran to piss it up the wall in the Nevada desert. Or so they must have thought. That's what usually happens.

It works out for Johnny, though. He wins the World Series of Poker in 1987 and 1988, the fourth man to win back-to-back world titles. In the 1988 tournament, there are 167 players and Johnny Chan reaps the grand prize of $700,000. The field includes some of the great names of poker history: Jack 'Treetop' Straus, Puggy Pearson, Crandall Addington, Jack Keller, Johnny Moss, 'Amarillo Slim' Preston. They're pretty much all from Texas.

Betty Carey is the only female player in the field. There's a story about the time she lost a big heads-up match to Amarillo Slim, after he tricked her by asking whether she liked her cup of tea. She said, 'Yes, sure, Slim, it's great.' And then, an hour or so later, during a big pot, he asked whether she liked her hand. And when she said she liked her hand, in a slightly different tone of voice from when she said she liked her tea, he knew she was bluffing and he took her money.

My sympathies are with Betty. I like a nice cup of tea at the table, too.

♠

In a dream, I am just in the middle of folding a 67 offsuit when I am tapped on the shoulder by another me. She is older, filled out in some places, slimmed down in others, still looking very comfortable in the card room.

She says, 'I'd have raised with that.'

I laugh.

'No kidding,' she says. 'It's a lucky hand.'

'So has it all turned out all right?' I ask.

'Pretty good,' she nods. 'You've grown up happy enough. You sometimes wish that you were still a teenager, but only because you've forgotten what it was like. You play poker all the time now, because there's nobody to stop you. The game has taken over your life. You've won a million dollars. You've been to the World Series of Poker. And Al Alvarez has sent you an email, congratulating you on becoming the European Champion.'

'What's an email?' I say.

'It's something that took over everybody else's life,' my older self replies.

I think for a little while.

'Have I got a husband and babies?' I ask nervously. 'And a nice house with a big garden?'

She has her own little think now. Maybe she doesn't want to scare me. But she also wants me to know that girls are more honest when they're older.

'No,' she says eventually. 'You could probably afford the house and garden, what with the million dollars. But you'll quite like your little flat. You won't especially want to move anywhere else. Husband and babies . . . you're in no rush.'

'When I'm *over thirty*?' I ask, in horror. 'Not married? No children? Aren't I incredibly lonely? Am I going to die alone?'

'You might,' she says. 'But you won't find it such a scary idea by then. And you're not lonely. You've got poker. You've got lots of people. You're not lonely at all – apart from occasionally, in an enormous, black, existential way, at four o'clock in the morning, when you are driven mad by the mind-blowing concept of finite human consciousness. And fifteen husbands couldn't cure that!' she chuckles.

There is a pause.

'But I'm not at school any more, right?' I ask.

And she nods.

I pick up my next hand, a pair of tens, and I think, well, that's all right then.

⌘

A PAIR OF JACKS

Two jacks! Often a trouble hand. And the trouble is: you're more likely to see an overcard on the flop than not to see one. So it can be kind of a relief if everyone passes before the flop comes down.

A pair of sevens, something like sevens, that's easier to play after the flop. You know fine well whether you want action or not. Jacks . . . not quite a big pair, not quite a small one . . . they have this horrible habit of continuing to look good even when they have gone behind. Frozen there, preserved: could still be as good as they look, or could be artificial beauty now. So hard to tell sometimes. The Botox hand.

How much should I raise with these jacks, then? All-in would be dumb. Let's not be dumb, on the biggest final table I've ever reached. My chip stack is too big to move in; anyone who called would have to be beating two jacks. Suicidal. And I don't want to chase away every hand that's worse than mine.

I don't mind one caller. I'd like one caller. Blinds 8,000 – 16,000. I'll make it 40,000. Enough to show I'm serious. But less than the full pot, give the weaker hand some odds. I bet 40,000.

Sid Harris re-raises all-in. Damn. I didn't want anyone to go all-in. I certainly didn't want Sid Harris to go all-in. Sid plays a hand once an hour or something. Aces, kings.

Hard to pass a decent pair, though. Haven't had a good hand for ages. Pairs are so pretty, so enticingly symmetrical. Two curvy jacks, like Christmas stockings hanging in a fireplace. Or two round, juicy queens, like quail on a rotisserie. Two spiky kings, determined and macho, like marching soldiers in profile. Two clean, sharp, pure aces. God, I love looking down at my hole cards and finding a pair of matching picture cards. Painted twins.

*Does Sid have a prettier hand than mine? 'Whores' or 'cowboys',
as the Old School parlance goes? I would never call them 'whores'. The
queens aren't whores. They are fat, proud, classy ladies. Like Mma
Ramotswe from* The No. 1 Ladies' Detective Agency. *And the kings
aren't cowboys. Cowboys are American, and America's a republic. The
kings look Persian to me. Noble Persians, from that ancient land where
cards were played in the fourteenth century. Carpets, cats and cards: what
a beautiful culture. Has Sid got kings?*

*I like Sid. He's Old School. He lives in Hove and writes books
about horse racing. Been playing for a long time. He's like a classic Vic
player. I've never actually seen him in the cash game at the Vic, but he
would fit right in. Looks right, talks right. Not one of these crazy teenage
Swedes. No mindless all-in, all-in, just for the sake of aggression.
Thoughtful, gradual poker. And he seems like such a nice man. I don't
really want to knock him out.*

*Wait, wrong thought process. I want to knock everybody out. No
pity, no mercy. No feminine. He's not a nice man, he's an obstacle to
victory. I want to knock Sid out. I want to grind him into the ground.
I want to send him home skint. I want every chip, I want him pleading
for the bus fare. I want to obliterate them all.*

*Crazy teenage Swede, of course, it's easy. I would call in about three
seconds. Less. Two jacks, raise, all-in re-raise from a crazy teenage Swede:
my chips are in the pot before Björn's even moved.*

*With Sid, you know, it's more difficult. I have to think about it.
The railbirds might disapprove of that. Let's say I call, cards come over,
Sid was making a move, I've got massively the best hand — then I
thought too long, it looks like a slow roll. But Sid doesn't seem to make
a lot of moves. He's a solid player. I respect that.*

*Then again, I can't pass. For this situation, I've got a hand. It's a
chance to knock out a player. More money. Good chips. He could maybe
do this with any pair, any ace. Even if he's got me beat, I'm not dead.
Five cards to come. Plenty of jacks in the deck.*

Well, two.

But you have to get lucky to win tournaments; got to give yourself *the opportunity to get lucky. And this is the most important tournament of my life. It's the final table of the London EPT, that magical week when the all-important European Poker Tour comes to my own home casino. My regular poker opponents are gathered on the rail, watching. Some of them have shares in my action, others just want to see a local player do well in the big event. $1,000,000 available as first prize. No woman has ever won it before.*

And I got to this final by being gutsy; can't switch that off now. Can't hide from chance. If I lose the pot, I still have chips. Not many, but some. I don't need to win the tournament anyway. It's enough just to have made the final. I've won tournaments before, but never made the final of anything so hugely significant. Just getting here, that's enough. I'm happy now.

What am I thinking about? I have two jacks and a man's gone all-in! It's Christmas! I call.

Sid rolls over two nines.

Poor Sid. It's a nice hand. He's entitled to be in front. He's entitled to a 50/50 against a couple of overcards, and he's entitled to be better off even than that. I raise a lot more often than he does. I've raised with some outright rubbish in this tournament so far, and got away with it. He's entitled to a pass from me in this spot. He's unlucky I've got two jacks.

Then again, no early cheers. Plenty of nines left in the deck. Two of them. Two fat apostrophes. Two evil hand grenades, waiting to explode out of the dealer's fist and kill my brave jacks. My vulnerable knaves. Poor boys. I will protect them. I will protect them from the nasty nines. Nina from Pasadena will not come flirting off the deck to wink at my helpless little jack tars, turn their heads and sink their boat. No nine!

The flop comes: K♦ . . . 4♦ . . . 10♣.

That's okay. No risky backdoor flush draw. Sid doesn't have the nine of diamonds. The curse of Scotland. But why have I let that card come into my head? Why did I even think about it? It's like I want it to come! I'm practically SUMMONING it out of the pack! Like I'm

URGING the turn card to give Sid a set! Go away, curse of Scotland. Focus. Jack of spades, jack of spades, jack of spades . . .

   K♥.

No problem there. Two pairs each. Mine are better. Blank, blank, blank . . .

   J♠.

The jack of spades! Just the fellow I wanted to see! Not that it makes any difference. A blank would have done. I don't need the full house. But I thought about the jack of spades and he just showed up, like sometimes when I'm thinking about my dad and then he rings. Always quite a comforting feeling. A good sign. Good omen. My dad ringing, likely to be a good day. Jack of spades showing up, maybe a good tournament.

Unlucky, Sid. Well played.

Wow. I seem to have quite a few chips now. The crowd is shouting encouragement as I stack them.

And there are only seven of us left.

2

THE CHIMNEY SWEEP

'Good luck will rub off when I shakes 'ands with you . . .'

– *from* Mary Poppins

As I deliver the punchline, I run a finger across my chest, describing an imaginary slogan on a T-shirt.

Then I tell the audience, 'That wasn't really a joke. I just felt like touching my tits.'

They fall about. I seem to have found their level.

'Well,' I continue, 'if you want something done properly . . .'

Another roar of laughter and a round of applause. I'm not actually being funny. I'm just exploiting the fact that it's 2 a.m., everyone in the club is drunk and a female stand-up comic is a bizarre curio, like a talking monkey. Throw in something rude, and they're in your pocket.

It is a good feeling. It seems unfair that butchers and doctors and electricians don't get applauded for doing their jobs, too.

♠

I have just left school and I'm so happy I could kill myself. Now to work out what to do with the rest of my life. I've been writing a 'teenage newspaper column' for a couple of years, and an agent got in touch to ask if I'd like to join a stand-up comedy show at the Edinburgh Fringe Festival. Why not? I'm immortal. Nothing could ever frighten me again, after walking into the school hall every lunchtime and wondering who to sit next to.

So I have chanced my way into this strange, counter-cultural, late-night community. It is a pure meritocracy: you can hold your own or you can't. London's little circuit of subterranean comedy clubs, packed and hot if there is an audience in double figures, is utterly seductive for the insecure. You can hide in a private world and prove yourself publicly at the same time.

It seems to be thought of as a man's business, with very few female comics in these clubs, and the idea that 'women can't hack it' is irresistible.

When I'm sitting around with a bunch of comedians in a room above a pub, after the shows are finished, drinking and listening to stories, I feel, for the first time away from my family, an epiphany of belonging. All the school rules are overturned. You can be fat here. You can be short or short-sighted, Jewish or Asian, useless at sport, baffled by sex – it doesn't matter, as long as you're brave and quick-witted.

In fact, the worse your social skills, the more you have to talk about.

♠

I play poker occasionally. Some of my brother's friends know a couple of people who run a private cash game in Archway, so I visit a couple of times. They are a nice, funny group. A couple of them are famous: Ross Boatman, who's in *London's Burning*, and Jesse Birdsall, who's in *Eldorado*. The others are just gamblers who haven't got to grips with life yet: Barny Boatman, who works for P&O; Chris Colson, who doesn't seem to do anything much; and Patrick Marber, a stand-up comic who's thinking of writing a play.

The games are Omaha, seven stud and hi-lo split. But the stakes are a bit rich for me. I love poker, but I'm bad at it. I lose £200 or £300 every time. I'm currently making £210 a week working in a shop, and £25 a time for comedy performances.

The only way to learn poker is to go to a casino (far too scary) or get fleeced in these expensive live games. I can't resist stopping by every so often for the fun, the scathing banter and the takeaway pizza, but I can't afford it more than once every few months.

♠

I tell my parents that when the year comes to an end, I'm not going to university. I think I've found a sort of vocation in comedy. I love the underworld, I love the screwed-up people, I finally fit in and I am happy. I'm not going to give it up to study T.S. Eliot and *The Wife's Lament*. I can't bear to re-enter the misery of my school years. And I sense that I'd never go back to comedy if I stopped to be a student for three years. I'd lose my nerve, and I can't risk that. Something finally feels right to me. I'm on my yellow brick road. So, I'm going to write to the admissions tutor at Oxford and say thank you very much, but they should give my place to somebody else.

Then I look at my father's face. I love him more than anyone in the world.

'It's okay,' I say. 'I was only joking.'

♠

Having saved up all my shop and comedy money, I have managed to swerve the expensive poker games for long enough to build a travel budget. Most of the girls from my school have gone to India, where they all seem to be getting spiritual and getting food poisoning. They consider this a big plus, since most of them try to throw up after meals anyway, but it doesn't sound like much fun to me.

I have no interest in 'discovering myself'. I want to discover America. My father travelled there in 1960 and spent two adventurous years studying American fiction, dating American girls, driving American cars across American landscapes, eating hamburgers and going on civil rights marches. From him, from the cinema, from *Huckleberry Finn* and *Moby Dick* and *Dallas*, I am in love with America, too. I keep a giant folded map in my bedroom, and take it out to stare at the redolent, romantic names: Hawk Springs, Dead Man's Gulch, Looking Glass Falls.

Over two tightly budgeted months, my friend Nicky and I take Greyhound buses all round the southern states, up via New York to Massachusetts and on across the country, all the way over to the west coast through Illinois, Iowa, Nebraska and Colorado. We hop aboard a shaky twin-prop flight to Alaska, taking the first train of the season from Anchorage to Fairbanks. We rent a car and drive around the Painted Desert, New Mexico, Arizona and the Grand Canyon. All there is left that we really want to see is Wyoming, the Dakotas and Las Vegas.

Unfortunately, we start in Las Vegas. I write in my journal:

Sunday 2nd June

Nevada is amazing. Right over the state line, in the middle of nothing but dusty hills and sand, there are huge pink and yellow casinos, and nothing else at all. After driving through empty hot landscape for ages, you think you're imagining them, that they're a mirage. It's like that old cartoon where the cars keep driving past the hotel and the man in the fez is standing outside saying, 'I knew we shouldn't have built it in the middle of the desert!'

Then Las Vegas is BREATHTAKING. Millions and millions and millions of neon signs and shiny hotels and pink plastic flamingos and adverts for famous people and sparkle and I ABSOLUTELY LOVE IT. We were going to stay at the Las Vegas Hilton where The Four Tops and The Temptations are appearing nightly, but the Desert Inn has Joan Rivers.

It's AMAZING what hotels give you for the money here.

The Desert Inn said they'd charge us $75 a night if we agreed to stay two nights, and for that we've got a STUNNING room with its own bathroom, seven free drinks each and millions of 'Buy 5 get 5 free' tokens for roulette and poker chips. It's so weird and amazing after all the youth hostels. They valet parked the car!!

Couldn't resist the casino and they couldn't resist us either – business is so slow that they only asked for ID once and my fake student card held up fine. So I was able to lose $5 on fruit machines and $47 on roulette. I was doing all right at roulette, but decided in advance that it was OKAY to lose all my winnings for the fun of playing. Tonight I'm going to try poker.

We never make it to Wyoming and the Dakotas.

♠

You wouldn't think there was anything especially character-building about eating cheese sandwiches and reading Milton under a tree. But my college is ambitious, heavily male-dominated, and our tutors approach English Literature with military discipline. They specialize in reducing new students to tears, stripping away our confidence, then gradually bestowing approval as we work longer and longer hours, until we hunch over the books all night with an obsessiveness born of Stockholm Syndrome.

I like it. Standing my ground with alpha males, not showing fear, trying to make them laugh, noticing their own vulnerabilities, aiming always to win respect – I've grown up with my father, and taken my chances with a rowdy Brixton club audience; this is fast becoming a comfort zone. Being shouted at by macho Yeats scholars (a construction which may sound oxymoronic to anyone who's never met the men in question) is a pleasure. The only terrors of university life lie in the bars and parties, the competition for social and sexual success. It takes two years to find a proper best friend, a quirky theologian called Charlie, who introduces himself to me with a bizarre puppet show and an enormous row about whether or not *Beyond The Fringe* was funny. Our relationship really takes off when it turns out he is head of the five-strong university cribbage society. Cribbage is much easier with six.

Until Charlie stumbles into the picture, apart from one intense, doomed love affair with an angry medical student, I spend most weekends back in London, hanging around in comedy clubs and stopping in occasionally at the Archway game to lose money I can't afford.

I miss the comic meritocracy. But getting older brings a self-consciousness which makes it quite impossible to go back on stage and shout 'Good evening!' at a bunch of sceptical strangers. I'm not scared of the idea, just embarrassed.

By the time I leave university, comedy has changed. It has developed an unexpected cool streak. Articles in newspapers are describing it as 'the new rock and roll'. Comedians have become sex symbols. They have groupies. They have managers and TV deals. They don't seem to be the community of outsiders that attracted me in the first place. They have become the in-crowd.

So, the natural path is to settle back behind a typewriter and try to craft my jokes from there. Broadsheet newspaper readers are far less demanding than stand-up comedy audiences. If you're appearing after 2,000 words of earnest opinion about Bosnia, they're happy if you can give them a single wry smile. And if they don't smile, what the hell? You're safely alone at home, not standing there like a lemon, being rubbed against the grater of public silence.

But there's no risk in it. No clench in the stomach as you walk to the microphone, wondering what kind of an audience they're going to be. No euphoric high when you hear the first laugh and know it's going to be okay.

And how can there be any community, any belonging, when

I'm alone at the typewriter? It's a good life, but there is something missing.

♠

I am standing in the doorway next to 7-11 in Notting Hill,
clutching a bottle of whisky. The door is opened by a delicate,
laconic little fellow with an explosion of black hair that makes
him look, somehow, as if he is a Victorian street urchin who's
spent the afternoon up a chimney.

He looks at the bottle of whisky, baffled. He seems as though
he is about to say something sarcastic, but doesn't. He takes the
bottle from my hand, mutters a thank-you and puts it down on
the stairs. I don't see it again.

He leads me up into a small room that appears very crowded
with people. I can't quite tell how they all fit round the table; it's
a Mad Hatter's tea party with dormice slotting into teapots. They're
eating sweets, talking, dealing, swearing. Hugo, the chimney sweep,
murmurs a couple of half-introductions, then gets bored and gives
up. There are a few journalists, an IT man, a sleepy second-hand
book dealer, a few undefined extras. And there is a slender, elegant,
quirkily dressed woman, the first woman I have ever seen playing
poker: Kira. A mutual friend has sent me to this game, amazed
by the coincidence of knowing two female poker enthusiasts.
Such unlikely specimens had to be introduced.

But there is no smalltalk; this isn't a dinner party. The hellos
take about eight seconds before I am asked for money, given chips
and dealt in. The entire conversation is about poker. There seems
to be an intense group fascination for each hand, each deal, each
variant, each card. If they're not talking about the hand in play,
they're talking about a hand that just finished or a hand that was
played last week. If it isn't a hand they played themselves, it's a
hand that somebody played 'in the Vic'.

The game itself seems easier than the ones I've played before.

The stakes are smaller. And although the conversation is saturated with poker, the atmosphere is more light-hearted than I am used to. No alcohol, no machismo, lots of junk food and giggling and double entendres and throwing sweets at people who win pots. There's nothing cool about it. It's somehow . . . *silly*. And yet it's completely engaged and engaging, involving and enthralling. Within an hour I am not just playing poker, I'm debating poker, arguing about poker, laughing about poker, inhaling poker. I even win some money.

'Thanks for having me,' I say, very sincerely, on the way out. 'I had a great night.'

'Come again,' says The Sweep. 'We play every Tuesday.'

A SUITED ACE

A♦ 6♦. That's a pretty hand. I'm fourth to speak, and I should probably raise. But I would have to pass for a re-raise, and I don't want to waste chips.

New players get very excited about lone aces. In the past, doing TV commentary on amateur or celebrity tournaments, I've invariably found myself shaking my head in despair as yet another player fritters his chips away by refusing to pass any hand with an ace in it. Just like me, as a kid, playing in that old teenage game with the boys, waiting for aces.

The problem is, everybody likes aces. If you bet with an ace, someone else will call or raise with an ace. In that situation, with A6 or A7, if you miss the flop you've got nothing, and if you hit the ace you're probably still losing. What a mess.

AK is obviously a big hand, though not as big as some kids seem to believe. It's no pair! But it carries a strong promise. Everybody loves AQ, too. AJ is moving into tricky territory – and A9 is not just a poisoned chalice, it's a goddamn beaker of arsenic.

Suited wheel cards, I like those. A2, A3, A4, A5 of a suit: you're drawing to a straight and a flush as well as two pair. And with the wheel cards, you don't tend to get all feverish if you only hit the ace. I love those 'spokes'.

Very big aces, great. Very small aces, focused goal. Middle-sized aces: like plastic lobsters in a Chinese restaurant window, they aren't nearly as tasty as they look.

So what shall I do with this A6 I'm looking at, then? If I'm going to raise, I won't want action. The ace is not just a plastic lobster, it's a red herring: I might as well raise with any cards at all. A6 could be a particularly bad choice, because my cards might well be counterfeited by any hand that chose to get stubborn. So I opt to be conservative, and pass.

Emad Tahtouh makes it 50,000 to go out of the small blind, and Michael Muldoon calls in the big blind.

Flop comes 8♥ A♣ 5♦.

I should feel regretful: my hand would probably have been good here. In fact, when Emad comes out betting 70,000, I'm relieved.

He's super-aggressive, this Emad. Probably the biggest threat on this table. He is a pro, making most of his money in the high-stakes games on PokerStars. I remember him from the World Series of 2005, he was one of the Lebanese-Australian crew who came out with Joe Hachem. I played a bit with Emad on the cash tables that year. Very nice guy. But I know his playing style.

A couple of days ago, in this same tournament, I made a deliberately small raise with AQ to trap Emad on the big blind. He was short of chips, but had just enough to make me pass for an all-in re-raise if I had a medium-strength hand. And I knew he knew it. I knew he'd move in if the maths were right. So I made the maths right, and he stuck it all-in with an 89 offsuit. To his annoyance, I called immediately – and to my annoyance, he hit a nine. The best-laid plans . . .

So now I feel like he's made this tournament on borrowed time, with my chips, and sooner or later it will be my job to knock him out. Like Batman in a multi-way fight, when it comes to the biggest challenge, with the personal twist – 'Leave this one to me.'

And this could have been the hand. If I had raised with my A6, and he had played back, and I had called, then I would probably be winning on this flop. My tactic with Emad is definitely to try and use his own aggression against him.

The problem is, just because he's a good, strong, aggressive player, that doesn't mean there's a law against him being dealt a good hand. Why can't he have a bigger ace than A6? Sure, if everyone passes to his small blind, he can raise it up with any two cards – but everyone on this table can play, everyone knows that you can raise with anything from the button or small blind when the others have folded. Poker double-think suggests, therefore, that people would actually be raising with real hands in these spots. Would I have wanted to play for all my chips, for my entire tournament, with a weak paired ace? I'm relieved that I passed. Michael Muldoon also passes.

On the very next hand, Peter Hedlund (a tall, tipsy, talkative Swede, who has seen his massive chip lead whittled away with each fresh beer) moves all-in with KQ, and is unlucky enough to find Michael Muldoon with AK in the small blind. No dramas on the flop, and Peter's out in seventh place. He wins £36,600. The next prize is £44,000 – so that pass of A6, however girlish and weedy, might have won me £7,400.

And we're down to six.

3
PIRATE SHIPS AND CACTUSES

*'The lowest pool hustler in the business is four times
more respectable than some of those humbugs in
Washington.'*

— Minnesota Fats

They talk about 'love at first sight', but who needs to wait so
long? I am in love before first sight: the new world champion of
poker is twenty-seven years old, six-foot-six, from Montana, and
his name is Huckleberry Seed. Word has come back from Las Vegas
of this lanky superman, who has beaten a field of 295 runners
in the 1996 World Series and won $1,000,000. *Huckleberry Seed?*
Can he really exist, or is this a daydream spread across the Atlantic
by a fan of Damon Runyon?

I need to find out. I imagine a poker champion as an ageing
Texan, body like a sack of sand, hands hairy and heavy with
jewellery, voice like a waterfall of cigarettes. This isn't conjured
from the air; that's what most poker champions are like. I've read
about them. But I've never met any. I want this glamorous young
pro to be my first.

I may have met some professional poker players without
knowing it. Who are those people in the Vic? Shadowy, gravelly,
never a smile. I daren't speak to them. I have no idea what they
do for a living, if anything.

♠

Ever since I came back from that first trip to America, five years
ago, I've had an occasional recurrent dream that there is a magic
walkway between my house and the Desert Inn card room. In

the dream, I am lying asleep in bed at home, but I wake up. That is, I dream that I wake up. And in my dreaming-awake state, I remember about the bridge. I don't need to save money, I don't need an aeroplane, I don't need fake ID. I just walk over the bridge and find myself in the card room. Even though it's the middle of the night, the place is buzzing and lively. I sit at a candle-lit bar, sipping a Martini and kicking myself for forgetting the bridge was there. I don't play poker. I just sit at the bar, excited to be there, anticipating action to come. It is a very, very happy dream.

And then my brother's friend Matt, who knows Al Alvarez, tells me about the Victoria Sporting Club. It is just across London, with a real-life poker room.

Matt drives me down to the Edgware Road and parks outside McDonald's. We walk into 'the Vic' and he signs me in as a guest. I feel sick and shifty at the desk, like you do walking through Customs – like I did going into those Vegas casinos, when I really was smuggling something. My underage self.

But this is perfectly legitimate. All I have to do is sign my name where Matt has written it in block capitals, and we are waved in with a smile. We check in our coats, because there is a dress code (no coats, no trainers, no jeans, no T-shirts, no hats, no carrier bags, no income tax, no VAT, no money back, no guarantee) and head upstairs to the card room.

It doesn't look like my dream. It doesn't look like the Desert Inn. It has a garish carpet and cheap fruit machines. The air is a soupy smog of B&H cigarette smoke, Middle Eastern aftershave and non-specific Man Smell. Everybody looks miserable. This is not a holiday casino at all.

We go into the card room. A gaggle of elderly men, dressed in collared Aertex shirts, slacks and nicotine-stained sports jackets, squint at me and look away again. Nobody says hello. I shrink a little closer to Matt.

We are here to play a £20 seven-card stud tournament. I sink into my allocated seat and don't speak a word all night. But, sticking to my traditional strategy (wire-ups, pairs above jacks, three suited connectors; fold everything else), I end up coming second in the tournament. I win about £250. I reckon I've got the game licked. This place may not be Disneyland, but I'm going to come here all the time.

♠

My second trip to the Vic is by myself. I've joined the club, which turns out to involve nothing more than filling in a form and waiting 48 hours before I'm allowed to play. Then I drive my own car down to the Edgware Road and sign myself in.

I wend my way through the siren calls of the slots, as far as the card room. I peep through the glass partition wall. There, just about visible through the volcanic cloud of smoke, is the same cliquey gaggle of old men. A couple of them peer suspiciously at me. My stomach clenches with fear. I go back down the stairs, find my car, and go home.

♠

I drive to the Vic. I park my car, I sign in, I leave my coat at the desk, I climb the stairs. I walk quickly and purposefully between the slots, up to the card room. When I get there, my feet stop by themselves. I peer in. The old men peer out. I might just as well leap over the barrier to the lions' enclosure at London Zoo.

I retreat to the roulette table. Roulette is different. The croupiers are chatty and friendly. There are women around the table, young Chinese women, elderly Arab women. They bet fast and furious, scribbling down the numbers in their little notebooks. I throw £30 onto the baize and receive a small stack of chips in return. I play for half an hour and win about £20. I leave, satisfied.

♠

I drive to the Vic. I park in Harrowby Street, say hello to the receptionist, sign myself in, leave my coat, walk up the stairs, hurry to the card room, get to the threshold, swivel without stopping and walk back to the roulette table. I win £50. I go home.

♠

I drive to the Vic. I park outside the Marriott, wave at the doorman, greet the receptionist, sign myself in, leave my coat, walk up the stairs and over to the roulette table. I lose £100. I go home.

♠

I drive to the Vic. I park in the underground car park, leave my coat in the car, walk up to the desk, sign, say hi to Karen, take the lift to the first floor, walk to the roulette table. I lose £200. I go to the cashpoint, get another £100. I fight back to −£40 and stop.

Next time, I'll win.

♠

I have started dreaming about roulette. At random moments during the day, I think I can hear the tiny 'click' which emanates from a croupier's marker going down onto a winning chip. Wheels spin in my head. Money spins out of my bank account. I am playing, what, three or four afternoons a week now. I know that if I want to make a living as a self-employed writer, I need discipline. But I keep knocking off work at lunchtime and going down to gamble with the stake I have calculated from this week's earnings, and next week's and the week after's. If I earn something once, I lose it three times. My bank statements are red. I have borrowed money from my brother, pretending it was for something else. This has got to stop.

♠

'Try the Stakis in Russell Square,' says The Chimney Sweep. 'I'm
in sometimes, if I'm not in the Vic. Roy Houghton runs the card
room, he's pretty friendly. We'll be there on Wednesday night for
a hi-lo tournament. Meet us there.'

And, finally, I start playing casino poker. Just once or twice a
month, to supplement the weekly Tuesday game. For a while, I
pop into the Stakis in the afternoons and play roulette there. But
eventually it gets bad, and it really does have to stop, and it does
stop, and it hurts, and I swear off roulette for ever.

But I get to know people in the Stakis card room. There are
usually about thirty players in there, just enough for a tournament.
I say hello to some of them, ask how they're getting on. And I call
Hugo and Kira sometimes, to find out if they are going to the Vic,
and I go when they're going. Turns out The Sweep was usually in
there all along, tucked away behind a pillar or a Greek. I become
one of a handful of semi-regular younger players, who are looked
on by the old men with indulgent amusement. I recognize their
faces now, know some of their names, but I never speak to them.

The Vic games are very tough. I'm a Stakis player, an amateur,
an occasional and recreational visitor. Maybe I'll graduate to the
Vic properly one day, but not yet. That's how it works: you play
your home games, and you play for fun sometimes in the Stakis,
and one day – if you don't give up or go broke – you graduate
to the Vic.

♠

Flying back into McCarran airport, this time 'of age' with a
genuine driving licence and an adult's right to play poker, I am
determined to win more money and meet Huckleberry Seed.
My friends have crushes on Robbie Williams. I have a crush on
a poker player I've never even seen. But I have a good excuse to
look for him: I can sell an interview with him to the newspaper
back home.

I'm not a proper journalist. I have never whipped late copy from a typewriter and cried, 'Hold the front page!' I've never shouted information down a sat-phone over the roar of gunfire. I have once bruised my fist by thumping it angrily on a coffee table while trying to explain a joke to a bored copy-taker on a crackly mobile, but that doesn't count. I write the light stuff, features and columns, more closely related to the crossword and horoscope family than hardline news. Certainly, I can sell an interview with a 27-year-old millionaire gambler. Poker is a tiny secret world that nobody on the outside knows about. It's an investigative piece, like infiltrating the Bilderberg Group. Most people barely know that poker exists. If I ever mention that it's my hobby, in a social situation, people are amazed and fascinated. Poker! Who knew that anybody plays that old game, any more?

♠

Being a rambling-gambling man, Huck Seed isn't easy to track down. I launch my quest from a cheap room at the Las Vegas Hilton. A list of defunct telephone numbers leads eventually to an old flatmate, who is less than encouraging. 'You know the movie *Forrest Gump*? You know the leaf that floats through the movie, never settling in one place? Well, that's Huck. Last I heard, he was playing at the Crystal Park Casino in LA.'

More phone research reveals that the leaf is indeed tossing around in the Crystal Park air, obstinately refusing to settle. I could drive to Los Angeles from here in about five hours, but what if he has moved on when I get there? Everybody knows him, everybody has just that minute seen him, nobody can find him. Surely, if he is any kind of gambler, he will be sucked back into Las Vegas sooner or later? I phone every day, until a sympathetic dealer advises that Huck has at last left LA and returned to the magical city where the hotels have theme parks inside them, restaurants do not offer 'all you can eat' but 'all you can imagine', and every gas station attendant would have been a millionaire if it weren't for a bad out-draw in 1973.

From a sizzling phone booth opposite the Mirage, I finally reach Seed and gabble my journalistic credentials at him. In a deep voice, slower 'n molasses in January, he invites me to his rented house a few miles west of the Strip.

Through the cab windscreen, the desert landscape grows unexpectedly prettier. The giant neon lions, pyramids and pirate ships of the town centre are gradually replaced by cactuses and flowers. I'm slightly disappointed not to have found Huck chain-smoking and re-raising on the Strip itself, but still I've got it all worked out: he will be James Garner, he will be Steve McQueen, he will be a hard-drinking, loose-living card sharp with electric-blue eyes and a cruel mouth. He will be The Cincinnati Kid.

He is a man in Bermuda shorts and a baseball cap who has just been to the corner shop to buy a carton of milk for his girl-friend. He's a boy who went to Caltech hoping to become a physicist, started playing poker with his friends, and dropped out of college when he started making money at it. He's a kid whose competitive streak was at its highest 'when I used to play Scrabble with my mom'. His family is respectable, educated; the kids' names are all clever combinations of the rural and the literary. Huck's sister's name is Caraway Seed, which conjures images of a woman just as strapping and Aryan as he is, all cornfields and improving books. Meanwhile, having won a million dollars in a poker tournament, he doesn't seem to have done anything with it. The apartment is sparse, spartan.

There are only two signs of Huck Seed's card-earned windfall: his girlfriend's son is cross-legged in front of a television eight times the size of himself, and the coffee table groans under a de luxe Scrabble set with gold-embossed tiles.

As we talk, Huck chews thoughtfully on a bowl of oatmeal

and discusses his interest in exercise physiology and nutrition. His dad sends him books about it.

This is not quite the risky rebel I expected. He tells me about his love of running and mountain-biking. He explains that he wins at poker because he has a good understanding of game theory, probability and statistics. 'Like if you were playing Scrabble, uh, you've just got to know which letters make more words, it's kind of like a percentage thing.'

Game theory? Who is this guy? Poker is about intuition and sixth sense, bluff and bluster, psychology and gut. It is about dusty landscapes, saloon bars, riverboats, gunfights, saucy molls and crooked cowboys. Huck Seed seems to be treating it as some kind of soulless science project.

♠

In the autobiography of Amarillo Slim, 1972 world champion, Slim writes: 'Women are meant to be loved and not to play poker. My wife Helen Elizabeth thinks that a king is the ruler of a country and a queen is his bedmate. A woman would have a better chance of putting a wild cat in a tobacco sack than she would of coming out to Vegas and beating me.' Even in 1996, among the bullets and balls of high-stakes poker, this is very much the prevailing attitude.

I put it to Huck Seed, who is cagey but not impossible to read. 'I guess I have my own ideas about that . . . I guess I won't comment on that . . . I guess men run faster than women and . . . it's an evolution thing.'

Evolution? Over the tree-swinging centuries, men somehow *evolved* a better ability to calculate their odds with the second nut flush draw and a gutshot? Take the maths away, and poker demands only an ability to know when you are being lied to; I say most women have plenty of experience. And what has running got to do with it? This is not a physical game. All you need is a fat butt and decent eyesight. I suppose men's larger fingers would give them an edge in a game of ten-card Omaha, but we don't play that even in the Tuesday game.

But I don't say anything. I am a guest in this guy's house. Besides, what have I ever won? Second place in a seven-card stud tournament, after a statistic-bucking deluge of wire-ups. Maybe he's right. But I will be good one day, I swear to God. When Huck tells me that Las Vegas is a boom town for young couples, 'where the guys play poker and the girls serve cocktails', my resolve hardens like quick-dry cement.

Maybe Huck feels grudging about women because he thinks they look down on him? He doesn't have a job. He plays an old-fashioned gambling game that offers no security and certainly no respect. He tells me, 'Women want to know what you do for a living, and when I say I'm a poker player they think I'm some kind of bum.'

♠

It is only when we talk about his winning hand of the World Series, when Huck beat a doctor from New Orleans called Bruce Van Horn to the title, that the music of poker language begins to trickle from his lips. 'He was on the button with king-eight suited. The flop comes nine-eight-four and I've got top two pair. I made a pretty good-size bet, he raised, I put him all-in and he doesn't catch his king.'

Oh, that music. Whatever my friends feel when Robbie Williams sings *Everything Changes But You*, I feel when I hear that unique mixture of past and present tenses, the suspense of the turn card, the narrative of a hand.

Not that I can make head or tail of the hand Huck's describing. Holdem isn't really my game, and I've never played a Holdem tournament. And I'm a rock. What are these people doing in a pot with 89 and K8? These aren't hands! But I am seduced by

the hypnotic sound of the story. I want to talk like that myself,
one day.

♠

When I have switched off my tape recorder, ordered a taxi and
started daydreaming about Bruce Van Horn, the poker-playing
New Orleans doctor, Huck Seed stands on his head. He explains
that he has bet a couple of guys $10,000 that he can stand on
his head for 52 minutes during the upcoming 1997 World Series
and must keep practising.

A prop bet? I love prop bets. They always make the best
stories. Amarillo Slim once won a lot of money claiming that he
could beat a champion racehorse over 100 yards. People fell over
themselves to take the bet, but cunning old Slim chose the course:
it had a turn in it, 50 yards one way, 50 yards back. Of course,
there was no way of explaining this to the horse, which was still
running straight in the other direction while Slim was collecting
his winnings.

People are always getting suckered by Amarillo Slim's prop
bets. Another time, he took on a professional golfer over the question of who could hit the ball furthest. Slim let the golfer go
first. When he took his own turn, he explained that he would
be choosing his own course here, too: a frozen lake. The ball kept
bouncing and skittering for miles.

With that kind of history, you'd think a champion ping-pong
player would know better than to accept Slim's expensive challenge to a match, along with a generous offer to provide the bats.
But no, the pigeon seized this opportunity, certain he could trash
any amateur and make a small fortune. Going to his car for 'the
bats', Slim whipped out two Coke bottles, with which he had
been secretly practising for months.

But it turns out there is no twist in Huck Seed's bet. He just
thinks he can stand on his head for a long time. He explains, 'I'm

training to run a 4.5-minute mile anyway, and it's good to let the lactic acid and blood drain into your head.'

I ask him about other prop bets he has made, and they are all very healthy. He has won money by floating in the sea for 24 hours, by halting a card game to run an immediate marathon, and (potentially) by staking $100,000 that his weight will not reach 250 pounds in the next 35 years. I expect he'll win that.

This is no Cincinnati Kid, with dark yellowish circles under his eyes that rested on his cheekbones where the skin was drawn tight, as if he might have liver trouble from too much drinking. Maybe poker is changing in America? Maybe the old romance is dying, and there's going to be a new spirit of living right, sleeping well, eating carefully, taking exercise, thinking about 'strength and focus' at the table? Or maybe it's just Huck.

Hell, he doesn't care about The Cincinnati Kid anyway. 'People have made the connection, but I haven't read it,' says Huck. 'I like books about chess.'

♠

I don't know if Huck Seed wins his $10,000 upside-down bet, but he doesn't win the 1997 World Series. The title goes instead to a screwed-up, debt-riddled drug addict.

It is a miracle. Stuey 'The Kid' Ungar won the World Series in 1980 and 1981 (back to back, just like Johnny Chan), then dissolved into a swamp of cocaine and hookers. In his first victories, he was a beautiful Jewish boy with rock star looks and a blazing poker talent. By 1997 he is broke, skeletal, mashed up with jaundiced skin and a disintegrating nose. His old friend Billy Baxter buys him into the World Series main event – one of 312 runners – and, incredibly, Stuey tears through the field to win it for a third time and collect $1,000,000. This is like a film. The old racehorse, the old athlete, washed up and crippled in early middle age, giving it one last shot and making it first past the post as the fireworks explode in the sky.

By Christmas, Stuey's done his share of the money on drugs and sports betting. A year later, he refuses to let Billy Baxter put him in the 1998 World Series, because he can't bear to show up in his state of collapse. He spends a few months wandering around the card rooms, begging for money from anyone running good. If he gets any, he spends it on crack. In November '98, he's found dead in a cheap motel room, aged 45.

I buy an old picture of Stuey, from the glory days of 1980, and put it on my bedroom wall.

A PAIR OF SIXES

So, with jacks, you are more likely to see an overcard on the flop than not to see one. With nines and below, it's pretty much a certainty. Your opponents might not necessarily have hit these overcards, but your own hand becomes much trickier to play.

The main reason to play small pocket pairs in a cash game is the chance of hitting a set: the economics of cash-game play mean that you can afford to see a lot of flops with the occasional big pay-off in mind.

In tournament poker, you can rarely afford to leave chips behind. You can't just throw a pair away because the flop brings nothing but over-cards. If you've raised pre-flop, you can bet out when anything comes – but, if the flop is unsuitable, you are now bluffing. You may be bluffing with the best hand, but it's still a bluff: pretending you like the flop, or that it's no threat because you started with a huge hand anyway.

Six-handed at a tournament table, a pair of sixes pretty much IS a huge hand. Before the flop, you're certainly entitled to believe that your hand is winning against the other five hands out there, at least until an opponent tries to tell you different.

So, what to do with these two sixes under the gun? It's annoying to be out of position. If I get a caller behind me, I'll have to act first on the flop.

Let's make a small raise, try to make my hand seem bigger than it is. If I'm forced to bet out later on a king-high flop, I don't want to have made this cripplingly expensive for myself.

Blinds still 8,000–16,000; I make it 35,000 to go. Just a little over the minimum. Emad Tahtouh calls in the cut-off, and the others pass.

Flop comes: 9♠ Q♣ Q♥.

Short of seeing an actual six, or some cute little 3 4 5 draw, this is as good a flop as I can hope for. There are only two cards for Emad to have hit – I'm going to assume that he'd have re-raised before the flop if he had a pair himself. The problem is, he could easily have called with something like TJ, KJ, KT, and decide to get busy with a straight draw. A clever little check-raise will keep him in line, if he has that in mind. I check.

Emad bets 50,000.

I make it 200,000.

He calls.

Hmm. I would have preferred him to fold there. His total chip stack is about 900,000 to my 750,000: he could afford to flat call with a straight draw to knock me out on a later street, but he might also flat call with a queen in his hand.

Turn card brings 10♦.

Now I hate it. With KJ, this card makes Emad a straight. With TJ or KT, he's made a bigger pair than sixes. Or he could have had a queen all along, or 9T, or K9, and has had me since the flop.

If I check now, that's giving up the pot without a fight. Aggressive Emad will bet with anything if I show weakness, and I'd have to pass.

If I make a small bet, he'll come over the top for the exact same reason.

If I move all-in, he can't call with only a nine or a ten in his hand. But he can call immediately with a queen, or a straight, so it could be a suicidal move.

I think I have to check and pass.

I check.

Emad moves all-in.

All-in! That's an unexpectedly big move. Now I start to consider calling. If he's got a full house, a straight, or three queens, why does he make such a huge bet to scare me away? I ask him this question out loud. He replies, with seeming frankness, that he's nervous of what I might be holding. I think that's actually true. He looks unsettled and twitchy. He is moving and talking a lot.

So maybe this is a total bluff? It's certainly sized like one. But then . . . bluffing with what? He's got to have SOMETHING. There's no flush draw there for me to beat, and with a straight draw he's probably paired the ten.

Now I'm onto my third thought . . . this all-in move is DESIGNED to look like a bluff. That must be it. He doesn't have a full house, but he knows that I don't either, and he thinks he's winning. Emad's got a straight, or at least three queens, and he's trying to do basic 'reverse psychology': an oversized bet to suggest weakness, hoping to find me with aces or kings and unable to pass them. I mustn't fall for that old trick.

I pass, with a flirtatious little sigh of defeat, intended to seduce him into showing me his hand. That works surprisingly often: if I smile enough, sometimes people feel sorry for me and flash their hole cards as they muck them.

It works! Emad flashes a KQ, saving me a gruesome half hour of wondering whether I missed a chance to double up. I don't really know why he showed the hand — maybe it was in a spirit of friendliness, or maybe a more calculated attempt to set me up for later bluffs — but either way, I'm grateful. Makes it easier to clear my head and concentrate on the next case. If my girly sigh was a factor in flipping the cards over, so much the better.

The following year, Australian Penthouse *(in an article about Joe Hachem and the Aussie poker crew) reports that I wanted to sleep with Emad more than I wanted to win the tournament. Goodness, who would have expected such sexism from an antipodean soft-porn mag? But I make a note to be more careful, in future, about my flirtatious tactical sighing. Sometimes I forget that there are people watching. And some of those people are idiots.*

4

TUESDAY

'Each atom of that stone, each mineral flake of that
night filled mountain, in itself forms a world . . .
One must imagine Sisyphus happy.'
                                        – Albert Camus

We're all talking about Robert's cock. We haven't seen it for ages.

'I miss it,' says James. 'It's been such a long time, I'm starting to forget what Robert's cock looks like.'

It can't be denied: 'There was always something reassuring about looking up after a bad beat and seeing Robert's cock pressed against the window.'

'His large, impressive cock,' says Trouts, dreamily.

'If you want to see it again,' says Robert, 'we'll have to play at my house.'

Quite why Robert should have a large wooden cock in his kitchen window is anybody's guess. But his flat, in a council block off Chalk Farm Road, is full of odd things that he's picked up over the years. Outside is all concrete, graffiti and pissy lift shafts. Inside is a cosy cave of antiquarian books, chess sets, obscure records, china bowls and hand-carved wooden items of no obvious purpose. Robert is a hoarder. If I'm ever trying to offload any unwanted Christmas presents, videos, crockery, random ephemera, he will always carry it away and squirrel it somewhere.

Yes, Robert's wooden cock, his inexplicable decorative cockerel. Not his penis. The other boys are not so comfortable talking about that. They all made retching noises earlier tonight as he told us, again, the story of the Italian waiter who promised Robert, one drunken Christmas Day in a local restaurant, that he would be able to give him an erection. Always open-minded, Robert gave him the opportunity right there at the dinner table. But the waiter was wrong.

'Come on, Robert,' says The Sweep impatiently. 'Imagine it was your turn to act – what would you do?'

It's been Robert's turn to act for about five minutes. He has a short attention span. It may be the drink. Robert plays tennis every Tuesday evening, drinking throughout, then turns up at the game with a beer tin clutched in his hand. He's about 50, probably. A good-looking man with thick silver hair, dressed in a stained old tracksuit as though he sleeps on a park bench. He does sometimes sleep on a park bench. Not because he's home-less, but because he'll sleep anywhere.

'I raise the pot,' says Robert. 'Blind.'

Everybody calls. Turns out Robert, who hadn't yet looked at his cards, has got the nuts. He scrapes in a generous pot.

♠

James is in a bad mood. He's been arguing with Pierre again. James runs a voiceover business and he made the mistake of forming a partnership with French Pierre, one of his 'voices'. This has caused nothing but trouble. James is tense all the time now. When Hugo complains that James's dog is farting under the table, James snaps at him. James loves that dog.

Pierre comes to the game, too. Pierre looks like a Goscinny & Uderzo cartoon. He has a walrus moustache, blazing tattoos and a comedy French accent. You'd think he was gay, if his conversation didn't make it quite so obvious that he isn't.

Pierre takes so long to act, he makes Robert look like the March Hare. But he's one of the stars of the game. He gambles like a lunatic. And J.Q. loves to be shocked by Pierre's tales from the sexual underworld. This week, Pierre is eagerly describing a Parisian fashion for urinating on a piece of bread for one's lover to eat. Pierre doesn't use those words.

♠

James cheers up when he remembers that he's got a new personalized number plate which looks a bit like it says 'poker', if you squint. We congratulate him on faring better than Gary 'The Choirboy' Jones, who bought the number plate P1OKER and showed it off with great pride until someone in the Vic pointed out that it looked like PLONKER.

I try to charm James further by complimenting his new, short haircut. The plan works. James starts humming the theme tune from *The Banana Splits*, and re-raises Hugo the pot.

'It's that fucking haircut,' says Hugo, angrily mucking his cards. 'He thinks he's Jean-Claude Van Damme.'

♠

Trouts, an IT support man who plays in a suit and tie, is doing impressions of Mr Burns from *The Simpsons*. Trouts loves *The Simpsons*. But not as much as he loves *Friends*. Trouts watches an episode of *Friends* every night before going to bed. He has seen them all a hundred times. He watches carefully until the last episode of the last series, then goes back to the beginning again.

Trouts eats meat. Only meat. No vegetables, barely even a potato. He likes a platter of beef, nothing on the side. Hugo, the erstwhile Sweep, worries for the state of Trouts's intestines.

The Sweep's own constitution is delicate. He is always either famished, or feeling sick because he ate too much. He'll say, 'I'm dying of starvation, when's dinner, when's dinner?', then take one bite and groan, 'I'm bloated.' He can't bear to play poker with anyone who has a cold. He thinks that if he sits too close to an open window, he might get polio. At our Christmas game, he always refuses to wear a paper crown because he says it gives him a headache. He thinks he's got a 'sensitive head'. Tonight he is nervous because his Creme Egg has got a hole in it, and The Sweep is afraid – genuinely afraid – that someone at the factory might have made the hole and injected liquid mercury into it.

♠

'I'm losing again,' says James. 'I can't believe Trouts will go home with another cheque of mine in his pocket. That's terrible.'

'It is terrible,' agrees Trouts. 'You must start bringing cash.'

♠

Dinner's ready. Pasta for everyone, but a defrosted meat pie for Trouts. I bring in the plates. Conrad says thank you; the others remain silent. I carry the plates out again immediately. They jump up and rush into the kitchen with compliments. They remember the time I was so irritated by the lack of thanks, I scraped everybody's dinner into the bin. They had to order a pizza.

But Conrad always says thank you. Conrad is awfully polite, very pukka. I think he might be related to an earl. He is easy-going and smiley, possessed of a genuinely optimistic temperament. God knows what he's doing playing poker. Must have taken a wrong turn one day. He runs a charity tournament every Christmas, to raise money for a cancer hospital. He's the nicest guy that ever comes here.

♠

Joe is teaching us a new variant. 'It's seven stud hi-lo, pairs wild for the low, leaners for the high, wheel's the low.'

The Sweep gets excited. 'We needed a new variant.'

It's the last thing we needed. As if split pots, multiple flops, wild cards and draws weren't enough, J.Q. has been keeping busy inventing new variants entirely; for weeks, we have been trying to get our heads around 'Middles For Diddles' and 'Poker Baccarat'. I'd like to see Huck Seed apply his Game Theory to those.

Joe cleans up, wins the lot. Who allowed a professional into this game?

♠

Ashley's a professional too, different sort of professional. He grinds it out, night after night in the Vic. Except Tuesdays, when he comes here. He plays online at home all day. I try to make a home-cooked meal every week, because Ashley is one of the people I worry would never get one otherwise.

Ashley always has a story to tell about someone in the Vic who annoyed him. Most people annoy him. He is a fiftysomething teenager. He wears a leather jacket and plays online under 'Iconoclast'. He's sarcastic, cynical and funny. He and The Sweep get along very well. They talk a lot about music. Ashley's off the drugs these days, but he needs a cup of coffee every twenty minutes.

♠

'My deal,' says James. 'How about regular seven stud, but if you manage to burp as you receive your up card, it's wild?'

'Banned,' I say. 'It's on the list with baseball, fiery cross and burning ring. No burping wild cards.'

'Oh,' says Robert, disappointed. 'I was just gearing one up.'

But he's soon distracted by a race with Kira to see whose Jaffa Cake can melt faster.

♠

Robert's asleep. J.Q. insists that we deal him in anyway, as he might wake up at any moment and want to bet the pot blind.

Val is watching sadly as Ashley felts Warren with two pair. Warren buys another stack of chips.

'I would have flopped a straight,' murmurs Val.

'All right,' says Hugo. 'No need to tell us your life story.'

Val is a journalist, a reporter of the old school. He is dressed like James Stewart playing a journalist in a film. Proper shirt, knitted tie, brown waistcoat and jacket. But his trousers are taped at the bottom, for safety on his bicycle ride home. He is nearly as patrician as Conrad, and hasn't belched or sworn in ten years at this game. But he always laughs at the others.

Val is feeling a little down because he has just published a book about his allotment, called *One Man And His Dig*, and The Sweep has told him it should have been called *Sunday Muddy Sunday*. His spirits are further lowered by spending three hours building up an impressive stack over a series of strategic Omaha coups, then blowing the lot in a single, terrible hand of Shifting Sands.

♠

J.Q. hasn't said much tonight. That's because he is trying to think of knock-knock jokes based on the choruses of popular songs. Last week, The Sweep turned up with

Knock knock.
Who's there?
Warrior.
Warrior who?
Warrior wanna make those eyes at me for . . .

And he sang the punchline. Ever since then, J.Q. has been obsessed with creating the longest possible sung punchline to a knock-knock joke. He is currently working on *Matchstick Men And Matchstick Cats And Dogs.*

He's got as far as
. *Knock knock.*
Who's there?
Andy, Payne, Ted, Matt, Chip, May, Nan, Matt, Chip, Cass, Anne . . .

But he's not happy with it. He thinks 'Chip' isn't quite right.

He's too stubborn to use the obvious Polish name Maçek. He thinks
that would be cheating. And Val is insisting that it's not 'matchstick'
in the song anyway, it's 'matchstalk'. This is very problematic.

♠

It is last week, this week, next week. It is at Robert's place, in
James's office, at The Sweep's temporary home in Waterloo, at my
flat, in all the future flats and houses we might inhabit. Within a
year of my first visit, whatever else happens on Tuesday nights
– birthdays, book launches, first nights, fire sales – the game is
where I am. Always Tuesdays, in tribute to the old Alvarez/
Holden/Spanier school of the 1980s.

Some of these players drop out of the game, some of them
are yet to come. They will get married, get divorced, get drunk,
have babies, end up in court over inadvisable business partner-
ships. James's dog, Skala, is going to die.

Well – we're all going to die.

But, until death comes, any of them could be back at any time.
They appear and disappear again, as Feste dips in and out of Illyria.

Still, the game goes on, always the same. Even the money's the
same, passed round and round and round the same group of people
from week to week and year to year. Same arguments, same jokes.
I call . . . was a very good horse. I call . . . was a very good horse.

KING QUEEN SUITED

This is a big hand, even at a full table. In their classic textbook Hold'em
Poker For Advanced Players, *Malmuth and Sklansky classify it as a
'Group Two' hand. Group One hands are AA, KK, QQ, JJ and AK
suited. Group Two hands are TT, AQ suited, AJ suited, KQ suited and
AK offsuit. All other hands are Group Three or lower. These lists are in*

rough order of where each hand falls in the group, too – it's worth noting that AK unsuited (so beloved of the aggressive modern player, who is too quick to shovel all his chips in with that hand before seeing a flop) has been calculated as statistically less lucrative than lower picture cards of the same suit. Malmuth and Sklansky are talking mainly about limit cash games – but limit or no limit, tournament or cash game, KQ suited is a big hand.

Chad Brown raises it up to 38,000, and everyone passes round to my big blind. I find K♣ Q♣.

He's an interesting character, this Chad Brown. He's an actor from the Bronx, who has had a few roles in TV shows and films including Basket Case 2. *I have actually seen that movie. Years ago, in my teens, I was a devoted horror fan. At least one night a week, my friend Jess and I would curl up on the sofa with a packet of Revels and a VHS in which teenagers with more sexual experience than us would take it in turns to be slashed, chopped, hanged, beheaded and otherwise despatched in grisly ways until one of them (usually the virgin) walked into the sunlight at the end of the film, usually on the arm of a friendly vicar (unless the friendly vicar had turned out to be one of the vampires/werewolves/slashers etc). For some reason, some time in my twenties, I completely lost the ability to watch horror films. Like rollercoasters; I lost my stomach for those, too.*

But I still remember a few favourites. Aerobicide: Working Out Can Be Murder *(in which the victims were killed off using various different items of gym equipment) was very much a classic of its time.* Rawhead Rex *was beautifully scary until you actually saw the monster in question, which was patently made out of Blu-Tack and safety pins. Then there was* Basket Case, *the motto on the box of which was 'Tisket tasket, what's in the wicker basket?' I don't remember what was in the wicker basket, but it was something pretty gruesome. And the motto of* Basket Case 2 *was, if I remember rightly, 'Don't you dare snicker at the thing in the wicker!', which sounded a little defensive, as if the producers had lost the courage of their convictions by the time they made the sequel.*

Anyway, Chad Brown is mostly known in America now as the

presenter of Ultimate Poker Challenge. *So he's a bit like me, maybe – working a lot in televised poker, presenting or commentating or interviewing the professionals, quite keen to prove that he's a proper player, too. Except he's got less to prove than me, since he's had quite a few cashes in the World Series of Poker and other circuit events, and he's been playing seriously since 1993. He's dating Vanessa Rousso, a professional player from Canada. The organizers of the EPT will be delighted that he's bringing some star quality to this final.*

Chad's been a bit quiet at this table lately. He came in as chip leader with 759,000, but he's lost a few chips since then and has been on the back foot. Ordinarily, I might re-raise with KQ of clubs, but I'm aware that Chad hasn't raised for ages and might have a big hand. Or he might feel obliged to show strength, whatever he is holding. I don't want him to get stubborn and four-bet all in. I have got a big draw, and would really like to see the flop. So I just call.

The flop comes 8♣ 10♣ A♥. There's a middle pin straight draw for me; if I were in position, I could bluff-raise with that, but it's silly to bet out first when Chad is supposed to raise me whether he's got an ace or not.

I check. Chad, surprisingly, checks behind. So he either hates the ace (maybe he's got some kind of pair like JJ or 99?), or loves this flop so much (AK? AT? A set, even?) that he's scared to lose me.

The turn comes Q♦. Well, now I don't need to bet. If Chad has a better hand than a pair of queens, he will certainly call; and if he's got a worse hand, he won't. I'm better off checking and calling, give him a chance to bluff it.

I check again, and so, obligingly, does Chad. Now I know he doesn't have two pair or a set, because only a basket case would check that twice.

The river is 9♣, and I check for the same reason I checked the turn. Now Chad bets 35,000. This seems a little curious. I guess he could have hit the nine, or he could just figure that I've shown weakness throughout the pot and be trying to pick it up on the end with nothing much. I'm only being asked to call 35,000 to win a pot already containing

119,000 — more than three-to-one my money, and it's a lot shorter than 3/1 that Chad's bluffing. I don't even need to think before calling.

Oh! He's got A♦ 5♦. That's unexpected. I wonder why he didn't bet the flop or the turn? I'm now especially glad I didn't bet the turn myself, because I would have lost more money. But I doubt that Chad would have called a big re-raise before the flop with A5, so hindsight tells me a more aggressive play was in order. The flat call . . . as that strange man from the bridge club used to say whenever someone lost a trick after playing a finesse the wrong way round: 'Not best.'

5

LATE NIGHT POKER

'Television brought the brutality of war into the comfort of the living room.'
— Marshall McLuhan

My father says it is a red herring to call the Miss World contest sexist. Last year, the 1998 competition was on terrestrial TV – it had been shunted off onto cable for years – and there was a lot of fuss about it. People said it was wrong to encourage men to sit there drooling over girls in swimsuits.

'They aren't drooling,' my father says.

He thinks that nobody is looking at the women's bodies with lust, or even much interest. His theory is that people just love watching competitions. They want to see winners cheer and losers cry. Or, in the case of Miss World, winners cry and losers cheer insincerely. He thinks viewers enjoy rooting for their home countries against others, regardless of what they're doing. We will get excited about curious Olympic sports we've never heard of, if Britain starts doing well at them. In the same spirit, my dad reckons, we are far more interested in the results of Miss World than the parading.

But my father is a very innocent fellow. He is gentlemanly towards women and he never underestimates them. He likes to hold doors open and stand up when women enter the room, but he admires their brains, enjoys their conversation and employed dozens of them as writers when he edited a magazine. He is proud that his wife is beautiful but prouder that she is a doctor. He doesn't leer at dolly-birds in swimsuits, so he doesn't believe that anyone else does either. He thinks the popularity of the show must have a different explanation.

I am not entirely sure that he is right about Miss World, but he is definitely right about *Late Night Poker*.

More than half a million people are tuning in to this cultish new programme, broadcast after midnight on Channel 4, and there is no way that more than half a million people in this country understand what they are looking at. Go into the Stakis or the Vic, or anywhere that poker is actually played, and you'll never see more than fifty people. The same fifty people.

Presentable Productions, the first company ever to try putting serious poker on television, have made it as easy to follow as possible. It is a competition rather than a cash game, to satisfy that desire to see a sole winner and a lot of losers. The betting is No Limit, so nobody has to bother calculating the pot size. The variant is Texas Holdem, which means the players only get two cards each. And there is a Perspex strip round the table, so these secret cards are visible to the players at home. When a devious maestro trap-checks his aces so the poor innocent fool with the jacks comes out betting, viewers can watch the whole foul plot unfold.

But this is not commissioned as a game show or a sports show, so much as a window on shady underworld life. That's why it is on at half past midnight: 98% of viewers don't understand the rules. They just stare at it, drunk, transfixed by the money and the cheery quips of Barny Boatman, the villainous leer of Koresh, the sheer bulk of Dave Welch.

♠

Poker on television! Week after week, for a whole series! The Chimney Sweep is so excited, he can't eat. He has always phoned me up if there is a glimpse of poker in the background of *Roseanne* or *EastEnders* (or, on one odd occasion, *Star Trek*) and these are shows where they play five-card draw, have stupidly unlikely hands and usually get the rules wrong. Even *The Cincinnati Kid*, which has a beautiful authentic spirit, has a preposterous final showdown.

This is real poker. Marginal hands against marginal hands. Real money: each player puts up £1,500, which is divvied up again as prizes. Nobody from the Tuesday game leaves his house when this is on. I curl up on my sofa each week, mesmerized, often with The Sweep at the other end of the phone, often without either of us speaking.

The average perplexed, intrigued, tipsy midnight viewer certainly won't have appreciated what's so funny about The Sweep's favourite episode – the one featuring Mickey Dane. The man at the table, using that name, is in fact the obscure American novelist Jesse May. Mickey Dane is the hero of his poker novel, *Shut Up And Deal*. Why use the pseudonym to play? Because Jesse May is also the series commentator. There is no mention of that in the programme at all. When 'Mickey Dane' raises with a losing hand, Jesse May says, 'What is that guy thinking? Maybe his hat's too tight.'

I would never have known what was going on, but The Sweep hung out with Jesse May in Vegas last year and recognized him immediately. The word in the Vic is that a decision to add commentary was only made after the tournament was finished, and there were no 'professional poker commentators' to hire so they asked Jesse May because he was the funniest player. When he got to his own match, he just renamed himself and pretended it was somebody else.

Meanwhile, I can follow the action but I'm baffled by the cards they play. Like T.S. Eliot on Margate Sands, I can connect nothing with nothing. I have played very little Texas Holdem myself. I'm playing hi-lo tournaments at the Stakis, seven-stud cash games (£25 buy-in, deal yourself) at the Vic and anything goes on Tuesdays.

Many Vic players have turned down invitations to *Late Night Poker* – Donnacha O'Dea, for example, the former Olympic swimmer, who thinks that poker on television will give too much away about the players' styles, make it too easy for novices to improve at the game. Novices like me. He needn't worry: I'm amused and impressed to see these guys raising with nothing, but I'd never dare do it.

Others are steering clear because they don't want to 'go public'. Poker is a shifty game played by shifty characters. Outside the two official card rooms in London, most games take place in illegal spielers with heavy rake money. Debts and revenges are rife, names are changed, multiple passports are not unheard of. The majority of regular players have no interest in advertising their lifestyle, their whereabouts or even their existence to tax inspectors, thieves, neighbours, creditors or old enemies. Television? You'd have to be a complete ice cream.

♠

There is very little bad behaviour in the Vic. There is a lot of complaining and ill-temper, the odd £5 chip scraped out of a pot by sleight of hand in the deal-yourself game, but that's it. Any genuinely threatening language would get you barred. And the playing of the game is bound by rules, specifically English rules, of careful etiquette. 'The moody rule' forbids any conversation about the hand while it is in play. No discussing the cards you may or may not hold. No showing cards until the action is finished. No encouraging an opponent to call or fold. No thinking for a long time before raising; that is definitely moody. No pulling faces of anguish if you have the nuts.

The rules are strangely *polite*. They are also baffling for any American player who happens to drop in. Americans think that 'anything goes', that showing one misleading card or acting up or making tricky statements about a holding are 'all part of the game'. Not here. We have these guidelines in place to keep it sporting.

I love it. The very essence of this game is trickery and deceit, yet the rules forbid particular kinds of trickery and deceit. This is a smoky, late-night, restricted-entry gambling cave, yet we adhere to a strict code of conduct as if it were the playing fields of Eton. There are people here who have done, or do, or would do, truly terrible things in the outside world; in here, they are horrified and shocked if a man says 'I don't think I'm ahead' and then tries to raise. Every instinct must be reined in, reined in, reined in. We are demonstrably here to take each other's money and we all know it, but we must not behave like it. The principles are as contradictory, quirky and illogical as the English language itself.

♠

So now I get to discover a little more about some of the Vic gaggle and what they do. According to the TV commentary, they are jewellers, businessmen, travelling salesmen. I am now brave enough to make smalltalk with the familiar faces in the card room, but I never ask about their jobs. It isn't considered polite, somehow. Conversation at the table is almost always about poker, gossip about who's winning and losing, debate about how particular hands have been played. Some jokes – topical stuff. Lots of talk about sport. And lots and *lots* of complaining: the food, the temperature, the dealers, the chairs, the state of the lists, the quality of the game. If there is ever an awkward silence (which there never is, and that's why I love it), you could just say, 'This sandwich is a bit stale,' or 'The air conditioning is faulty,' and everyone will join in eagerly for hours. But they don't seem to talk about their working lives, their private lives, their home lives.

I think they avoid these areas because knowing what the money means to somebody, how they earn it and why they need it can make you feel bad about taking it off them. Like Alice in

Wonderland saying that when she has been formally introduced to a pudding, she feels rude eating it.

Or maybe it's a London thing. Keep it impersonal, at arm's length.

♠

The first series of *Late Night Poker* is such a surprising success that another is commissioned the very same year. This time, they are desperate to slot more female faces into the 42-player line-up. They manage to get six. There are three poker wives (Tina Jordan, Somkhuan Harwood and Debbie Welch, whose husbands appear on the series alongside them), and two other ladies called Vanessa Rogers and Andrea 'Babydoll' Sterling.

And me.

Obviously I accept the invitation. They must have got my name from asking around at the Vic. I am excited less by the tournament, which I have no idea how to play, than by the chance to get to know these other players properly.

But I'm not paying the £1,500. It's an insane amount of money. I wouldn't pay £1,500 to enter a poker tournament and I wouldn't pay £500 – I've never paid more than £50. So I persuade the *Sunday Times* to take an article about the experience, in return for the buy-in money. I tell them it will be a great story if I win it, and I have every chance.

I am lying.

♠

Arriving nervously at the studio, I immediately recognize a handful of Vic players I've never spoken to. One of them I remember in particular, because I've been told a story about the time he fell out with someone during a poker game in Amsterdam. After a nasty series of accusations, the riled opponent followed him back to his hotel and shot him in the nuts.

He turns out to be very friendly, striding over to shake hands and say hello. He has only a slight limp. He's a lot more relaxed than I am – which is to his credit, because I've never been shot in the groin by an angry Dutchman.

These people, who seem so unapproachable in the Vic, are much more open here. It must be the adventure and adrenaline of being on TV. Each player is only required to show up for a single heat (and potentially the final) but most of them are here all week to watch the other games and lark about. They are simultaneously excited and nervous about the cameras. Their faces turn ashen when they're asked to go into make-up. For the poor make-up lady, it's like trying to give 42 cats a bath. They literally run away and hide.

♠

I am lurking in the corner of the studio with a list of the other players in my heat, trying to work out which is which.

1) Bambos Xanthos

He must be a Greek Cypriot. Half the Vic players seem to be. You often see two or three players gabbling away to each other in Greek, to which a passing cockney usually mutters, 'Easy for you to say . . .'

2) Jan Lundberg

I know which one he is because he strolled over to introduce himself, looking like a friendly walrus. But walruses can be dangerous if you get too close, and I suspect the same may apply to Jan.

3) John Kabbaj

So that's his name! I've seen this guy often in the Omaha game at the Vic – a bigger game than I'd ever play in – and people refer to him as 'Cabbage'. I get the joke now. Sophisticated. In the absence of any further information, I assume that he's the best player at the table. He's unlikely to get in a pickle.

4) 'Big' Badar Islam

An even simpler nickname; he must be that guy over there, who can barely fit himself onto the sofa. But he looks rather impressive, in his flowing robes.

5) Peter 'The Bandit' Evans

I ask Rhiannon, a reassuring lady who works for the production company, and she points to a fellow whose face is almost entirely obscured by a baseball cap. He's been drinking all afternoon. He seems like too much of an old-timer to have any tells, so I wonder if the low-brimmed hat is intended to hide his bloodshot eyes from the cameras.

6) Howard Plant

That's the chap from Blackpool I met last night. I like him. He's extremely friendly and very flirtatious, but I think he's just teasing. He wears a Hawaiian shirt and makes terrible jokes. He reminds me faintly of Ted Bovis from *Hi-de-Hi!*. He told me that he booked two rooms at his hotel: he sleeps in one, and the other is the venue for a secret round-the-clock cash game, staffed by two dealers Howard brought with him from Blackpool. There are 42 enthusiastic poker players in town, why waste it? Howard invited me to play. I went along and watched for a while. But I didn't play, not with my tiny bankroll and a heat to worry about in the morning. I just watched the money change hands, and laughed at the furtive way they tried to disguise what was happening when a waiter came up with room service. Then they tipped him £50, just in case.

♠

Jesse May, now firmly installed as commentator and not playing, is running a book and offering me at 10/1 to win the heat. I'm deeply offended, and tell him so. I should be 66/1.

'Don't worry,' drawls Jesse, pocketing another wad of money bet on Cabbage, 'you'll go right out by post time.'

I am awestruck by Jesse May. He's such a Damon Runyon character: a handsome, giggly, gambling-crazy New Yorker in ridiculous shoes. I am also a little shy because *Shut Up And Deal* is one of the greatest things I've ever read. It's so intense, so enthusiastic and bitter and real. In person, he crackles with love of poker and excitement about the forthcoming games, but I know from the book that there are no stars in his eyes. This is an honest, unconditional love.

He writes, 'People always want to know what's going on, and what's going on is people are going broke. There are no guys and there is no peer group, just a bunch of desperate lonely souls trying to make a few bucks for themselves by fucking over others.'

I have ventured out of the Tuesday game and into the card rooms just enough to get a sense of what he means. I also know that my own game is flawed by the weakness of compassion. If somebody comes into the card room drunk, or loses a big pot and goes on tilt, I can see my opponents' eyes light up. I see them offering to buy more drinks, or talking about the fatal hand to keep it in the atmosphere. But if I see a player sliding helplessly down the greasy ladder of uncontrolled loss, I don't really want to win his money. The situation is supposed to spell opportunity, but it just makes me sad.

The other commentator, Nic Szeremeta, editor of *Poker Europa* magazine and one of the *Late Night Poker* founders, gives me some kindly advice about tournaments. He tells me to play tight at the beginning, and start gambling or getting aggressive later on. I smile and make a note, knowing perfectly well that I'll be playing tight from start to finish. I've never done anything else. But I appreciate Nic's advice and I'll try, I'll try.

Nic also points out that I don't have a nickname and I need one. He suggests 'Sticky Vicky', on the grounds that he once knew a Thai stripper with that name. I decided to soldier on without.

♠

I play pretty horrible in my heat. I'm super-tight anyway, and the whole situation is so terrifying that I feel sick whenever I consider playing a hand. I can't think about entering a pot with anything less than a pair of nines or I might actually throw up on the table. So, helpfully confirming every prejudice the guys have about female players, ignoring the advice they all gallantly gave me before the match, I allow myself to get quietly blinded down – taking an absurd and pointless pleasure in not being the first one out, after Cabbage gets boiled within half an hour.

Part of me knows it is a classic novice's mistake, being glad not to go out first. Who cares? The winner of this heat will go through to the final, the runner-up will go to the semi-final; every other place is meaningless. Of course it's better to go down in a blaze of glory than pass your way to an ignoble third or fourth. But my fingers are frozen, I'm like Eric Bristow with dartitis. I just cannot move my chips without a huge hand. I'm soon down to only five £50 chips, and I'm desperate to avoid putting them in the pot.

Two hundred and fifty quid! It's half my mortgage payment for the month! But here, it means I'm nearly skint.

You can't cash in your chips during a tournament. It's a knockout. In cash poker, you can get up and walk away whenever you want. In a tournament, you must remain at the table until you have every chip in the room, or none of them.

When I am obliged to put in nearly half of my precious remaining chips on the big blind, and look down to find 10♥ J♥, I sit worrying about what to do if anybody raises. I know I am not supposed to pass. But I have no ace and no pair! Thank God, I get a walk. Thanks only to this particular line-up of players overestimating my ability to grasp pot odds, and therefore failing to raise my big blind, there is no footage out there of me passing 10♥ J♥ with half of my entire stack in the pot already. Because I would've done.

And then – what do you know! – I find aces. Well, hello, little fellers. What a beautiful, calming sight. This is the premium starting hand in Texas Holdem, and your odds against finding it are 220/1. That means, in a Holdem tournament, I am always 220/1 to find a hand I am actually happy to play. So I am suffused with relief to see them: my twin saviours have finally arrived. I stick it all in and get called by Bambos with Q♣ 9♣.

Bang, bang, bang, three clubs come down on the flop, and that's the end of my first experience with televised poker.

♠

Deep down, I know I must blame myself for getting so low on chips that Bambos was happy to call and gamble with his hand. But I still complain about the 'bad beat'.

I am comforted in the kitchen of the TV studio by Jonas, a Slovenian talk-show host who's playing tomorrow. He is wearing a vicar's outfit.

'I have bad boy image in Slovenia,' he tells me. 'I play cards, ride Harley and have lots of women.'

So the vicar's outfit is presumably a joke about his reputation. It would be perfect, if only the show were going out in Slovenia. I suspect a UK audience is going to be puzzled. Then again, this programme goes out at midnight and the viewers are all drunk. Half of them are sitting in their underpants, wondering what happened to the ice hockey. They might not even notice.

Jonas tells me about PlanetPoker.com. It is a website launched by Mad Mike Caro, which offers people the opportunity to play poker on the internet.

It won't catch on, Jonas explains. Poker is all about face-to-face interaction. Banter, cash moving back and forth, handling chips and cards, the narrowed stares and the reading of body language. Mike Caro of all people, author of the famous *Book Of Tells*, should know that. It can't work as a computer game. Besides, very few people would ever be prepared to type their credit card details into the internet. What are they, straight off the onion boat? Poker players deal in cash, and suspicion.

But where the internet can be useful, Jonas advises, is to discuss the game with other players around the world. You can already do this on 'forums', and Jonas visits these regularly on his home computer in Slovenia to argue hands through with his peers.

'But you don't want everyone to know how you play,' he tells me. 'I, personally, choose to pose as an Albanian.'

♠

By Sunday, Cardiff is getting hot. The local Stakis casino has never seen such big action, Howard's secret cash game is thriving, the £1,500 tournament buy-in is starting to look like loose change for the Coke machine. Players who have been knocked out are hanging around to soak up the fun of the TV cameras, funk for their friends and play extra poker on the side.

Stepping into the hotel lift, en route to the studio for the morning match, I see it is already occupied by an elderly couple and a tall, faintly sinister man in a long black leather coat and rose-tinted sunglasses. He winks at me.

I recognize that wink. It was played in slow motion over the closing credits of the first *Late Night Poker* series. It was the wink of the winner – a man who, I discovered from the white letters on the screen under his name, was a professional jeweller. From the gossip this week, I now know that he is not a jeweller, he just bought a pawnbroker's shop after leaving prison. I have learned that this notorious character started from a rough background in Hull, spent a few years as a criminal, did his jail time, was 'a star' (i.e. a regular loser) in cash poker games around the UK but is now reborn as a tournament hero. He calls himself a jeweller on TV because it doesn't sound very respectable to say he plays poker all the time.

But what's to be ashamed of? He has not only won *Late Night Poker*, he has won a bracelet at the World Series of Poker.

'You're the Devilfish,' I stammer.

'Yes I am,' says the Devilfish.

The elderly couple must think we're both insane.

We share a cab to the studio and Dave 'Devilfish' Ulliott lets me hold his WSOP bracelet. It is a heavy, chunky, golden circlet of triumph. In return, I spend the evening making him cups of tea. The Devilfish tells me about the terrible occasion when he once had to make his own tea.

'I rang my wife to ask where I'd find the spoons. She said they'd be in the dishwasher. I said, "What fucking dishwasher?"'

But that's fine with me. There is a time and a place for feminist statements, and midnight in the kitchen of a television studio with a poker champion is neither.

♠

I can't bear the week to end. I have been so desperate to know these people better, and now I do. I've had seven days of total immersion: watching poker, discussing poker, even briefly playing poker, with the best in Britain. I love the way the games end in the studio and everybody moves to the Stakis casino until it closes, and then to Howard's private cash game until the morning, and then back to the studio. I love eating room service hamburgers at 3 a.m. I love the salty talk and stupid nicknames.

The players don't feel like strangers any more. I know who they remind me of. They remind me of the lost family, the cousins I used to see at weddings or funerals, and the ones I never met: Fat Sam and Ginger Phil, violent Great-Grandpa Dave, Dunkirk Uncle Sid.

When the waiter arrived at Howard's door with room service and they all hurried to hide the money, it was just like Grandpa Sam when my parents got home.

♠

Back in London, I finally find the courage to start going to the Vic on my own, whether The Sweep and Mrs Sweep are there or not. I start greeting players by their actual names and they seem to know mine. Like spiders in the bath, maybe they were as nervous of me as I was of them? Not of my poker skills, obviously. But I must have looked unusual.

I get to know Mr Chu, the ancient Chinese man with one very long fingernail. There's Terry, the meticulous Bulgarian who is always asking questions like 'What means this . . . *pie in the sky?*' There's Michael Arnold, the grand duke of the card room, who snoozes through every hand like another dormouse at another Mad Hatter's tea party.

Mr Arnold wakes up occasionally to grab his cards, shout 'Pot!' and go back to sleep again. If he is neither snoozing nor raising, he likes to beckon people over, imperiously, for a chat. When I line up to pay court, I am six years old again, going to visit Great-Grandpa Harry, Sam's father, at his house in Lordship Lane in the wilds of North London. Harry expected to be visited by the family on weekends. He was a big fat fellow who didn't get up out of his chair; we walked over to kiss his whiskery old cheek, then sat quietly while the elders talked about fish prices and old times.

I don't kiss Mr Arnold's whiskery old cheek. But I go to shake his hand, when he peeks sleepily over the lid of his teapot.

Then there's Scottish Pedro, who always carries a selection of miniature fans and bottles of essential oils. He is a giggly, affectionate little fellow. He's always trying to diagnose me with something – anaemia, a cold – and dispensing immediate herbal remedies. Sometimes, Pedro gets himself some fish and chips on the way to the Vic, wraps them tightly in paper and hides them in the bushes outside. That way, when the casino's closing and all the takeaways are shut, he knows he can still collect a tasty supper to take home.

I might look at that bunch and think that they are all a little peculiar, but God alone knows what they must think of me.

I'm a woman. I'm an unmarried woman, who seems happy to go out and play cards on her own without a care for the important job of husband-seeking. I have no children. And I've got a posh voice. Professor Higgins might spot the tell-tale North London twang, but compared to most of the Vic regulars I speak like Princess Margaret.

Mr Chu might have one inexplicably long fingernail, Terry might mangle the language to a bizarre degree, Mr Arnold might snore and Pedro might wave Oil Of Midnight Snowdrop at anyone who comes near him, but – to them – I am probably the weirdest person in there.

ACE KING

If you are a newcomer to poker, let me give you some advice: AK is a very big hand. It's even-money to beat almost any pair, and a good favourite against every other hand. You must play it strongly.

If you have been playing poker for a couple of years, contesting a lot of tournaments, watching the game on television, wondering whether to start calling yourself 'a professional', let me give you some advice: AK is not that big a hand. It's no pair! Stop moving all-in as soon as you see it! Play it with some finesse, for heaven's sake!

I'm down to about 500,000 in chips when I find A♦ K♠ on the button. Everyone passes round to Jules Kuusik, the shaven-haired Swedish pro in the cut-off. He makes it 45,000 to go from a stack of about 250,000. What to do? I could flat call, encouraging Kuusik to move in on the flop. But there are two problems with this move. One is that I would be allowing the blinds to enter the pot with random hands; I don't want to give Emad Tahtouh (in the big blind) any excuse to get clever on me. The other is that I might miss the flop, and feel reluctant to put in 200,000 more with no pair.

I have no idea what Kuusik is holding, but he can't knock me out because he has fewer chips. I'm happy to let my hand play against his over five cards, at a total cost of 250,000. But if I miss the flop and he bets again, when I only have two cards to come and my odds against a pair are drastically reduced, 200,000 might feel too expensive.

I'd rather put the whole 250,000 in now. No need to raise any more than that: betting Kuusik's total stack will signal to the blinds that I am attempting to knock him out by myself. They oughtn't then to get involved without a really big hand, so there's no point betting all my chips when one of them might actually have aces or kings.

I make it 250,000 to go. The blinds pass, and so does Kuusik. There are cheers from the crowd at this display of 'power poker'. God bless them, my fellow Vic players, who have gathered in the seats around the TV table and are rooting for me to do well. They know that any money I win at this event will stay in the room. But they are also genuinely behind the local player, and some of them are good friends of mine. Seeing their familiar faces, and hearing them make an encouraging noise, helps me to be brave.

Of course, in this case I had a real hand. They can't see the cards. They are cheering the strong play, and the possibility that Kuusik was stealing from the cut-off (which he must have been, to put in a fifth of his stack before passing) and that I was re-stealing from the button. Actually, I wasn't. Maybe it would have been better to play my hand slower, and invite Kuusik to knock himself out?

6

CELEBRITY LATE NIGHT POKER

There's a shotgun in the drawer.

♠

I riffle £1,000 through my fingers. Martin Amis clears his throat. Click-clack-click go the shiny £50 discs. I select a few hundreds' worth and chuck them across the table. There is a pause. 'Call,' says Stephen Fry. And I must, surely, be asleep.

♠

It's July 2000 and I'm playing a lot of poker by now. I'm starting to get my head round Holdem tournaments, though I still don't know how to bet with no hand. But I'm in the Vic or the Stakis a couple of nights a week, the Tuesday game has moved to my flat, and I've got a new occasional Friday night school with a bunch of journalists including my great friend John Diamond.

John has cancer. The diagnosis has encouraged him to embrace hedonism: he's bought a motorbike, figured out how to inject champagne directly into his stomach, and had a royal diamond flush tattooed on his arm. John is young, in his mid-forties, with a wife and two small children that he adores. You'd think a terminal illness would cast an air of tragedy over him. In fact, he brings an air of life-affirming joy to every party he graces. And he's gracing a lot of parties. He has also unveiled an impressively sick love of gambling; not just poker, but generous helpings of casino blackjack on the side.

He is both a good and bad influence. I've been adapting his

newspaper columns into a play to take to the Edinburgh Fringe Festival. I'm so obsessed with it, I spent Millennium Night at my desk and failed to notice the new century until it was several hours old. John is an inspiring person to know.

On the other hand, I am close enough to the line between 'recreational gambling' and 'compulsive disorder' to be better off without a friend who loves blackjack and knows he's going to die. It is not a combination that spells caution.

Thank God, my old roulette habit has been channelled into poker, which offers the same adrenaline but can, slowly and gradually if I study the game, be controlled by skill and judgment. Poker still offers the masochist a tantalizing promise of tearing his or her money away at the whim of ill fortune, but there is a deeper pleasure in the opportunity to force chance under control: a good player will lose the minimum when fate puts on the black cap, win the maximum when it's exchanged for an Easter bonnet. There is detective work, calculation, psychology. I have dismissed roulette as a mug's game.

But there will always be an element of muggery in my soul. John and I have been meeting up in the afternoons to play blackjack for stakes I just can't afford, especially if I'm going to devote this year to working in fringe theatre. The only reassurance is that I have managed to stay off roulette. Plan A was to avoid all table games, but I have decided that I'm allowed to have a spin on the blackjack as long as John keeps employing that evil twinkle and telling me it's his last wish.

On Fridays, I've been organizing a semi-regular home poker game for mutual friends, all hacks with a natural attraction to louche hobbies. Most of them are new to the game. Roger, my editor at the *Observer*, has particular trouble grasping the principle of bluffing. He keeps flat calling on the river, then chuckling 'I've got nothing at all!'

They all love poker but they turn up mainly for the opportunity to spend time with John, and because his wife Nigella, a beautiful journalist who has launched a new career as a cookery writer, occasionally sends him along with a home-made cake. Nigella comes to the Stakis blackjack sessions sometimes, which improves our edge because the goggling male croupiers are liable to pay us out by mistake. When the Dark Marilyn takes her seat, they start dropping cards on the floor and forgetting how to count. The boys are very disappointed that she doesn't come to the poker game, but they settle happily enough for the cake.

♠

Finding myself opposite Martin Amis at a surreal celebrity poker table, I'm wondering whether my brain has been affected by all this social gambling, enough to make me dream about it. Where else but in a dream would I find myself sitting around an over-sized baize oval in the middle of Wales with the author of *The Rachel Papers*? To my left sit Stephen Fry and the now celebrated playwright Patrick Marber. To my right are the comedian Ricky Gervais, the jetlagged royal biographer Anthony Holden, Amis the child prodigy turned fully-fledged Brit Lit star; and my hero, the pipe-chewing poet, critic and mountaineer Al Alvarez.

It is not a dream, it's a miracle. I have been trying to save up £1,500 of my own money to buy into the new *Late Night Poker* series, but it's like running up a down escalator. I win small sums at poker, lose bigger sums at blackjack. At the last minute, just when I was giving up on the hope of experiencing that magical week again, I was invited to play in a one-off 'celebrity curtain-raiser', with Channel 4 putting up £1,000 per player.

By July 2000, the series is widely known. I have only appeared in that one match, losing to Bambos with aces, yet already a policeman, ticking me off for a piece of illegal parking in Camden Town, has winked, 'I suppose you'll pay the fine with poker winnings . . .'

That does not make me a celebrity. But poker, although it is

now popular viewing on TV, remains an unusual hobby. Many
people are watching, nobody is actually playing. Asked to come
up with a celebrity special, the production company had trouble
finding seven people who write, or do the odd bit of television,
and know the rules of the game. They weren't expecting to get
Madonna.

Al Alvarez and Anthony Holden can travel by bus without
undue attention, too, but they've both written poker books. They
are old cronies (Holden's *Big Deal* is dedicated to Al) and I know
they are danger at the table.

Ricky Gervais is a young comedian from Reading who appears
on *The Eleven O'Clock Show.* I've met him a few times before,
through friends who work on that programme, but I never heard
that he played cards. I find this reassuring as I assess the opposi-
tion: truly devoted players can usually sense each other in a room
and fall into poker chat. Like gaydar, they pick up the vibe and
within minutes they're onto the flops and bad beats. If I have
met Gervais several times and poker has never come up in the
conversation, I decide he must be the least serious threat.

Indeed, Gervais's first words when we arrived in the lobby of
the Cardiff Hilton were: 'I've never played this Holdem game
before.' I smiled conspiratorially at Patrick Marber and murmured:
'That's what we like to hear.' Gervais seemed genuinely annoyed,
so I knew he wasn't hustling, and we sat down in the bar for a
quick whip through the rules just to be sporting.

I played with Patrick Marber in the old Archway game and
a spin-off version at Chris Colson's house. He was in that gang
of sharks who gobbled all my college money. But Patrick finally
finished that play he was going to write, and it went very well.
These days he is back and forth from New York, acting, writing,
winning awards and directing his own work on Broadway, so I
reassure myself that I have more chance to beat him now. He is
far too busy to spend his nights playing cards in a smoke-filled
basement full of sick gamblers and stale egg sandwiches, which

is where I have the advantage over Patrick Marber. If you don't stop to think about it.

♠

The real celebrities at the table are the two that I have never met before, but deeply admire, Martin Amis and Stephen Fry. With nothing to go on but Amis's public image, I decide to put him down as a loose-aggressive player. I am guessing he likes poker for the atmosphere and fellowship, so probably enjoys a gamble. I assume from newspaper stories about his book advances that he is probably comfortable with high stakes.

I know that Fry has played socially at the Groucho Club in London. My instinct is that he would take the game (and victory) less seriously than Amis, but his razor-sharp brain could be cause for concern. When I raise in middle position with A♦ 10♦ and Fry calls, I realize my problem immediately: having no idea what standard of player he is, I don't know what he'd call with. Is he dazzled by weak aces? Would he slow-play a big pair? It's a mystery.

The flop comes 5♣ 10♣ 3♥. This looks like a great flop for me. I bet my pair of tens strongly to protect them, but Fry calls. What on earth does he have? It could be anything. And I'm not exactly a Holdem tournament specialist myself. When the turn card pairs the three, I check nervously and so does Fry. The river is a blank; I check that, too, and Fry makes a small bet. I have to call, and he turns over a pair of fives. The *Jeeves & Wooster* star has a full house! If he had raised on the flop (when he hit his set), I might well have folded. In flat calling and betting small on the end, he squeezed another couple of hundred out of me. So either he undervalued his hand or he's a much craftier player than I've given him credit for. Still, it's funny how tight we both play with someone else's money.

Ricky Gervais, meanwhile, clearly loves action and calls with almost anything. For a time, his confidence pays off as the more experienced players fold against him. He calls with 62 offsuit, hits sixes and deuces on the flop and makes money. But, probably not knowing why he's winning, he doesn't know when to change gear. If you keep calling with 62 offsuit, you're going to start losing. Sure enough, his chip lead is gradually whittled away and he's the first out. He doesn't seem happy about it.

'What am I supposed to do now?' he asks.

'There's a shotgun in the drawer,' says Stephen Fry.

Things seem a little prickly between the two comics. Stephen Fry is the next player out and the two of them end up in a cash game back at the hotel. I hear that Fry gets the better of Gervais again, is not above a few cheeky put-downs when he wins the pot, and Gervais snaps, 'I might be bad at poker, but at least I'm not gay.'

You hear some pretty sharp gibes at the poker table, and when word of this barb gets round the professional players, they are surprised and amused to hear that the celebrity game threw up as much needle as a real one. But these players are not familiar with the ironic trend in late-night Channel 4 comedy. Gervais must have been joking. He must have been.

I get unlucky with AQ against Anthony Holden's AT. The inevitable ten comes down to seal my fate, and I walk away wondering whether to be a pessimist (I had two bad beats on *Late Night Poker*!) or an optimist (I had two free shots at *Late Night Poker*!).

Amis is hitting ace after ace, but he's also drinking a fair bit and the two old muckers Alvarez and Holden soon have the novelist's chips off him and play on heads-up until Holden emerges triumphant. But Amis certainly wins the prize for looking most like a Hollywood movie gambler, having mastered the art of rolling cigarettes in one hand while holding his cards with the other. Everybody smokes on *Late Night Poker*, but Amis does it best.

♠

When the celebrities leave town, I hear that Stephen Fry did not notice the difference between me and Kate Szeremeta, daughter of Nic the commentator. He chatted to her in the cash game, assuming she was the same girl he played with in the tournament. Fair enough: two gambling blondes, we're similar enough. But we have different tastes, admire different men and express our admiration in different ways. I'm a little embarrassed that Stephen Fry has left Cardiff thinking that it's me who has Ben Elton's face tattooed in four colours across her stomach.

♠

I'm definitely sticking around for the rest of the week to watch the main tournament. Since I've been away, the Tuesday night players have organized a satellite game so that one of them (apart from me) will represent the others in the TV series. Ten of them put in £150 each, and James wins the satellite. I'm so delighted to see him when he turns up. This high-stakes world is still daunting for me, and it's lovely to see a fraternal Tuesday face.

James does great, getting heads-up with Mike Magee to finish second and make the semi-final. Sadly, he is knocked out of that pretty early. But in the commentary, Jesse May pays James several compliments – while also referring to him throughout by his surname, which Jesse mispronounces. The Sweep loves the mispronunciation. It makes his year.

♠

Once the celebrities leave town, it is business as usual. Cash games on the side, yelps of protest about going into make-up, nerves about being filmed. Bambos, Howard Plant, Peter The Bandit, they are all back again for the new series. Malcolm Harwood has returned, having had a heart bypass and been warned by the doctor to 'avoid too much excitement'. We all hope he doesn't flop quads.

Malcolm's wife and fellow player Somkhuan has taken to phoning the temple back home in Thailand before big games, pledging money to Buddha if she wins and asking the local priests to curse her opponents with misfortune if they knock her out. The night before her heat, she pops into the bar to check the spelling of Ram Vaswani's name. Luckily, Ram gets knocked out before she does, thus saving himself from a plague of frogs.

But when Dave Devilfish Ulliott turns up, in his trademark red shades, I think: that fellow seems like one of the celebrities, not the normal players. He has a certain charisma, a certain air of expectation, of *droit de seigneur*. That's as well as being a memorable character, a funny storyteller; I think he'd be right at home on *Parkinson*. I am pleased to see him, even though he stares immediately at my chest and says, 'There's a couple of things I wanna talk to you about.'

When I say 'celebrity', he's more of a Bernard Manning than a Cary Grant.

♠

Devilfish is not the first to test me with cheeky puns and saucy comments at the poker table. I've lost count of the number of players who try to turn the conversation round to 'big pairs'. But few of them make actual passes and I'd never accept. I'm not a one-night-stand kind of girl, and I'm certainly not looking to get romantically involved with one of these shady gamblers, all questionable cash payments and sunglasses indoors.

I love the game, but full-time poker is a different world and

I'm perfectly happy with the divide. I don't want to screw any of them, date any of them or marry any of them. I have no interest in embracing life as a gangster's moll, a gambler's bit of totty; I don't even want to play bigger myself. I am happy to be here among the high rollers again, but I remember my comfort zone when I see them joined by James from the Tuesday game. He and I are recreational players, hobbyists, in it part-time for the fun, not the money.

I know there are tournaments around the world, but they cost too much, they happen too far away and I'm just a writer who likes playing poker in a couple of local London casinos. A small profit on my hobby, that's all I want. The rest is Wonder-land and it can stay there.

♠

At the end of the week, a black Porsche 911 draws up outside the hotel. The number plate is JOE 911. Its driver, Joe 'The Elegance' Beevers, is a cocky young Londoner with slick hair and an Armani suit. I smile to myself at the number plate, smile to myself at the nickname, shake hands with this new player, and tumble down the rabbit hole.

JACKS AGAIN

Here it is again: the Botox hand, looks better than it is. Lovely on its own, but hard to play after the flop when there's an overcard, which is more likely than there not being one.

I find JJ under the gun this time. When I found this hand earlier, I raised, Sid Harris went all-in and it worked out pretty nicely for me. But I want to mix my game up, so now I decide to limp. I flat call the big blind, 16,000.

Chad Brown passes, and Emad Tahtouh gives me the stare. He obviously has some sort of hand.

'Be careful,' I tell him. 'I'm limping to re-raise.'

Michael Muldoon, the Irish player on the button, helps me out by commenting, 'The last person who said that folded!'

I look upset, and tell Michael that it's completely against the rules for him to make this comment. Actually, it isn't; he hasn't acted yet. He can say what he wants when he's still in the hand. It's only the players who have passed their cards who are banned from making remarks about who's got what. If the old 'moody rule' was still in play, my hand would actually be dead because I've made a comment about my intentions.

Wow, remember that rule? I'd forgotten all that etiquette we used to have, before so many Americans came here, before we had the international competitions and the moody rule got scrapped because it confused too many newcomers. I used to love it, the way all these natural rebels obeyed that rule with such care, such discipline.

But now there is no moody rule, so I might as well exploit it by warning Emad to be careful. I want it to look like I'm nervous about my holding.

It all pans out nicely, and Emad makes it 70,000 to go. Muldoon, Jan Sjavic and Jules Kuusik all pass. I make it 240,000. Emad looks annoyed.

'What?' I say. 'I told you I was limp re-raising!'

Emad grumpily passes and that is fine with me. I have picked up an extra 70,000, along with 24,000 from the blinds, without having to play an enormous pot against an unknown hand.

Neil 'BadBeat' Channing beckons me over to the rail. He is holding a cup of tea.

'You shouldn't talk so much,' he says. 'You're giving too much away.'

People always tell me that. But then they sit down at the table and misread my hands completely. I have more control over what I am 'giving away' than they think. I wanted Emad to think I was weak and he did, he raised and gave me the chance to win a chunky pot without seeing a flop.

Having said that, Michael Muldoon's comment certainly helped. Maybe I am getting a bit close to the wire. If Michael had remained silent and Emad had read the situation right, he might have flat called the 16,000 and out-drawn me or muscled me out on a difficult flop.

'Joe Beevers just texted from Spain to find out how you were getting on,' says Neil. 'I told him that you were on the red wine and talking a lot.'

'The wine is helping!' I say. 'It gives me confidence!'

'Confidence to shop your hand,' mutters Neil.

He shows me Joe's reply on his little Nokia screen: SHE DOESN'T EVEN LIKE RED WINE. TAKE IT AWAY FROM HER AND GIVE HER A CUP OF TEA.

What am I, a six-year-old?

Then I remember that Joe has won more than a million dollars worldwide, taking the Irish Open title at Holdem and the British Open at Omaha, making more televised finals than any other British player; that he has made a living from poker for more than ten years and known me for as long as I've been trying to play the game at a serious competitive level. In fact, if I had never met Joe Beevers, I wouldn't be in this giant EPT tournament in the first place.

I take the cup of tea and go back to the table.

PART TWO

7

DOWN THE RABBIT HOLE

'In another moment, down went Alice after it, never once considering how in the world she was to get out again . . .'

– Lewis Carroll

Joe and I watch Hemish get busy on the roulette. It is an impressive sight. He bets like a fallen Shiva, arms at top speed, chips all over the layout, shouting for the hosts to bring him more ammunition. No money changes hands. Hemish seems to have unlimited credit at the casino. I have no idea whether he is in front or behind, but I expect they know.

Hemish is not a tall man. Nevertheless, he seems able to reach all 36 of the numbers from wherever he is standing, and pile great towers of coloured chips on most of them. It is almost as though, when the wheel starts to spin and the croupier says 'Place your bets,' he actually *grows*.

When Hemish has exhausted himself with all the spinning and stretching, signing and pressing, winning and losing, the three of us retire from the gaming floor to the restaurant. Joe orders champagne to drink with dinner, a new indulgence that I love immediately. It makes this random Wednesday night feel like Christmas; no gambler can resist a rebellion against timetable.

But that is not the only unusual thing about this evening. I have never been on a first date with a chaperone before.

Neither have I been on a date at a casino, but that makes sense. Joe is the first person who has ever admitted to my face that he is a professional gambler. When he rang up to ask me out, some time after we met on *Late Night Poker*, I was not surprised when he suggested dinner in the old Barracuda Club on Baker Street. I knew of the Barracuda, which was once a big rival to the Vic; they no longer run a poker game there but I have always been curious to see it. Besides, I thought, if I'm going on a date with a gambler, it might as well be in a casino.

When I arrived, I found not one but two gamblers waiting for me. Standing next to The Elegance was a shorter, plumper, darker fellow in a suit. He looked a little like an accountant, but there was something in his eyes . . . a twinkle, a mischief, a restless hint. He introduced himself as Hemish Shah.

Joe explained, as if it was quite natural, that he had arrived half an hour early to find that he was barred from the club. He used to play professional blackjack with his father, years ago, and was barred from many British casinos – an occupational hazard for the expert card-counter. It's a terrible injustice, Joe explained, that as soon as anyone gets good at this particular game, they're banned from playing it, or even from entering premises on which it is played. But it is a ubiquitous gambling principle, Joe said. He warned me that if a bookmaker is happy to take my action on horses or football, it means I'm a loser. His sports-betting friends use false names, or third-party accomplices, because winners are not welcome at the bookie's.

Joe stopped playing blackjack ages ago and has been removed from most casino blacklists. But when he arrived tonight and tried to use his membership card at the desk, the computer bleeped and he was denied entry.

The Elegance doesn't invite girls out and then change the plan late doors. So he phoned Hemish Shah and explained his dilemma. Hemish is a big gambler. London casinos fall over themselves to please him. They are desperate for his action. Like the joke about what you call a gorilla with a shotgun; every casino manager in town calls Hemish 'Sir'. So Hemish came down to Baker Street and told them Joe was a friend, and the casino manager was quick to agree that any friend of Hemish's was a friend of the Barracuda's. If Hemish had wanted to bring Fred

West in for dinner, the manager would have offered the Gloucester monster a complimentary hors d'oeuvre.

It was a lot of information for the first five minutes of a date.

♠

I tell them over dinner that I have never seen anyone bet so high or so fast as Hemish. Joe says the amazing thing is, Hemish is actually very tight with money. The tightest person Joe's ever known. This strikes me as an odd thing to say with Hemish sitting right here, but no offence seems to be taken at all. In fact, Hemish nods proudly at the accolade. When Joe points at Hemish's shoes and says 'He's eked out that single pair for seven years,' Hemish cackles 'It's not even an expensive pair! Only high street!'

They both sit chuckling at Hemish's curious savings. One time, I am told, Hemish drove all the way to the Vic from his home in Temple Fortune to borrow Alan Abraham's European plug adaptor before going to a tournament in Paris. Hemish had calculated that the petrol costs for the seven-mile round trip would be marginally lower than buying his own adaptor at the airport.

Gambling tens of thousands, while driving for an hour to save £2, seems to be one of many strange contradictions in Hemish's lifestyle. Despite his love of casinos and their late-night atmosphere of Jack Daniels, B&H and giant steaks, he is a vegetarian who doesn't smoke, doesn't drink, lives with his mother and honours their Hindu religion. Apart from the gambling bit. He waves away the champagne, asks for water and eats a salad. But he seems itchy to get back to the roulette wheel.

♠

The quirky, lovable Hemish is a welcome diversion on a date where I might otherwise have been quite shy. I have never dated anyone like Joe before: all confidence and finesse, sports cars and champagne. During the chat about Hemish's cheap, enduring shoes, The Elegance tells me that his own nickname comes from his notorious penchant for Armani. Joe says, 'I like to wear a nice suit and a dress watch.' I don't know what a 'dress watch' is, and the only boyfriend I've ever had who wore a suit was my childhood sweetheart Daniel in his school uniform.

Joe gives me a lift home. I have to duck to get into the low-slung car, trying to remember something I once read in an etiquette guide about 'bottom on the seat, knees together, swing legs in'.

It feels quite glamorous to be this close to the ground, speeding along in a torpedo of leather and fuel. I tell myself very sternly, 'You are *not* the kind of girl who's impressed by a Porsche.' But the whole night is kind of head-spinning. It's just different, that's all. Just different.

♠

On our fifth or sixth date, I go back to Joe's place. He has a flat above a bank in Hendon Central. As we climb the dark concrete stairs, I pause for breath.

'Only one more flight!' encourages Joe.

I have paused outside a doorway covered in stickers. You can't see the wood for the slogans. They overlap with each other, some of them repeated. They say BEWARE OF THE DOG, NO TRADESMEN, KEEP OUT, PROPERTY ALARMED, WIPE YOUR FEET, NO SMOKING and about a dozen other warnings.

'Ah, so you live above a nutter,' I say.

Joe says, 'That's my mother's flat.'

♠

My previous boyfriends have been artistic left-wing types, who played guitars and liked Steven Berkoff. I am amused and excited by the Otherness of Joe, who doesn't read much (I give him Paolo di Canio's autobiography for his birthday; Joe abandons it halfway through) but his maths and savvy are as sharp as a paper cut. He runs a lucrative private cash game, he knows about stocks and shares. There's something of the East-End City boy about him, but he's a North Londoner. Then again, he's a West Ham fan.

Joe tells me straight that I should have no problem with him going to lapdancing clubs because 'It's just like going to an art gallery – only, instead of paintings, it's topless women gyrating round a pole.'

His particular combination of simplicity and sophistication is the direct opposite of anyone I have ever gone out with before. Still on the fringes of the professional poker scene, such as it is, I don't really have any friends like that either.

Joe is focused, disciplined and disturbingly patient at the poker table, not so disciplined away from it. He likes a drink and a laugh, once fell asleep at 5 a.m. in the middle of a hand of high-stakes Pai Gow.

Soon, I am less excited by the flash car and the champagne than I am by the way he is solid and trustworthy, safe and sweet. He wears a Santa Claus outfit at Christmas.

♠

We go to tournaments outside London – France, Holland, Luton. I finally start to grasp the important differences between cash and competition poker, as well as getting to know the small crowd of British players who travel regularly to these events. They don't find me weird, now that I am a player's girlfriend; suddenly, I fit like a jigsaw piece. I have a defined role overnight. It is understood that I will be girlish and deferent, politely blind to the presence of any mistresses or hookers, sweetly yet undefiantly shocked by any bad language or behaviour, ready to peel off and chat with the other girlfriends and wives if they are in attendance. I don't mind. It isn't important to be treated like a player, as long as I can play.

It is a small scene. Tournament fields are usually less than a hundred runners. The big main event of a festival is £500 or £750. The decision to go is taken the day before – at most, the week before – based on cash flow.

In the winter, we go to Paris for a festival of poker at the Aviation Club on the Champs-Élysées and I play my first multi-table Holdem tournament. The buy-in is 1,000 francs, about £100. I get nowhere, but I love the place immediately. It's an old, wood-panelled airmen's club, full of cigar smoke and paintings of old planes. Everything moves at a civilized, gentlemanly pace. The tournament stops for a two-hour dinner break so that everyone can repair to the Aviation restaurant for a subsidized four-course meal with wine.

As Grandpa Sam would have said, 'It'd take a lot of this to kill ya.'

I am getting a sense of how the mood changes at various stops on the circuit. The boys take their wives to Vegas (with children, if there are any), their girlfriends to Paris (for shopping and champagne) and nobody to Amsterdam (where there are big nights out at the Yab Yum brothel). I manage to tread the diplomatic line in both of those European locations, but even I don't want to go to Moscow. Christ alone knows what they get up to there.

The Aviation Club has a piano in it. During dinner, Devilfish leaps to the piano stool and bangs out old Elvis numbers. Outside, it's late and even the Champs-Élysées is quiet. I think of that early scene in *Some Like It Hot* where Jack Lemmon and Tony Curtis walk through a silent, empty shop, a secret door swings open, and suddenly they're in a packed, noisy room with people gargling bourbon and smoking cigarettes and singing songs. It feels like that, behind the door of the Aviation. I wish my father could see it. *Some Like It Hot* is his all-time favourite film.

Joe's closest friends in poker are Ross and Barny Boatman, who I remember from Archway, and Ram Vaswani, a former snooker player who turned to poker because 'It's similar really – going around, hustling where you can.' They all met in the London cash games, they travel together to tournaments in Baden or Atlantic City, they lend each other money and swap shares of each other's action. They refer to themselves light-heartedly as 'the Poker Rat Pack' or 'the Hendon Mob'.

I like the second nickname, better. The idea of Hendon, a trafficky suburb of North London where a couple of them live and where they all play poker in various private games, garnering a few hundred here or there, gives their little gang an Ealing Comedy flavour. When I was a kid, I used to watch Disney films at the old Classic cinema in Hendon Central. A collection of bagel bakeries under a flyover, it just couldn't be less scary. Hendon: the mean streets of NW4. The gateway to Edgware.

Joe, Ram and the Boatman brothers have ideas about how to do something with this mob concept, something that could take poker to another level. With the success of *Late Night Poker*, they think there is further potential in TV and foresee a growing audience for this colourful world. Nobody really listens to them. But it's good to keep having ideas.

♠

We go to private cash games in streets that appear on the more obscure pages of the A–Z. There's one at The Whacker's house in Finchley. The money is big, the tension is high, the windows are dark . . . and The Whacker's mother pops in frequently with cups of tea. One day, The Whacker will get married and have a child. But he'll put them up in a flat, and carry on living with his mother.

These games aren't like the Tuesday game. Most of them are professionally run fixtures with illegal rakes (a form of house tax), women hired to provide meals and drinks – possibly more, I don't ask – and dangerous credit available.

There are plenty of funny stories about games like this. Tall Alan from the Vic likes to talk about a night when several players turned up with money that was strangely singed around the edges. Nobody commented on these damaged bills. The next day, local newspapers reported that a safe had been blown up in the post office. I'm not sure the story is entirely true, but it could be.

They have dark edges, these private games. They are built around rich losing players who are phoned, flattered, encouraged to visit, smiled at and pampered at a tiny cost. The atmosphere is like a friendly social event, but the underside is cut-throat. The idea is to get every penny off the wealthy fish, then give them unlimited credit so they can lose some more. The game is so heavily raked and taxed, it would be impossible to make a profit without these hapless donators. However much money they have, they can go broke in these circumstances.

Joe can't. He is much too smart, always a winner. And I can't either because I play super-carefully, mostly taking the opportunity to watch and learn, and to eat fried breakfasts at four in the morning. I am learning a lot.

I learn that I am playing against the players not the cards, that I must identify who can be bluffed and who can't, who will pay me off and who won't. I learn about position, playing stronger round the button than from the blinds. I learn that funny little hands like 56 suited can be used for re-raising purposes, and that they are better and 'fresher' than picture cards if you get called.

I learn that bluffing is about representing a particular hand, not just 'pretending to have something', and that semi-bluffing is better still. I finally relinquish Matt's old adage 'Don't disgrace an ace'; I start throwing weak aces away. I stop calling with draws, and start betting them. I begin to grasp the concept of pot odds, and to stop folding when they're in my favour. I look for tells, count my outs, and watch hands even after I have passed, to spot the other players' betting patterns. I learn to look for 'situations' where my cards aren't even relevant. I'm starting to become a player.

I'm playing bigger, too. It's inevitable, the action is infectious. I learn to create a proper bankroll, separate from my living money. Buying-in for £500 rather than £50 starts to feel normal. Playing carefully, watching, waiting, studying, I start to win. It is small, but it is winning.

♠

Sometimes, we go to a place round the corner from the Vic that stays open all night after the casino has closed. Joe has to deliver a password at the door, to gain our entry into a fuggy little room where people sit playing poker and backgammon. Or they just sit, gazing into space, smiling vacantly. Until our first visit here, I hadn't known it was possible to smoke heroin. Not that I would touch it myself, and Joe certainly doesn't. Quite apart from anything else, he always keeps a clear head for the game. But some people use it as a drug shop, others as a private loan emporium, and others for gambling. Amazing that they have only a password for security.

We go to a bigger private game in Europe which is fitted out with CCTV cameras trained on the driveway and men with guns in the hall.

♠

We're watching the Grand National. I've chosen five horses and bet £20 each way on all of them, rather than my traditional £2. It makes me giddy, but that settles soon enough.

Still, it's not much fun watching the Grand National with Joe. He doesn't pop down to a local betting shop in the morning and then shout at the television throughout the race, as my father has

always done and I always will, but 'trades' on the horses – betting
and laying from start to finish, by phone and on internet betting
exchanges. The prices are better, but I don't want to do it that
way. I like handing over real solid money, and (on a good day)
getting real solid money back again. I don't mind taking the bad
prices, for the romance of doing it the old way. Joe finds this
exasperating.

I ring my dad after the race, without mentioning how much
I bet, to find out how he has fared. Terrible. His horses never
finish anywhere. One year, he couldn't quite be bothered to go
down to the betting shop and my mum was disappointed because
she particularly wanted to bet on Minnehoma, Freddie Starr's
horse, which was running at number eight. My mother likes the
number eight. So my father said he'd lay the bet himself, and
Minnehoma romped home at 16/1. That was the only bet my
father had in the whole of 1994: that Minnehoma would not
win the Grand National. And it did.

16/1 was only the starting price. My father laid it at 20s.

♠

By now, I'm carrying £50 notes around. Having barely seen one
a couple of years ago, I now have ten of them in my pocket at
all times, because I never know when I might be going to a
game. The cashpoint limit is £250 a day (not enough, if sudden
action broke out) and, besides, you feel silly counting out £500
in tenners. Smaller wad, bigger bills, that is the way forward. It
all seems very high-roller.

One night, we get back to Joe's place, after a game where
he's won several thousand, to find the flat in darkness because he
hasn't paid the electricity bill.

♠

I learn more of the language. Suddenly I'm finding pairs of treys, roufs, nevises, Tom Mixes. And sometimes, these days, I'm even betting them.

I start referring to sums of money as a pony, a bottle, a carpet or a monkey, quite unselfconsciously. Probably sounds ridiculous in my posh voice. One time, in the £50 game at the Vic, I try to bet a cockle and (once the word has crashed against the accent barrier and slumped unconscious on the baize) it goes as a call. Stupid really, since I'm the only one who actually pronounces the 'ck' in the middle.

But this is the language, it feels normal to use it. I can't sound any funnier than Bambos does when he bets 'sirillo'. Three, or three hundred, or three thousand = a carpet, because people used to get a carpet in their cell if they were jailed for three years or more. And there used to be a carpet manufacturer called Cyril Lord. So when Bambos, in his heavy Cypriot accent, bets 'a sirillo', everyone knows exactly what he means.

The last two communal cards in Holdem are 'the turn and river'. I have always used the old-school phrases, fourth street and fifth street – to be followed, in many of the variants I have played, by sixth street and seventh street. But 'the river' is beautiful. It is the last card you are going to see in the hand, yet the language reassures you that it's not really the end. It's just the river flowing. The game courses on, a single body of water, always changing but always the same. An ace might be floating downstream on this particular hand, but it could be a three at the conclusion of the next one. Just one long river. One single, fluent, eternal game.

♠

On a big desktop computer in his study, Joe has downloaded something called Paradise Poker. It's like Planet Poker, launched a couple of years ago by Mad Mike Caro: card games on the internet. You can buy chips on your credit card, and play 'live' against real people, at their own computers all over the world.

Now I actually see what internet poker is, I am mesmerized. No dress code and no time restriction, no travel time, no danger, no social awkwardness, a potentially infinite supply of opponents . . . and all these pretty little cartoon cards! Most days, I beg Joe to let me come round to his flat with sandwiches, make a cup of tea and play on his computer.

I wonder what effect this will have on the tiny international tournament circuit and the private cash games of Hendon and Finchley. If it's this easy to find opponents without even leaving your house, why worry about casino rules, opening hours, dangerous credit and illegal house taxes? Maybe these are the last days of the roaming empire. Maybe we will never go abroad to play again.

'Do you remember Slovenian Jonas, from *Late Night Poker*?' I ask Joe. 'The one who dressed like a vicar? He said that nobody will play online poker because it's not safe to type in your credit card details, and there's no face-to-face confrontation so it's not a proper game.'

'Nah,' says Joe. 'I think it's going to be big.'

ANOTHER WEAK ACE

A♣ 3♦. That's much uglier than the A♦ 6♦ I found before, but my position is better here. I'm in the cut-off, one before the button. You can play far more hands in late position than you can in early position, because you get to see what the other players are doing before you make a decision.

When Michael Muldoon, Jan Sjavic and Jules Kuusik all pass, I think the chances are that I've got the best hand on the table at the moment. The problem is, everybody knows that you can play a wider range of hands in later position, and a raise from the cut-off can look like a steal. Players are tempted to re-steal by re-raising – and although I wouldn't exactly be bluffing if I raised (my ace high may very well be good against the only two remaining players), that doesn't mean I want to call a big re-raise or stick all my chips in with this vulnerable hand. And if they flat call, I'd rather have an even weaker hand – a 67, or a 45 – because then at least my cards would be 'fresh', unlikely to be duplicated by anyone who gives me action. If I'm forced to play a big pot, that may well be because there's a bigger ace behind me, and that would leave me with the old pickle: I don't want to miss the flop, and I don't want to hit it either. I remember learning all that in the old cash games with Joe.

I wonder how they make a living now, the people who ran and raked those spielers? I knew the internet would kill them off. Live poker never died, of course, it got massively, massively bigger, but who goes to big raked private games in people's houses any more?

I pass my A3, and Chad Brown makes it 50,000 to go from the small blind. I am briefly jealous that he is playing a gutsier game than I am. He's happy to try and nick a pot when everyone else has passed, and the blinds and antes are big enough to make this absolutely worth while.

Ah . . . but Emad Tahtouh, in the big blind, immediately re-raises to 160,000. Well, exactly. Aggressive Emad, knowing how easy it is for someone to raise in this situation with pretty much anything, is putting the pressure back on. There's the problem in a nutshell. If Chad has a hand like mine, he will have no idea if he's miles behind or being bluffed. He passes, and I'm relieved it wasn't me who just lost 50,000 in the pot.

Over the Tannoy, I hear Mike Masuris being called for a cash game downstairs. It makes me smile. I'd forgotten I was at home. With the audience up here, the announcer, the cameras, I'd lost sense of the fact that it's still just the Vic, my regular home casino, business as usual in the card room.

I once had a stand-up row with Mike Masuris – The Mad Monk – because he called me 'Rubenesque'. I told him that no woman wants

*to be called fat, not even by a Greek man who means it as a compli-
ment. The Mad Monk said it was a compliment not only to my figure
but my poker playing as well, 'because you must be winning the lot, if
you can afford to eat that much'. Then it got noisy.*

    *But I love Mike really. I love everybody in this place. The thought
of him taking up his seat in the £50 round-of-each, ordering a lemon
tea from Sandra, possibly a sandwich . . . it reminds me of where I am,
relaxes me. It's just a poker game. I know how to play. And I can get
as lucky as the next man.*

8

FACT AND FICTION

The blue whale's tongue is as big as an elephant.

It is a cold, wet, fog-bound day in a place where the sheep have four horns, the cats have no tails and the people believe in fairies. I have travelled here alone, by road from London to Liverpool and then a stomach-churning, rain-lashed ferry over the Irish Sea.

The Isle of Man, where superstition is king, suits the game nicely. Poker players spend half their time explaining that it is all about maths and skill, pot odds and prices, the other half panicking because they can't find their lucky gnome. Poker is a blend of luck and judgment, in a world that mixes fact and fiction. If there are four-horned sheep, why not fairies?

In a tournament at Brighton a few weeks ago, green chips were brought to the table after the break. These were bigger denominations, so we all wanted them for their value. And yet half of us feared their colour. I was sitting next to Steve Bovis, who said miserably, 'I have no chance in this tournament anyway – just look at my glasses case.' He snapped it open to reveal a bright green lining. We both shrank back from its ill-fated glow.

That was a normal tournament, £50 buy-in, a few hundred quid for making the final. This one on the Isle of Man has a freakish £6,000 buy-in and the first prize is £1,000,000. A British competition of that size is an incredible experiment. I am not going to play it, of course I'm not, I'll play a few cash games and maybe a small side tournament. But they seem to have found

150 people prepared to put up this crazy entrance fee, and I am definitely going to have a look at them.

The journey made me feel like an old-time gambler: hours across country and over the waves, to find the action. Road and sea travel is always romantic, especially alone, which I am because Joe has gone ahead by plane. The landscape unfolds, telling you its story, connecting place to place, but an aeroplane just teleports you from one soulless terminal full of Tie Racks to another. Tarmac and water, compared to air, are like natural birth rather than a caesarean. It has taken me the best part of a day to be delivered here, but it's better than flying. My fear-of-flying counsellor has just been killed in a plane crash. If anything's going to make you superstitious, that will.

♠

We are in Douglas for the biggest poker game ever held outside America. That is why poker champions from all over the world, from Vegas, from Vienna, from Paris, from Sydney, have descended on this windswept isle. That's why Manx shopkeepers, who might not usually see a customer for hours at a time, are now doing business with giant Texans in snakeskin hats and fearsome Frenchmen in long black coats, who take out wads of £50 notes, fat as phone books, to pay for their cigarettes.

Even Chris 'Jesus' Ferguson, the new world champion, is here. He has just won the 2000 World Series, which was played by 512 runners (poker must be getting more popular; 393 played last year), for a prize of $1.5 million. Amazingly, the same money is promised as first prize right here, on our own little weird offshore island.

Also here are four young men in black suits, striding purposefully along the darkening and deserted seafront, heads full of plans, pound signs where their pupils should be. The Hendon Mob have come for the million.

These boys have small bankrolls and big dreams. Joe, Ram, Ross and Barny are more certain than ever that opportunity is in the air for anyone gutsy enough to reach out and grab it. The way they see it, alcohol and cigarette companies sponsor people to play snooker, why not to play cards? They have now officially named themselves 'the Hendon Mob' and would be happy to drink Jack Daniel's at the table, or wear Old Spice, or print FERRARI on their jacket pockets, if these companies would pay them to do it.

Other players laugh at the idea. Sponsorship! Corporations! Poker is not a real sport, nobody will ever pay the players to show up. But I think there might be something there. The final of this 'Poker Million' is going to be broadcast live on Sky Sports. More televised poker is surely coming. And these guys make a good, memorable team, each bringing something different to the mix, like a cool, North London, male, gambling Spice Girls.

Ross is the famous one, from the nine years he played a fireman on *London's Burning*. When he walks down the street, people still shout, 'Where's the fire?' He is charismatic, macho and sexy. Only a couple of years ago, he was offered a part in a new film called *Lock, Stock And Two Smoking Barrels* – but he didn't take it, because he had just played the lead in a movie called *Hard Men*, and he was lined up for a stage play which he didn't want to turn down for a small role in a risky British film that in all likelihood, Ross reasoned, nobody would ever watch. Acting, you see, is also a gamble.

Joe is The Elegance, with his designer suits and his Porsche and his cannily managed bankroll. For anyone who fails to find the hopeful, hand-to-mouth, Ealing Comedy life appealing, Joe represents a different sort of ambition. Luxury, smoothness, status. It is a different way of being self-employed. He is an aspirational figure, like a Thatcherite entrepreneur.

Ross's brother Barny is the best talker: quick-witted, funny, clever, unusually sophisticated for a poker player. He speaks fluent

Spanish, and knows about architecture. He's dyslexic, but he's one of the most articulate people you'll ever meet. He makes his way in this hard world, tough as he needs to be, but he put it all on hold to look after his sister when she was ill. He is complicated and wonderful. If televised poker has a future, it will be because of characters like Barny. He is booked to commentate on the Poker Million final, so television is already spotting his potential – though he is a little less sparkly and jokey than usual today, because he wishes he was playing. Still, £6,000 is a lot of money. Barny can't put that up out of nowhere.

Then there's Ram, the ex-snooker hustler, quiet, beautiful and crazy for gambling. Ram has all the moves. He wants to play bigger all the time, seize chances and capitalise on them. There is not enough money in the world for Ram. He is ever so handsome and the lady croupiers get lost in his big dark eyes, but Ram doesn't seem to notice women. If the dealer was topless, Ram would still look at the cards. He once had a girlfriend who asked Ram to write her a love poem. He wrote, 'On the moors there's heather and bramble, but all I want to do is gamble.' They are not together any more.

When Barny tells me that the boys want to promote poker but not gambling in general – that 'Scratchcards are too accessible to kids and people without money; it's a tax on desperation and stupidity' – Ram thumps the table and says, 'Fuck! I forgot to buy my Lottery tickets. I was going to get a hundred quid's worth.'

♠

Amarillo Slim, the old Texan legend, is telling everybody in earshot that an Englishman has no chance of winning this Poker Million. 'What the Brits smell cookin' ain't on the fire,' he says.

I am very excited to see him. Slim, a wizened icon who's been 'swoopin' into gamblin' towns like a vacuum cleaner' for more than fifty years, is the world's most famous poker player. He won the World Series in 1972 and embarked on the American talk-show circuit afterwards. Before *Late Night Poker*, he was the only player that anyone had heard of.

Slim has been hired to promote this tournament, and he's giving the money's worth. 'I play the golden rule,' he insists. 'The guy with the gold makes the rules.'

During the promotional push, this ancient card sharp turned up to do a Radio 4 show in London and stood next to my father in the foyer. The researcher came downstairs, looked at my father waiting next to this skinny giant in his snakeskin boots, pearl-white cowboy hat and gold jewellery, and asked 'Which one of you is Amarillo Slim?' My father was delighted.

♠

The Hendon Mob are playing in a £100 super-satellite, trying to win seats in the big tournament which begins tomorrow. American champions have jetted into town with great thumping bankrolls of cash, ready to fork out the £6,000 no problem. But the Hendon Mob are not millionaires, just guys who try to make a living playing cards. Sometimes a very nice living, sometimes a meaner one. When Joe goes to a poker game, he calls it 'going to work'. He told me once that most people treat poker as a hobby, like golf, and 'while they're having a good time, we're collecting our wages'.

Of course, I am one of those other people myself. Poker is still in the golf category for me, not the job category. I'm not even having a spin in the satellite.

The women in this building can be counted on one hand. Naturally there aren't any women playing; few of these bumpy-income loners have serious girlfriends, and there are no glittering hookers in the bar of the Hilton Hotel & Casino, Isle of Man. But Devilfish is doing his best to soften the atmosphere by singing

Try A Little Tenderness into the tournament director's microphone.
He really is a kitten after all.

♠

While I'm here, I'm making notes for a magazine article about
the giant tournament. As I sit scribbling in my notebook, the
producer of the Sky coverage beckons me over to the bar. He
says, 'We're going live for the final on Sunday and we really need
an attractive woman to interview the players, someone who
knows her stuff and would look good on camera, and we suddenly
realized it would be obvious to ask you, Victoria . . . can *you* think
of anyone?'

He wasn't kidding. The job goes to my old friend Carrie Frais,
a reporter on the Sky News channel.

♠

The Hilton bar is full of betting: 12/1 an Irish winner of the
million. What price an Italian? They argue about what happens
if the winner is born in one place but lives in another. The whole
bar is debating the definition of nationality, like a political think
tank but with more high-stakes backgammon in the corner. There
is an interesting feeling of European unity, where it doesn't matter
if the winner is a Brit or a Frenchman or a German, just as long
as we beat the bloody Americans.

It is not a big field. There are only a few from each country
who travel round the international tournaments, so they all know
each other. I know many of them too, now. It's like going to
school: at first it seems like a crowd of unlearnable faces, but
familiarity soon thins it out. Except, unlike school, there is real
camaraderie. I ask Ross how he feels about chatting and drinking
in the bar with people whose money he will be trying to take
tomorrow.

'Well, it's inevitable,' Ross says, 'because the same faces travel the poker circuit. You arrive in a new city and there are the Birmingham crew, the Irish crew, different mobs from different countries. We're out to get their money, and they're out to get ours, but here we are shaking hands, "How's it going?", "Are you winning?", and we're genuinely happy to see each other.'

There is no dress code here. Casinos on the mainland have a dress code but it only means no jeans or boots, so people show up in all manner of nasty Aertex shirts, B&H-scented sports jackets and scuffed shoes. Joe The Elegance likes to play in a designer suit, but tonight he is dressed down in an old orange jumper. Jesse May admires his 'retro chic'.

But fashion is no comfort when you're losing; none of the Hendon Mob wins a seat in this super-satellite. Three of the boys have only come here to play the tournament, and they still don't know if they'll be able to. It feels worst for Joe, who takes tenth place in the satellite when there were nine seats available as prizes. Finishing on the bubble has happened to Joe a lot recently.

'You're knocking on the door, man,' says Jesse May.

'I've been knocking on the door so fucking long,' replies Joe, 'I'm beginning to think there's nobody behind it.'

♠

Fat hailstones are spattering noisily onto the Isle of Man promenade, but you wouldn't know it inside the Hilton. A spaceship might have landed on the seafront for all the gamblers care: Ladbrokes has just announced an additional £250,000 prize money for runners-up and now there is too much value to miss. Joe, Ram and Ross start selling shares of their prospective winnings, a traditional tactic for the hard-up gambler who has a good shot to win but lacks the bankroll to buy in freely. These Hendon boys have got impressive tournament records – between them they have won competitions in France, Holland, Germany, Austria, Finland and Slovenia – and other players, with more easy cash available, are happy to buy shares and gamble on them. So they're in the big game.

Their friend, the fast-talking, sharp-witted London sports gambler Adam Heller, is betting with former world champion Johnny Chan ('The Orient Express') that an American will not win.

'The Yanks here are the cream,' says Adam, 'but they haven't come up against the Hendon posse.' He is only half joking. And you should pay attention, because this is a guy who knows how to make a bet.

Looking at the prices for the different nationalities, I ask Adam for a tip.

He says, 'Never sneeze when you're hiding.'

♠

Ten minutes to go before the start. Ross is worrying about a radio interview he has just done. As an actor, he gets nervous about appearing as himself. Ram is busy telling everybody that the blue whale's penis is as big as a man. 'That's why we call him The Brains,' says Joe. 'He knows this stuff.'

'The Brains is not a nickname, it's just a fact,' Ram informs me sternly. 'And the blue whale's tongue is as big as an elephant.'

Five minutes to go. Barny comes in, breathless, holding a pink tournament ticket. He must have borrowed money from everybody in the building and sold every share he could think of, but by hook or by crook he got his hands on £6,000 with minutes to spare.

'I just realized there was no way I could not play,' he says. 'No way.'

Life is often like this for Barny. He only went to the World Series this year because he had enough air miles for a free flight.

He used his case money to play a super-satellite when he arrived, and won a seat in the main event, where he finished 16th for $40,000.

'Then I went and did the lot playing craps,' says Barny. 'Came home with what I took over there: nothing.'

There is loud laughter. What could be funnier than Barny losing $40,000 on the dice?

'The point is,' says Barny, 'I'd almost won the world championship and then hadn't, so what's another $40,000?'

'Yeah,' says Ross, 'he'd already lost a million dollars.'

And once again, here on the Isle of Man, Barny has tilted in at the last minute and all four boys will fight for the £1,000,000.

'Now we have to get in there,' says Ram, 'and go to war. We're here to nick the million. This is going to change our lives.'

♠

There's a brief window of sunshine across the Manx coast, unseen by the players tucked inside the casino. This is Day Two. Half the field went out yesterday, including many of the US champs, but the Hendon boys are all still in action. Ross and Joe are survivors, thought of as rocks; they don't take too many chances. Ram and Barny are wilder, more likely to accumulate chips, more likely to lose them again.

Ram went out drinking last night till four in the morning with a friend who'd done all his money, thirteen large. Ram couldn't sleep anyway, because he was preoccupied with 'all them moves . . . can't stop thinking about the moves'. Joe slept very soundly, which he puts down to his exercise regime, but he told me when we woke up that he'd dreamed he knocked Ross out of the tournament. Now he is worried to learn that Ross has actually been moved to his table.

Poker is not a team game. The Hendon Mob must and will play against each other when they're on the same table. They trust each other, travel together, help each other out when they're in trouble, and give each other 5% of money won. If one of them wins £1,000 in a tournament, the others all get £50. And 5% of a million is £50,000. Fifty large. And yet they're all here to win it on their own: if Joe has to knock Ross out of the tournament, that is what he'll do.

Without a tournament to play, I wander off and take a drive around the island, but I can't find anything at all so I wander back again and find that Ross has been knocked out. Not by Joe, but by former world champion Phil 'The Brat' Hellmuth from California. I'm barely through the door before I get the story. 'The money goes in on a flop of A 4 5, I've got AQ against A3. I light up inside when I see the hands. But Hellmuth hits a deuce on the turn to make a straight. I'm absolutely gutted.'

I don't know what to say. There's never anything you can say. But Ross isn't in too bad a mood, compared to some. He's still smiling. He says, 'I'd rather go out like that than by making a mistake. I trapped the world champion, I had him by the absolute bollocks, but he had a few outs and he hit one of them.' He heads off to the media room and starts a cash game with the press. Soon the combined sports staff of the *Mirror*, *Daily Mail* and *Observer* are paying his wages. I join Sasha, married to Bambos who knocked me out of *Late Night Poker*, to sit on the rail like a proper poker wife.

At 5.30 p.m., Ram is knocked out, having also got his money in with the best hand. He disappears immediately, to gamble elsewhere.

And at 10.15 p.m., it's goodnight Joe. The flop is 7 J Q and Joe (with a pair of kings) calls an all-in bet from his old friend Simon 'Aces' Trumper, a businessman from Guildford who won the second series of *Late Night Poker*. But Simon has a secret pair of sevens and the flop has given him a set. Joe smiles, stands up and says, 'Well done, Simon,' and Simon says, 'Thank you' – not for the chips, but for the graciousness in defeat. Joe walks out, elegantly, and waits till he reaches the bar before he beats himself up about whether he made a bad call.

'Maybe I just don't have the stamina,' he says. 'Next time I play in a four-day tournament, I have to get back in the gym first.'

The field has narrowed to 20 players. Only one of the Hendon Mob is left, and it's the one who wasn't going to play.

♠

Day Three. The final will be six-handed, broadcast live on Sky Sports. When they get down to nine players and one of them is Barny Boatman, the people from Sky are a little worried. Barny is supposed to be their commentator. Everybody in the room who is not from Sky, or married to one of the other eight players, is rooting for Barny. Oh – except the security staff. Beefy Simon Trumper, with his shaved hair, gold necklace, big watch and karate black belt, is the bouncers' favourite.

But Simon goes out 9th. Ali Sarkeshik, a fun-loving high-roller of independent means, is 8th. Barny is getting no good cards, but he wins a big pot by making a clever call of a bluff, and a couple more by bluffing himself. The people's choice is hanging on.

♠

The audience has its own gambling to worry about. This is Saturday, and thousands of pounds have been bet on football. 'Mad' Marty Wilson, knocked out early from the tournament, is wandering around with a sign on his back that reads, 'I had £6,000 . . . now I have nothing.'

Mad Marty from the Midlands is a popular face on the circuit, a revered storyteller, joke-cracker and song-singer. He sells himself as a dedicated ducker and diver: the buy-in money has always come from a cunning plan, like the time he picked up a bag of acorns outside Las Vegas and sold them individually as 'acorns from Sherwood Forest'. Another time it was stolen whelks.

I have no idea which stories are true and which aren't, which makes me an ideal target for Marty. He gets me every time. I nod sympathetically when he tells me that he got knocked out by an Arabian player who had scars all over his wrists. Then Marty adds, 'I said, "So you won your appeal, then?"'

I walk with Marty to the reception desk so that he can order a taxi and go looking for a betting shop. 'The name's Wilson,' he tells the receptionist.

'For now?' she asks, picking up the phone.

'No,' he says. 'It's always been Wilson.'

Even so, *even so*, I believe him when he tells me that he used to be a taxi driver himself. And then he says, 'I gave up in the end. Couldn't stand people talking behind me back.'

When the cab arrives to whisk Marty off in search of bookies, I go back into the casino to see what everyone else is up to. Hemish Shah, my first-date chaperone, wants to play some serious roulette. He wants to put £25,000 on red, but the maximum bet allowed by this casino is £500. It's ridiculous that they won't open a bigger table, when you think how people fall over to please Hemish in London. If you run a gaming room, with a massive house edge in roulette, and you know a man who wants to bet £25,000 a spin, wouldn't you offer him a decent welcome?

Lyle Berman, an American casino-owner, tells Hemish he will take the bet privately, so they shake hands and watch the wheel. It comes up red for Hemish. Sadly, he cannot resist repeating the bet three times, and ends up £50,000 down.

Ross is missing his little daughter, Alabama. Fondly, he remembers her first full sentence, spoken down the phone when he was in France: 'Daddy in Paris, play poker, get money, buy presents.'

And there could well be presents coming to Alabama. Middle Eastern mystery man Mohamed Bakhtoul is knocked out 7th, winning £6,000 and a small consolation trophy that doesn't mean much except that we are at last down to six players, and Uncle Barny is in the final.

♠

Of the players sitting down in front of the cameras to play for £1,000,000, Barny has the lowest chips by a mile. He needs some luck.

Ross is going to be presenting the live coverage for Sky and is skittery with nerves but, he says, 'Over the fucking moon for Barny. He's played fantastic.' Ross has just phoned their mum, proudly, to report Barny's success and tell her that all their visions of poker celebrity and poker security are coming into place.

The crowd, spivved up now in suits and ties, are gathering in the bar for the final. I can't wait for it to start. It is bizarre to see the cameras being rolled around the room, microphones being tested, production crew rippling with the adrenaline of live coverage, as if this were an FA Cup Final rather than a poker game. Maybe the boys are right and it really is going to be big? I never considered playing this tournament, it's way beyond my level, but I'm happy just to be in the bar for what is starting to feel like a historic game.

I can see every poker player I've ever heard of. I can smell the shampoo on the freakishly clean hair of Chris 'Jesus' Ferguson, the world champion. The nickname is simple: with his rake-thin frame, waist-length locks and beard, he resembles the Messiah. Except when he puts on his big black hat, and then he resembles all four Horsemen of the Apocalypse rolled into one.

When Ferguson crosses the bar, Mad Marty leads his fellow gamblers in a chorus of 'We don't care if it rains or freezes; we've got a friend in Lo-ord Jesus!'

Barry Hearn, the promoter of the event, comes out to read the names of the six finalists. There is polite applause for each, but a deafening cheer for Barny Boatman. Half the people in this room have bought shares in his winnings, the other half just love him.

Barny seems very tired. He's coming down with a cold and he should really go to bed. 'I'm losing my voice,' he croaks to me and Joe in the bar, 'but I'm enjoying this situation. Everyone's shaking my hand, giving me advice, wanting interviews.' He admits, 'I'm a bit of showman anyway, and I'm in my element.'

The good thing is, he isn't nervous. He says, 'I've made a last-minute decision to play in this thing, and whatever happens now, it's been great.'

♠

On Monday morning, *The Times* reports: 'John Duthie, a TV director from Wandsworth, South London, has won £1,000,000 in Britain's biggest poker tournament. Londoner Barny Boatman was the first to be knocked out, losing his chips within five minutes.'

What's a man to do? Barny had the shortest stack. He went all-in when he found an ace, and got knocked out by Ian Dobson, a tattooed Black Country croupier turned pro. He was led out by Carrie Frais who, weighing up the chances of the remaining five players, asked, 'Where's your money now?' Barny replied: 'Back on that table in there.'

But he has reason enough to be happy. Barny won £14,000 for 6th place, and about £20,000 more in bets and shares with other players. Not bad for a man who came into town without even the money for his entry ticket.

We have breakfast on Monday morning before the 6th-place finisher and his brother head off to the airport. Joe's coming back with me on the ferry. I tell them I still have no idea what you're meant to say to someone who's just been knocked out of a huge tournament.

'Sometimes we might discuss the hands,' says Ram, 'but this

is too big for that. When Barny came out, I just gave him a little hug, a little handshake and said "Well done."'

And Barny doesn't seem too down, as he doles out 5% shares to his fellow Mobsters, in keeping with tradition.

'These are early days for us,' he says. 'Right now we're still ducking and weaving. But we all made it to the second day, and the others were knocked out through bad luck, not bad play. I think we've proved that the Hendon Mob are up there with the best. We're at the start of something absolutely massive.'

'Next year,' adds Joe, 'we'll all be in the final.'

AND ANOTHER WEAK ACE

A♥ 4♥. Now this is pretty: suited wheel cards. Spokes. And this time everybody has passed round to my small blind. This time I absolutely cannot pass. If I throw this away, with only one hand behind me, it's like I don't want to play. I might as well not have bothered to leave my house this morning.

I make a minimum raise to 40,000. I'm pleased with this play. It's a little tester raise, to see how much the big blind likes his hand. It leaves room for manoeuvre: if Chad Brown (who has the big blind) re-raises, and I think he's stealing from me, I have enough chips left to move in over the top and he has to pass most hands.

As it happens, he just calls and we see a flop of 2♥ 10♥ 5♥. Happy Valentine's Day! Look at all those beautiful beating hearts. They're beating Chad Brown, anyway.

I've got the nuts, the best possible hand, the top flush with a straight flush re-draw. I bet out 60,000: three-quarters of the pot. When I watch the televised coverage later, I hear John Duthie, who won the Poker Million in 2000 and now runs the whole European Poker Tour, shouting 'Don't!' when I make this bet.

I know why he would say that. I've got the nuts, why should I risk scaring away my customer? But there's a reason. Chad Brown knows that there are only two of us in the pot, and that he has not shown any strength. I would have to make a 'continuation bet' on the flop with any two cards at all. If I check, it's actually more suspicious than betting.

The plan works nicely: Chad Brown raises me to 120,000. I have a little dwell, then flat call. Why? Because I'm trying to represent the bare ace of hearts. I want him to think that I don't believe I'm winning but I'll stick around to hit another heart. The truth is, I'm actually gambling the opposite way – gambling that another heart DOESN'T come to kill my action.

Doing my absolute utmost to represent the bare ace, I check the turn 'in the dark'. That is, I check before the card has been turned over. The turn is 9♦ but Chad doesn't fall for it, and checks behind. The river is 3♣, giving me an unnecessary straight to go with my flush.

I think about it. If I check here and Chad has no hand, he may believe me for a busted flush draw and bet out to chase away an ace high. But what if he has a pair? If he has a pair (and he should have something for his pre-flop call), then he can just check behind and hope he's winning. I'd hate us both to check and then he turns over AT, a hand which would have called a value bet.

So I bet out 100,000. It's less than a third of the pot, how can he resist?

He does resist, pushing his dark hand over to the muck. Dammit, I should have checked to let him bet. But I've picked up 160,000 in this pot, and now I'm in much better shape. Rory Liffey gives me a thumbs-up from the rail.

9

SONGS OF INNOCENCE
AND EXPERIENCE

'And I watered it in fears
Night and morning with my tears
And I sunned it with smiles
And with soft deceitful wiles . . .'
— William Blake

Ah, Luton. Spiritual home of the hat trade. They don't make hats here any more, but they've got the big Vauxhall factory. Sadly, Vauxhall has just announced it will be closing in a few months. What does that leave? The Arndale Centre, the airport and the casino.

On a glowering January morning, Luton is not a beautiful place to visit. Thirty miles north of London, twenty minutes up the M1 from Hendon at the speed Joe drives, it's hard to see exactly where the motorway ends and Luton begins. The casino is in the middle of a car park, under a flyover, next to a supermarket.

This is not the most romantic spot for a day trip with your boyfriend. But Britain doesn't have a Las Vegas, a Monte Carlo or even a Reno. The hotspots for poker, apart from London, are Luton and Walsall. No disrespect to the people who live in those towns, but it would be hard for the tourist board to market either with much enthusiasm.

Still, they loom large on the poker map. Nearly 200 people have come here to play the £100 Pot Limit Holdem tournament, creating a £16,000 first prize if everyone has the re-buy. It doesn't compare with the Poker Million, of course, but this is normal poker. Cash games are the bread-and-butter, tournaments are the dream and £16,000 is a hefty payday. Everyone from the Vic has made the trip.

♠

I play the tournament all wrong. Since *Late Night Poker*, I have told myself sternly and regularly not to fold my way out of any more competitions. The problem here is that Joe and I are driving back tonight and he's got lots of chips, so I'm worried about getting knocked out too early and having nothing to do. This makes me play cautiously and, inevitably, fold my way out of the tournament. I end up doing a crossword puzzle in the bar.

But Joe makes the final, finishing 4th for £2,200, so it's all worthwhile. We have a drink afterwards with the man who came second, a Midlands veteran called Mickey Wernick.

He looks like one of the BeeGees. Or rather, he looks like one of the BeeGees might have looked if they had lived a harder life. He has the long thick hair and the generous beard, without the smooth tanned skin and manicured nails. His nickname is 'The Worm', which doesn't sound like a great nickname to me.

'In the Sixties, they called me The Kid,' chuckles Mickey. 'But not any more.'

This chap has been playing poker for a long, long time. As a young man, he helped his father run a joint that was part poker den, part nightclub. Mickey would deal the games, stay calm when the police raided, and watch his father losing money to local hustlers. But Mickey could see that this should be an easy game to beat. He had an affinity for the cards, and nobody seemed to play very smartly. So he started going to the old Rainbow in Birmingham and other clubs around the area, looking for tourists who were in the game 'for fun', and turning a nice profit.

He started going to Vegas and taking on the American pros. He played heads-up with Doyle Brunson, one of the great icons of American poker, and won the lot. He even played with Stu Ungar, the James Dean of poker, who won those three world titles and died in a cheap motel room. But Mickey Wernick is still here.

'That is what it's all about,' Joe tells me in the car home. 'Surviving. Mickey doesn't get greedy, doesn't get silly. He's kept his head above water for forty years in this game, covering his expenses, making his money, not getting into trouble. Looking after himself. That is the first thing you have to do, learn how to survive.'

♠

In the normal run of things, a trip to Luton is the height of excitement and potential lucre. My usual poker is the £50 round-of-each game in the Vic, the Tuesday game and lots of $10 tournaments on Joe's computer.

But, one day, we find ourselves playing cards on the deck of a luxury yacht moored off Marbella. A tangle of girls in rubber catsuits lie lazily around the table, purring. And a camera crew from Channel 4 is hounding a man to tears. Television is back again.

The Catman has a black ponytail and a lapdancing club called Sophisticats. Now he is starting to sniff out opportunities in the spread of poker, and has got himself into the cast of a documentary about British gamblers. I don't know how the producer found him, but I know him from the old Russell Square casino: we were both regulars in their Wednesday hi-lo tournaments.

For the documentary, Catman has hatched an ambitious plan. He has decided to hold a charity poker tournament in aid of Breakthrough Breast Cancer, on a yacht moored at Puerto Banus. Because of the TV cameras, he has persuaded Yamaha to donate a £15,000 motorbike as first prize. Because of the prize, eminent poker players have come to his tournament. Thus, in the programme, he will be seen lavishly entertaining the top pros, on a glamorous yacht, with lapdancing lovelies at his side. And it will all raise money for an important charity! Purrfect.

♠

I'm not especially interested in winning a motorbike, but Joe loves the idea of a poker tournament under such glamorous circumstances and this is my first chance of a sunshine holiday with him. We're sharing a rental apartment with Barny, we have eaten fresh fish on the quayside, I've also got a ticket to the tournament and I am fascinated to see a group of strippers, poker pros and media people come together. What an Olympics of scepticism and cunning.

All four of the Hendon Mob are here, along with Devilfish and Simon 'Aces' Trumper. Prowling around between Catman, Aces, Elegance and Devilfish are the girls from Sophisticats: Autumn, Ginger and Purrsia. I think I'm the only person on this boat still using the name she was born with.

The Devilfish, famed for his intimidating red shades and rough talk, looks charming with a tiny pink breast cancer ribbon pinned to his lapel. He has got hold of a guitar that he strums as the sun goes down, singing *Sylvia's Mother* and *Are You Lonesome Tonight?* exactly as Elvis would have sung them, if he'd grown up in Hull.

Devilfish is a great character for television, but difficult for TV people. At the filming of tournaments, they want his off-colour jokes, his old-fashioned machismo and his aggrandizing speeches (he talks about himself in the third person, like Othello; he can warn an opponent 'Don't mess with the Devilfish' and not laugh doing it) – but not too much. They don't want him to swear. They don't want him to offend anyone. They don't want him to pinch a researcher's bum, or say anything racist. And yet they want his salt and his danger.

Dave Ulliott was not born into a world where egos were

soft and bruisable. He spent his teenage years on the streets of working-class Humberside in the 1970s, leaving school with no qualifications, working tough jobs, moving into a flat 'which I took because I was hungry and you could eat the mushrooms off the bathroom door'. His only real pleasure came from betting on horses, and from what I can tell, he's sick on the races to this day.

There were fights, guns, prison stretches, all the juicy stuff of British drama. But when stories come out about him burgling off-licences with his teenage gang, Devilfish is quick to distance himself from the allegations. As the first winner of *Late Night Poker*, with the potential to become an international face, he certainly doesn't want to be known for knocking off grocery stores. 'It makes me sound small-time,' he says anxiously. 'We did bank jobs.'

His new life has come about by chance. A few games of cards in the back of a pool hall led him deeper into a shady and underground pastime. A good run in a few tournaments got him invited into the first, experimental *Late Night Poker*. There were many good players but Devilfish won, and is thus becoming the first British poker celebrity. He hasn't paused for media training along the way. He never even got his O Levels.

These days, having taken the long journey from a council house 'so small that we had to paint furniture on the walls' to a deluxe televised poker tournament on board a yacht, Devilfish is different but the same. He lives within the law, he loves a bit of bling, and his seven children enjoy luxuries he never had. But whatever TV can do for him, however famous he might become, he's never going to behave like a boy scout.

Personally, I am starting to love the guy. I invaded his world, he didn't invade mine. I don't care if he stares at my chest and murmurs, 'There's two big things we gotta talk about.' It's okay to laugh. He likes making people laugh. I am seeing his softer side on this Marbella trip; the hard surface is genuine but, equally genuine underneath, he cares deeply what people think. He may want to dazzle and impress, but more than that he wants to be liked.

Besides all of that, he is clearly a gifted, brilliant poker player. If he displayed the same flairy genius in chess or football or music, nobody would blink at his quirks of personality or speech. I'll say this for Dave Ulliott: he's a lot nicer than Bobby Fischer.

Anyway, I've got my own dangerous streak. Catman got terribly cross when he caught me smoking a cigarette over the side of the boat. 'Put that out!' he shrieked nervously. 'This yacht is borrowed!'

♠

So we sit playing cards, eating fish, singing along to Devilfish's guitar, excited about being on television. In theory, I am 'from the media' myself – I'm earning a living from writing, and come from a writing family – but I feel like one of the poker crew here, not one of the press. I'm Joe's girlfriend. I'm backing vocalist to the Humberside Elvis. I'm eager to play the tournament. We are all in a holiday spirit, treating this as a sort of *Late Night Poker* summer special, naively assuming that the TV programme will be discreet and sympathetic.

But apparently that's not the story they're looking for.

♠

Everything is fine until we're down to a final table. We have been playing the tournament in open air, on board this yacht, and it's all pretty light-hearted. I bluff Devilfish out of one pot, and he is so exasperated to fold for a girl's bet that he snatches my hand from the muck to examine it. This is severely out of order in a poker game and I'm confident enough by now to shout at him, but it's a sign of the holiday spirit that it's not a big scandal. I shout, he makes a sheepish quip, the whole table laughs and we go back to the action.

As night falls and the remaining players move inside the boat, the mood tightens. There is less chat and laughter, more focused concentration. But the quiet is broken when Agnieszka Piotrowska (the director, camera-woman and 'brains' behind the TV documentary) thrusts a microphone towards Catman, who is dealing the cards, and asks whether he bribed the players to attend his tournament.

We all look up, shocked. Bribery? Catman is the most shocked of all. He may be a poker player, but a single snide question has transformed him into a mass of tells. Not the tells of a duper, but of one who has been duped.

Suddenly, Catman is seeing the whole picture. He isn't the hero of a glamorous TV show. He is the gull of media people hoping to rake scandal and skulduggery from the poker gutter. They want to hear about bribery, not charity. They want to make us all look like crooks. That is the story they came to tell.

And they have weeks of footage already. They have been to tournaments all over Europe. They have been to the cash game in Jac Arama's basement. They have filmed Jac's children. Catman has opened his heart on camera about the recent deaths of both his parents. And he, they, we, are going to be stitched up.

This is not the sort of show that Catman promised Yamaha when the motorbike was donated. A small world is crashing. The fear – of the bike being withdrawn, of embarrassment on television, of being insulted in front of his fellow players – is colouring his whole face. This is *Alice In Wonderland* in reverse: the smile disappears and the cat remains.

So shocked is Catman by the false allegation of guile, so exhausted by the nervous weeks of arranging the tournament and the terrible year of losing his parents, so crestfallen at the crumpling of his hopeful TV vision, that tears come coursing down his cheeks. Right here at the poker table, Catman is crying.

I don't know what to do. This is the ultimate test for the unfazeable company of lapdancers, poker professionals and TV crew, all, in their own special ways, in the business of making grown men cry. I fail the test; I put my arms round Catman as if he were a child. But the girls keep purring, the cameras keep rolling, and Ross says: 'I'll bet the pot.'

♠

The following spring, Joe and I break up. He is ready to settle down, I'm not. He needs a woman who can work around his quirky lifestyle, who can run a home and look after children while he's away, or travel with him and be the supportive spouse when he's putting in the long tournament hours. Someone who will flirt with him, make him laugh and cheer him up when he's knocked out, who brings with her the fresh air of a poker-free world. I adore him, but I know that I am not the right girl.

I bet that Joe will be married soon enough. Somewhere out there is his perfect partner and all he has to do is go looking. He is a natural for marriage and children. I'm not so sure about me.

It is all as amicable as a break-up can be, our friendship survives with the valiance of Mickey Wernick, and we get together on the evening when the documentary is due to be broadcast. Eight per cent of Joe's mind is hoping to see himself look good on TV; he won the tournament and the motorbike, although it has not yet been delivered.

But we both know it is not going to be that sort of programme. Sure enough, Catman's tearful premonition comes true for everyone involved. We all look seedy. There's a grim scene involving Jac Arama, the travel agent who runs a furtive private game in Earls Court, and his mate Garry 'The Whacker' Bush, who failed to spot the microphone which recorded them discussing the price of hookers on a trip to St Petersburg. Their whole conversation is broadcast, with subtitles for extra effect. Catman is shown crying at the table in Marbella, with Agnieszka's nasty question replaced by a voiceover (done by Agnieszka herself) claiming, 'Why Catman is upset remains a mystery.' He looks like a lunatic.

My own face appears under the dramatic statement, 'There are a couple of women here, no doubt trained by their men, but they don't stand a chance. Whatever anyone else tries to tell you, I promise: this is the last bastion of male dominance. Women are just crap at poker.'

Quite apart from the assumptions about my poker skills, I am not delighted to see myself, unidentified, appear so close to another statement that it is 'a world full of prostitutes'.

The motorbike is withdrawn. Joe and Catman come to a private arrangement.

♠

This is a world with sick corners and bleak edges. Bad things happen in poker. People are cheated, threatened, lied to, beaten up and occasionally shot in the nuts. Foul words are spoken, people are insulted, belittled, humiliated. I have heard about a man, in a private cash game, reaching into a pot and taking back money that he had lost, then threatening his protesting opponent, who backed down in fear of his life. I know a man who, winning a large sum at casino closing time, was invited to continue heads-up in a hotel room where he was set up by moody dealers and moody players and left with nothing. I have played in games where heroin was smoked in the corner and games where gunmen stood in the hall. I know players who have borrowed and lost and borrowed and lost, then done terrible things to get the money back. Premises are burned down. People disappear. Usually they're in prison. That's what you hope, anyway.

And what has Agnieszka seen? A pleasant bunch of people playing guitars on a seafront. Friends, brothers, lovers enjoying a poker holiday. The happiest, friendliest, most playful end of the game. At worst, a bit of money trickled into the Russian sex economy. I suspect this was not what she promised the broadcaster at all. But if Agnieszka wanted to find the heart of darkness in poker, she'd have had to stick around a lot longer than a couple of months.

After this, there will be no more television without questions, meetings, contracts. And there will be no more excitement about being on screen. Even *Late Night Poker* seems less like fun and more like business; people start turning up for the tournament, trying to win the money, and leaving after they get knocked out. No more sticking around after defeat to cheer for friends in other matches, no more all-night games in Howard's hotel room.

That Spanish trip is where we lost our innocence, because we still had it to lose.

A PAIR OF EIGHTS

The garden gates. Another pair, another beautiful piece of symmetry as the matching eights cuddle together, curving and twisting like twin egg-timers. Earlier tonight, I lost a big pot after raising with a pair of sixes, but I still believe I am entitled to think a pocket pair is good against only five opponents. The sixes were winning last time, after all, and it's not my fault that Emad flopped trip queens.

Everyone passes round to Jules Kuusik's small blind, and he raises to 60,000. I make it 200,000 immediately. I'm not messing around here. This re-raise is a commitment to the hand, and he knows it. If he's found something better than eights in this spot, good luck to him. I'm feeling the determination. I'm betting because I mean it. I'm actually becoming a stronger player over the course of this single tournament.

Kuusik decides that he doesn't have aces after all. After a bit of Hollywood thinking, he folds, and I'm happy enough with that.

10

BRACELETS

'Passengers are reminded that professional gamblers
are reported to be frequent travellers, and are warned
to take precautions accordingly.'

— The Lady Eve

As the players walk into the main card room at Binion's for the 25th event of the World Series, the tournament director congratulates us all on looking so lovely. There is loud applause and several wolf-whistles. Only one of us can win the bracelet and $41,000 first prize that's at stake here, but we all get a red rose and a silver trinket as a present just for turning up.

Cards in the air. Two players immediately start talking about how nervous they are of making a mistake. Two other players admire each other's outfits. Everybody's smiling. And I'm thinking: this is bizarre. It's like the opposite of poker.

Where is the swearing, the growling? Where is the smalltalk about starting prices at Cheltenham or the Knicks' chances this season? Where is the rumbling baritone chorus of 'This tournament's got my name all over it' . . . 'I'm in the zone' . . . 'Nobody else stands a chance' . . . ?

Instead, there is a general shy murmur: 'I just don't want to do anything stupid' . . . 'I hope I'm not the first to be knocked out.' Weird, weird, weird.

This is the first tournament I have ever played, or seen, at the WSOP. I have been to Las Vegas before, but never at this magical time of year. My dazzled, jetlagged, heatstruck brain is already struggling to confront the immensity of actually being here, at the famous Series itself, which I have dreamed of ever since Matt talked about it 13 years ago, and the added strangeness of a tournament peopled only by women is slightly too much to take.

The Ladies' Tournament is a novelty event, held every Mother's Day to entertain the girlfriends, wives and mothers of the real players, introduce them to this funny game that so engages their men. But I can spot one or two among the 100-strong field who may, like me, be taking this seriously.

Nani Dollison has already smashed through an open field to collect a bracelet in this year's $2,000 Limit Holdem. And although some of my opponents are giggling and showing cards to their neighbours, some of them are playing sharply. But they don't behave like it. The conversation is . . . I don't know . . . *intimate*. One dazzling redhead scoops her Vietnamese neighbour's entire stack of chips with a fiendishly hidden set of eights, slow-playing her clean out of the tournament, while asking the question, 'Are you still seeing that construction worker? He seemed cute.'

The small blind asks the button if she's dating anybody right now. The button, calling a small raise on the flop, chats about an ongoing fling with an office colleague and some fears about commitment. The small blind, betting three-quarters of the pot on the turn, expresses the view that this is normal and that the romance sounds promising. The button, mucking her hand in disgust, compliments the big blind on her blouse. The big blind smiles, and provides details as to where such a blouse can be acquired locally at reasonable cost.

This is making my head spin.

♠

Since Joe and I broke up, I have been playing far less poker. The Tuesday game still runs every week and I pop into the Vic every so often, but there have been no more tournaments or online games. I've been busy with work, catching up with friends outside the poker scene, dating another guy who would feel threatened if I spent too much time at the casino. I found myself at the World Series of Poker completely by chance.

Well, not *completely* by chance. Like all the best poker situations, it was manipulated chance. My old college friend Charlie and I have been working on a book about the sex industry and we went to do some research in the San Fernando Valley, California, heart of the American porn trade. We started trying to contact local moguls at Christmas but, by the time we had gathered enough positive replies, we ended up flying out to the West Coast in May. World Series time.

I persuaded Charlie that if we were really going to immerse our polite English selves in a sea of international sleaze, we should pop over the state line into Nevada. Las Vegas is the city of lost souls, after all. He agreed, we drove through the desert . . . and what do you know? The world's biggest poker tournament was going on! Charlie was delighted.

Having got him here, I needed to distract him while I slipped away. So, spotting a newspaper advert for a local gun shop which offered potential customers the chance to fire an Uzi, I deliberately drove him past it. I knew Charlie would be unable to resist that bait. As he wandered awestruck into the shop, I raced downtown to find the WSOP. What I actually found was Barny Boatman, and kicked off my trip with several cocktails in the midday sun on the hottest May 9th in Las Vegas since records began. I have spent the last four days in bed with a blinding headache and horrific nausea.

But I was feeling better today, and Charlie still isn't speaking to me after luring him into the desert on false pretences. I bumped into Joe on Fremont Street and he said that if I wanted to play the Ladies' Event he would buy a share of my action. So: here I am, contesting my first-ever world title.

♠

This particular event may be a novelty, but so is the idea that any of the tournaments offer 'world titles' anyway. The name of this annual collection of poker events was originally copied from the World Series of baseball – which itself was so christened simply because it began as a series of matches sponsored by the *World* newspaper. It doesn't mean 'international' at all. And 'world champion of poker', a title that goes specifically with the $10,000 No Limit Holdem tournament at the end of the series, is especially arbitrary. That is just one competition of many – there are seven-card stud tournaments, Omaha tournaments, hi-lo tournaments, limit and pot limit and no limit, there's a 'Seniors' Event' as well as the Ladies' Event – and each one offers the winner a prize bracelet on top of the purse.

Nobody gets selected to play the main event, the last one, the one that creates the ultimate 'world champion of poker'. You can win your way there or you can buy your way there, but it's perfectly possible that the greatest poker players have never taken part. Freddie from the Vic, for example. He's never even been to Vegas.

Nevertheless, for want of an alternative, these are the tournaments we consider to be offering world titles. WSOP bracelets are the most sought-after trophies in all of poker. To many, they mean more than the money. Win a bracelet, you have it for life. Win money, it'll be gone with the next rainy day.

♠

Despite the gallant applause as we filtered into the room to take our seats, we don't all look so 'lovely'. Table 6 look like a bunch of truckers, don't worry about that. There's a lady on Table 7 in size 20 dungarees who should really have considered wearing a bra.

Nani Dollison, who already has a winner's bracelet from the $2,000 Limit event, is dressed comfortably for a long day's action in a T-shirt, trousers and professional-looking sunglasses.

But most are decked out as if it were Ladies' Day at Ascot. There are bright colours, floral prints, glittering necklaces, high-heeled shoes, gold clutch purses and cute little hats. Susie Isaacs, a well-known Southern belle, is wearing a jacket covered in sparkly aces, teamed with a pair of special dice earrings.

I always dress up for any poker tournament. Everyone dresses up for the televised events, but when there are no cameras the guys are usually in slacks and sports shirts, sometimes jeans if there isn't a casino dress code. But I like to be smart, like Barbara Stanwyck in *The Lady Eve*.

Barbara Stanwyck was not a beautiful woman. In a generation of stars like Vivien Leigh, Lana Turner, Betty Grable and Lauren Bacall, she was quite an ordinary-looking girl. But in *The Lady Eve* – where Stanwyck plays a cruise-ship hustler on the high seas – she is beautifully turned out, wears her hair nicely and flirts effectively, all of which is a useful distraction from the fact that she is a *brilliant card player*. She's easily capable of winning back Henry Fonda's lost $32,000 in about three hands. (This film is Henry Fonda's first attempt at playing the lover of a surprisingly able female poker player. He does it again in *A Big Hand For The Little Lady*. Twice in a lifetime, good work, Henry.)

So: I wear a dress or skirt, cute, sometimes fitted, sometimes a lower neckline, but always quite modest. High-heeled shoes or boots. Black tights in a European country, no tights in Vegas. Clean hair, lipstick, but not full make-up or I'll feel like a clown. Pink or gold watch, sometimes a little bracelet, usually a necklace.

If it's a televised tournament, there might be close-ups of my hands engaged in the constant obsessive shuffling and reshuffling of chips, so I might give myself a French manicure. Brightly coloured or scarlet nails are too vampy. But bare nails are risky because little bits of green baize are quick to accumulate under them, and I don't want to look like I've just finished weeding the garden.

There is a routine, then, before a tournament. Have a bath, wash my hair, dress nicely but not immodestly, add an unobtrusive slick of make-up, sometimes a couple of coats of nail polish, a trace but not a full rattle of jewellery, a hint of perfume but not too much. Then take a deep breath, hide the nerves, go out there and smile. Sometimes, it makes me feel less like a poker player and more like an agency hooker.

♠

I still don't have a nickname. *Poker Europa*, a magazine you see in racks around casino card rooms, once referred to me as 'Poker Doll', and The Sweep has used that nickname with ironic delight ever since. But I can't. It would be embarrassing now, and goddamn poignant when I got past fifty.

Ashley suggests 'Call Girl'. It would certainly suit my playing style, but I don't think I have the guts to pull it off.

♠

I once read an article in a glossy magazine about how to tell if your girlfriend has a sideline as a high-class prostitute. The signs were:

1. She stays out very late at night.
2. She carries a lot of cash.
3. Her mobile is rarely on before noon.
4. You get replies to your emails at 4 a.m.
5. She refers in passing to dozens of people you've never met.
6. She goes away on 'trips' not holidays, flying alone or with people whose full names you don't know.
7. She always seems able to take a day off work at short notice.

8. She has lavish spending phases and sudden frugal phases, which seem completely unconnected to her day job.
9. Even if she arrives home at dawn, she's never been drinking.
10. She has travelled widely in Europe, but never seen any of the sights.

That was the great thing about going out with Joe. I never had to explain any of it.

♠

I was so happy to bump into him on Fremont Street.

Downtown Las Vegas, in WSOP time, is nothing like the part of town I have seen before. Films and postcards always show you the Strip: giant themed hotels, wide streets packed with cars, enormous multi-coloured fountains. But downtown, Fremont Street, is small, pedestrianized, under a magic roof that plays electronic films and pumps out music. Buskers, jugglers and stall-holders jostle for attention. They sell T-shirts, trinkets, packs of cards, lucky dice and confusing Buddha money-boxes. Strippers beckon from doorways. And everywhere you look, there are poker players wandering back and forth. Standing there for five minutes, I saw ten or fifteen people I know from Europe. The little hardcore of travelling players is always in Vegas at May time for this series of events, and the baking-hot glittery street feels somehow *villagey*.

Binion's Horseshoe, the rickety old casino where the tournaments take place, is soaked in romance and history. As soon as I walked in, I felt like I've been coming here for decades. Dark, grimy, smoky, fervent, jingling with hope and slots, it looks exactly as I imagined from reading Al Alvarez's book.

As I stood on its grubby, momentous doorstep, I saw Jac Arama, the travel agent who was stitched up in Agnieszka's documentary, hobbling out of the Golden Nugget looking terrible. I was amazed to see him at all. Two weeks ago, he was mown down by a cab driver at Hyde Park Corner. The mystery cabbie knocked Jac unconscious in the road, then drove over his arm to get away. (Cab driver? Hyde Park Corner? Chances are the guy was in a hurry to get to the Vic.)

But you can't get between a man and his poker addiction. Standing there in the 104-degree heat, Jac explained that he limped onto a plane to contest the Vegas tournaments with two broken ribs, a punctured lung and a metal plate in his ribs. He hasn't won anything yet. He'd better hurry up; after the ladies' tournament, there is only the main event left.

Then I saw Joe sipping an iced tea on the corner and hurried over for a full rundown of British news. He told me that Devil-fish has had an impressive two runner-up spots, in the $1,500 Pot Limit Omaha for $167,035, and the $2,000 Pot Limit Holdem for $193,800. I can guess that the double near-miss has got him gnashing his teeth in frustration, but the prizes will keep him in diamanté knuckle-dusters for a while. And one UK player has snatched a bracelet: our old friend and chaperone Hemish Shah.

Joe told me that the win was remarkable for two reasons. First, it was in the $5,000 Limit Holdem event. Limit poker, in which the betting is capped for each round, is considered to be an American specialty; we Brits play pot limit. Second, Hemish was taken ill during the match.

Just before the final table began, Hemish developed terrible stomach cramps. In the breaks between levels, while rival players supped drinks and planned strategy, Hemish was doubled up in his chair. Joe tried desperately to find him a doctor, but Hemish wasn't keen: US doctors cost a lot of money. Hemish doesn't drive across London for a discount on a plug adaptor, then throw his money away on an unsubsidized health service. He struggled back to the table, outplayed the Americans, made the final, won the title, collected that beautiful winner's bracelet, pocketed a

$312,340 prize, then caught an early plane back to London and went home to bed.

I've only just missed him; he went back yesterday. Joe says he's going into hospital for tests. Most people are blaming the air conditioning. There is an air conditioning phobia in Vegas. Everybody is always ill here – it's called Vegas Flu – and they always blame the air conditioning. It must blow germs around. Nobody blames the fact that they get no sleep, they're stressed, they're eating rubbish, they're hunched over a table for 17 hours a day and they only take breaks to sunbathe or play golf in 110-degree temperatures. Ill? Must be a fault in the air conditioning vent.

Hemish, the teetotal vegetarian, lives a far healthier life out here than most, so who knows? Maybe it was the air conditioning.

♠

With only two World Series tournaments left to be completed, Hemish could be the only British bracelet-winner this year. To double our medals, either a Brit will have to fluke the main event, or this ladies' title must go to me or Debbie Berlin.

'The Debbiefish', wife of Luton player Dave Welch, is the only other British woman in the field. We wave at each other across the coiffed, gossipy room.

This is not the first time I've seen a woman across a poker table. My Tuesday life began with an introduction to The Sweep's wife Kira, who co-hosted the game when it was in Notting Hill. Currently, it is floating around between The Sweep's house in Vauxhall, Robert's flat and mine.

There's Kate Szeremeta, the one with the Ben Elton tattoo on her stomach. There's the handful who play on *Late Night Poker*, including The Debbiefish. And several women turn up to play Conrad's annual charity poker tournament, the Holdem 100, for a once-a-year Christmas spin.

But a whole tournament full of women, women on every table, women in front of me, women on either side, women in my peripheral vision . . . This is something else. It's like science fiction. It's a vision of how the world could have been, if somebody stepped on a butterfly and it all turned out different. Men looking after children, discussing emotions, fighting for the vote; women watching football, putting up scaffolding and playing poker.

Susie Isaacs gives me a copy of her book, which is dedicated to her 'poker friends Darlene, Peggy, Marge, Joanie, June, Barbara, Annie, Fran and Mary Margaret'. Wow. My poker friends are all called Dave.

Or Pantelis.

♠

There is no reason, of course, why women can't play as successfully as men. It's not a weightlifting competition. Even the smallest hands can hold two cards — or four, or six. When Amarillo Slim said, 'A woman would have a better chance of putting a wild cat in a tobacco sack than she would of coming out to Vegas and beating me,' he wasn't talking from a coolly scientific perspective. Neither was Huck Seed, that day he muttered to me about evolution and I was too shy to challenge him.

Men and women are not sufficiently different, psychologically, for either gender to be 'naturally' better at poker than the other. I am not saying that gender differences don't exist. It is only women who have headaches without telling anybody, remember arguments verbatim, re-use cotton wool, worry about the problems of characters on television, or have close and long-standing friendships with people they don't like. And it is only men who get excited about military hardware, blow their noses on their hands, say 'Can't we talk about this tomorrow?', have any interest in watching Michael Caine films, think seriously and carefully about what they would do if they encountered a bear (or a shark, or a dinosaur, or Hitler) while carrying only a candle-stick, or take out a pint of milk, sniff it, make a face, then put it back in the fridge.

But none of these things is a factor at the poker table. If the differences between men and women are relevant to the game at all, it should be true that women's traditional qualities of craftiness, patience and guile should balance out the male instincts of aggression, bluff and bluster.

In fact, the kind of men who have told me directly that women can't play poker are the same kind of men who whine 'I don't understand my wife – she's always saying one thing and meaning another.' Well, that should be her first natural advantage at the table.

But women just don't seem to be drawn to poker in any significant numbers. It's not about ability, but attraction. Men are quicker to care deeply about something that a sensible observer might say is 'just a game'. They are more likely to be overtaken by it. They are readier to forget the existence of family, or the potential for it, while gripped by an all-night, or all-life, gambling rush. It doesn't make them better poker players. Certainly doesn't make them better people. It just makes them more comfortable with the spirit and the lifestyle, more vulnerable to that particular addiction.

♠

At the Vic, there are rarely any women in the card room but me and 'the other Vicky'. To her, of course, I am the other Vicky.

Vicky Lincoln is a cash Omaha player, a girlfriend of Alan the sex mogul. I love Alan. He is one of those men who are softly spoken but very macho, tough but funny, bald with a lisp, well suited to smoking a cigar at the wheel of a Bentley. His particular car is big and gold, with the number plate XXX 1. I've won a

fair bit of money betting against people who assume Alan's Jewish.
Never bet on facts: the jack is always waiting to spit cider in your
ear. All I have to do is turn the subject round to the disproportionate success of Jewish players, chat idly about the mix in the
Vic, wait for Alan's name to come up and then say, 'Is he? I reckon
he isn't. I'd have thought he was Turkish or something.' If you
ever question a gambler's opinion, he'll be quick to get his money
out. ('No, I'm sure I'm right . . . Let's make it a carpet . . .')
And I know this fact in advance, so I can't lose.

   Anyway, Vicky is a beautiful, super-glamorous Yugoslavian
blonde who started off watching Alan play poker and developed
a knack for the game herself. We often have little chats in the
ladies' loo, the most peaceful place in the Vic. Almost anywhere
else in the world, a ladies' loo involves queuing and waiting,
drumming your fingers and thinking 'What are they *doing* in
there?', while a gents' has a fast, efficient turnover. But not the
card room loos in the Vic. If I see one of the cubicle doors already
shut, 10/1 on it'll be Vicky in there. If not, it's out of order. They
probably only have a ladies' because they are legally required to.
Terrible waste of gaming space, really.

   On tournament breaks, the Vic card room is a zoo. There is
always a great herd of players milling around and waiting for the
gents' to empty out, moaning that the break's too short for them
all to have a leak, using the wait time to phone in and check
their sports bets, or yell for the waitresses to bring a sandwich,
or tell uninterested bystanders about their bad beats, or try to
sneak their names illegally onto the list for a cash game in case
they're knocked out, or ask around for chewing gum, or do a
quick bottle on the roulette – all of it with Pedro, Mike Masuris
and Mr Chu trying to get on with a £50 round-of-each in the
middle.

   But the ladies' is silent, empty, calm. I'm either alone, or
washing my hands next to Vicky and asking how her luck is
going. I once burst into tears on her shoulder in there, when I

was having boyfriend trouble. 'Does he beat you?' she asked sympathetically. I replied with an impressively middle-class, 'Oh God, no! He just isn't very forthcoming with his emotions.'

♠

Sadly, I am not to be the 2001 ladies' champion of poker. The title goes to Nani Dollison for the second year in a row. That, on top of her Limit Holdem victory, makes two bracelets in one Series, an incredibly rare achievement. Maybe I'll play as good as her, one day.

And there's no British victory in the main event either, though Barny Boatman has another near-miss. There are 613 runners (a 100-strong increase on the year before) and Barny finishes in 33rd place for $30,000, the highest-placed Brit in the field.

But I don't see any of the main event. I am reunited with Charlie, getting on with our book research.

One night we watch *The First Wives Club* on the hotel TV. It opens with Stockard Channing, a wife who has just been abandoned by her husband, throwing herself off the top of a building.

'Of course, that would never happen to me,' I tell Charlie. 'That's the beauty of the thing: I will never need to be sat at home, staring at the wall. I can go to the Vic. If my husband dumps me for a younger woman, my life won't be empty and meaningless, I'll just go and play poker.'

'Plans, plans,' says Charlie. 'You have to find someone to marry you first.'

♠

I don't think I will play the Ladies' Event again. A special women's competition sends out the wrong message, as if we're admitting we need some kind of help. I want to get better at poker and take my chances in an open field. Of course I want to win a tournament one day, but I don't want it to be a handicapped event. I want to win a real one.

But it was amazing to see so many women playing, and hold my cards in a completely different atmosphere. True, most of the field was just stumbling blindly through for the fun of it; they weren't the sharpest bunch. I flew the flag with a big glittery Union Jack on my blouse and they still asked where I was from. ('Australia?' asked one dolled-up grandma.) But it was sweet, it was funny.

And the more serious players – I liked them a lot. Any woman who plays regular live poker, in this overwhelmingly male environment, is odds-on to be a little quirky, a little rebellious, unafraid of looking competitive, capable of standing her ground. She's likely to be earthy, with a decent sense of humour.

At the end of the day, every player took home her silver trinket and her red rose. There may have been some tough and serious players among the grandmas and the girlfriends, but nobody minded the cute stuff. In fact, it went down rather well, among the wolves in leopardskin clothing.

If this really were an upside-down world where all the gamblers were women, poker would be a much friendlier game. But I am not sure I want it to be. The games in Vegas are all friendlier than I'm used to, and it makes me a little uncomfortable. They ask your name, how you are, what you do. In the Vic, I would no more ask somebody how they make their living than I would enquire after the medical history of a fellow passenger on the underground.

Let's be honest: everyone is here to win everyone else's money. Everyone is thinking, when they see a new face, 'I hope this guy can't play. I hope he loses every last penny he can get his hands on tonight, and I hope I take it off him.'

In a faraway place, on a holiday break in the middle of a research trip, it's been fun to play amongst smiles and cocktails and firm friendly handshakes. But it isn't real. After five days of people beaming warmly while they take my chips, I am yearning to get back to the damp, sarcastic, cynical city of London.

T7 OFFSUIT

No woman has ever won a competition on the European Poker Tour. And no woman ever won this particular tournament, the European Championship in London, even before it was part of the EPT. This flickers through my head as I keep remembering that I am on the final table. It seems odd to forget, but I am thinking about the cards, the situations. Then, every so often, I feel a small shiver at being in the final.

I should be tired, but I'm not. This is my third long day of playing poker, with only short sleep breaks in between. I didn't sleep at all last night. Three days of concentrating this hard on anything else would be exhausting, and boring. Not when it's poker. Each new deal brings fresh hope, fresh excitement, new opportunities, and adrenaline. That's true in any poker game. Let the river run. And I'm down to the last six of a 400-runner EPT tournament, in my own home casino! I'm guaranteed to win lots of money whatever happens.

T7 under the gun is not exactly the 'fresh hope' I was looking for. That doesn't mean I can't raise with this hand – you can raise with anything, and under the gun (i.e. first to speak after the blinds) is a nicely deceptive position to do it from. But I don't need to. I pass, as do Chad Brown and Emad Tahtouh. Michael Muldoon makes it 65,000 from the button. Jan Sjavic folds, and Jules Kuusik goes all-in from the big blind for about 200,000 more.

Michael Muldoon calls and shows A♥ J♥. Jules Kuusik miserably rolls over A♣ 5♠. He must have been hoping this was an empty button steal from Muldoon, but it wasn't. See earlier warnings about weak aces . . . Kuusik is in bad shape, dead to a five or a running straight.

The flop comes 2♥ . . . 10♣ . . . J♠.

This is a great flop for the rest of us. It feels cruel to funk against somebody – to want them to feel the pain and disappointment of being knocked out – but at this stage, it's impossible to want anything else. Every exit brings us higher up the money ladder and closer to the title.

Turn J♣ . . .

That's it! Jules Kuusik is drawing dead, and leaves the tournament in 6th place. Poor Jules. I don't wish him ill. But this defeat earns everybody an extra £13,000, and takes us down to five.

11

THE VIC

Of all the card rooms in all the casinos in all the world, I had to walk into yours . . .

'You vuggin' sheet!' Stavros is screaming. 'You vuggin' cun', you tell me wha' I can' do?'

Each word is punctuated by a sharp stab of the forefinger, propelled by the full weight of angry Greek bulk behind it. Rumour has it that the myth of the Minotaur began when Stavros lost his temper during a weekend minibreak in Knossos.

A young Jewish kid is looking nervous. Turns out it was he who inspired The Bubble's rage, by complaining that Stavros spent too much time on the slot machine when his seat was locked up at the poker table. A gaggle of regular cockneys, who think the same thing but know better than to say so, maintain a diplomatic silence in adjacent seats.

I'm fond of Stavros. He's so glowering, so grumpy, that I laugh just thinking about him. And he's always terribly polite to me. I suspect that a woman at the poker table plays havoc with Stavros's brain. He wants my money, like that of any other player, and he certainly bullies me with his bets. But he treats me very gently and carefully. Which, in Stavros terms, means that he doesn't swear at me or throw his cards at the dealer if I beat him in a hand. In fact, he calls me darling. In a grumpy sort of way.

Pedro, the tiny Glaswegian master of low-stakes poker and alternative medicine, attempts to cool the situation by waving a miniature electric fan in the Greek's direction. This drives Stavros into greater spasms of fury. I duck backwards from my vantage point near the bar.

Jeff Leigh, the crop-haired, iron-muscled card room manager who once beat a semi-professional boxer half his age in a circuit-training competition, holds his hands up for quiet. Jeff can always manage trouble without backup – which is lucky on this occasion, because his two colleagues are tied up at the desk, where Dave Binstock is making a long complaint about something completely different.

'It's absolutely appalling, Brian,' Binstock is saying. 'We pay ten pounds an hour, and they tell me the Sunday roast is finished when I've only come in at half past five . . .'

'The what?' says Brian. 'Sorry, David, I wasn't listening.'

With an explosion of curses, Stavros stamps past them both towards the stairs. A waitress coming the other way is forced to stop suddenly, spilling a cup of dark orange tea all over the carpet and perilously close to the robe of a nearby Kuwaiti. Stavros has probably been asked to leave for the night; nobody ever leaves permanently, except Dave Moseley, who spat in a dealer's face. Throughout the encounter, the ripple of cards and riffle of chips has remained as constant as the ticking of a clock.

Peter Benson hasn't even looked up from his game of Mythical. I feel a wave of joy and relief, as if I have come home.

I'm not really one of the family. Or not yet. But, gradually, gradually, breaking through the initial suspicions on both sides, I can see that it *is* a family, and that for some people it is home. It might be like home at the tail end of Christmas Day, when tempers are frazzled and rows break out, it might be full of as many irascible old uncles as lovable cousins and as much jealousy, feuding, suspicion and hatred as there is respect, humour, history and trust; it may reverberate with black sheep and prodigal sons, but it is no less a family gathering for that.

♠

In the first week of September, another *Late Night Poker* kicks off in Cardiff. The televised tournament is so successful now, they're doing two a year. Hemish, who must really be in the zone, won the spring series. He is bang in form. But he's not going to play the autumn series, because he's still feeling unwell after the stomach cramps in Vegas. He's in hospital in London, having tests.

This time, there are no celebrity specials and no newspaper stories, so no free seat for me. But I've decided to invest my own money. I've been playing bigger stakes in the cash games and winning some money. Charlie and I have been working very hard on our diary of the sleaze business. Why shouldn't I splash out on a treat?

There's no real justification for it, from a professional player's point of view. I still haven't got my head round tournaments. I understand a lot more than I used to, but I know that I'm too tight and (as a cash player) I haven't completely grasped how to keep recalculating the value of my chips as the blinds increase. I know that I have to do it, I just don't know how.

I also know that I am not offered a seat on *Late Night Poker* for my tournament skills. I am invited because this is a character-driven show, they need women in the line-up, and I know the rules of the game. That's about it. I have no tournament record to speak of.

In general, my tournament poker has improved. I have learned how to look for situations, rather than having my outcome determined entirely by the cards dealt. But the vital, and for me fledgling, elements of instinct and perception shrivel under the gaze of the half-dozen cameras. When I sit down for my heat, I'm so nervous I can barely think, never mind analyse. Once again, I find myself waiting for big hands. And then I forget how to play them.

After a while, I discover a pair of jacks. Good: a proper hand. Better still: The Whacker is short-stacked and moves all-in from my right. I call immediately.

Stupid, stupid, stupid. I shouldn't have done anything immediately. I should have given myself a chance to think, and then I might have got to the correct play: moving all-in myself, over the top. It just didn't occur to me. Didn't enter my head. After my flat call, Surinder Sunar is priced in to call from the button with a weak ace. He hits the flop and knocks us both out. I really am a moron.

♠

There is still some fun to be had in Cardiff. On the second night, I go out for a Portuguese meal with a group of players including Phil Hellmuth, who may now be giving Amarillo Slim a run for his money as the world's most famous poker player – or rather, the one poker player that some people have heard of. Phil holds the record as the youngest player ever to win the World Series main event, which he took in 1989, beating Johnny Chan heads-up at the age of 24. He is known as 'The Brat' for his histrionics at the table and his fury at bad luck, a John McEnroe for the sedentary. Last year, he won the third series of *Late Night Poker*, scoring an irritating victory for America in an almost exclusively British field.

Phil appears to have a giant ego, but most poker players do. And there's no denying he is one of the greatest multi-table tournament players of all time. It would be most un-American of him to pretend otherwise. Self-effacement is not one of his more obvious qualities but, unlike those who are truly ego-driven, he is a phenomenally perceptive reader of people. I don't know him well enough to know if this applies away from the baize, but his ability to smell nerves, deceit, confidence, trickery or hope in an opponent means that there must be a big dollop of empathy in his emotional mix. You just wouldn't think so to hear him shrieking for an hour about a standard bad beat. If he has any empathy regarding what people want to hear over a relaxing post-tournament drink, his next best skill is blocking it out. ('And then the king came down, boom!', 'Did it really? . . . Crisps?')

Hellmuth is a wholesome fellow, a little like Huck Seed. He's towering tall and healthy-sporty, with an unusually settled domestic life. Phil's wife is a child psychologist, to the joy of poker rivals who say she would need to be. They live in Palo Alto, California, with their two sons, Philip III and Nicholas. Like Huck Seed, and like Johnny Chan, Phil dropped out of college (in his case, the University of Wisconsin at Madison, the town where he was born) when he discovered a fondness for poker – and, like those guys, he is making it pay.

During our Portuguese dinner, it becomes clear that Phil has also got something in common with the Hendon Mob: ambitions beyond the card-playing itself. Like Joe and Barny, he is a dreamer and a visionary. He is alert to a feeling of spring in the air, of poker budding and sprouting and sending little shoots above ground. There is a new fad for social Friday-night poker tournaments in people's homes, *Late Night Poker* trickling down at last into social habits, and Phil believes that real money is going to lie in diversifying, in business deals, in the fame that may come with further TV exposure. He just hasn't worked out how to make it specific. But he has plans.

'I'm going to release an album,' he tells me cheerfully over the piri-piri. '*The Phil Hellmuth Poker Album.*'

'Oh, you sing?' I ask. 'Like Devilfish?'

'No, I don't sing. Other people will sing.'

'You're a song-writer? You're going to write songs about poker?'

'No, no.' Phil waves this suggestion away. 'This is how I figure it. Singers, when they make an album, they never use all the material they have prepared. There's always a couple of songs they don't use. I will gather up a few of those songs, and put them on an album.'

'Well . . . then . . .' I'm puzzled. 'What makes it your album? What makes it a poker album?'

'Because I will have *collected the songs*,' says Phil impatiently. 'And I'm a poker player. The songs will be the choices of Phil

Hellmuth the poker player, that's what makes it *The Phil Hell-muth Poker Album.*'

'I'm sorry, Phil,' I say – respectfully, because this is a former world champion – 'one of us is missing something here. If it's just an album of songs, rejected by singers from their own albums, which aren't written or sung by you, on a selection of different themes, then it's nothing to do with poker. It's irrelevant. You might as well gather up a bunch of animals, put them in a field and call it The Phil Hellmuth Poker Farm.'

Phil sighs, exasperated, and turns away to chat with 'Poison' Pascal Perrault, the pharmacist and French champion. Perhaps PPP will see the potential in Phil's plan. Clearly, I am no visionary.

♠

Another of the French players is remarkably handsome and flirta-tious. Late on the third night, we are drinking wine in the hotel bar when he suggests a walk in the grounds. This year, the players are not staying at the Hilton, the grounds of which are a pedes-trianized shopping street filled with light-hearted Welsh drunks, but a more rural outpost with trees and a duck pond.

Determined though I am to date no more poker players, I can't see the harm in an innocent little moonlight stroll with a particularly good-looking French one. We wander about, holding hands, chatting; it's very romantic. Not necessarily in the sense of a love affair developing between us – I doubt either of us can see a future in it – but romantic in its randomness. It makes me feel like a truly travelling poker player, out after midnight in a place I would never be, kissing a man I would never have met, without the game. It's an adventure on the road.

Maybe I ought to spend the night with him? A truly emanci-pated, independent, travelling-gambling chick would definitely have a one-night stand with the hot French player she might never see again. I bet Barbara Stanwyck would. But one-nighters have never appealed to me. That is where I stop being a tomboy. Just like a proper girl, I think of sex as part of a love affair, exciting for the intimacy and communication and discovery. Thrashing around in a clumsy one-off tangle with a passer-by is no more tantalizing to me than a game of squash. And I really hate squash.

Kissing and 'what might have been', yes; sex with strangers, no.

So I arrive back at my hotel room alone, some time around 2 a.m., to find a note under the door. It's from Joe. It says CALL ME, DOESN'T MATTER WHAT TIME.

His voice on the phone sounds distant and terrible, though his room is only down the hall.

'What's happened?' I ask.

Joe says: 'Hemish died.'

♠

On 5 September 2001, Hemish suffered a cardiac arrest and died in hospital at the age of thirty-three. They never found out what was wrong with him.

At the *Late Night Poker* studio, the jolly festival mood fizzles and goes black, as the news spreads amongst the players. A gold-embossed Get Well Soon card, which had been lying on the table and covered in friendly messages to the last series' champion, is quietly disposed of.

Megan, Chris, Sian, Rhiannon and everyone else from the production company are as shocked as the players. They have only just finished editing Hemish's fourth series victory. Nobody knows what to do. The games continue in silence. Some players refuse to wear microphones, because they are afraid they might cry in the middle of a hand.

Ram is playing today. When he hits a lucky card on the river, he looks up and whispers, 'Thanks, Hemish.' Hemish himself was the most superstitious of men, especially smitten with the colour red and the number seven. Cynics scoffed, but he was the only man who was ever asked to stop playing roulette in the Vic because he was winning too much money.

When I sent him flowers in hospital, I was warned 'No green in the flowers! Green is unlucky!' I know that, but it's tricky to find flowers which don't have green leaves.

Hemish drew strength from his superstitions. When I watched him play the final of *Late Night Poker* series four, his game transformed at midnight like Cinderella's pumpkin-coach in reverse. Clang went the clock, Hemish changed gear and sped to victory. It turned out that when midnight came, it had become Hemish's birthday, the seventh of April. His 33rd birthday: double carpet, lucky again.

In keeping with Hindu tradition, Hemish's funeral is announced immediately. It is to take place in two days' time, clashing directly with the big last day of *Late Night Poker*, the day of the semi and the final. Presentable Productions is a small regional company making a low-budget late-night show, there's a tight schedule and no money for extending the filming days. But the 'hard-bitten players' in the studio don't care about losing the £1,500 they have paid to play, or the £100,000 prize money on offer. They are going back to London to pay their respects. It's a stalemate. Presentable is looking at a poker final with no players.

Well, they've got one player. Henry 'Nugget' Nowakowski, a German semi-finalist, tries to argue that he will be turning up at the time and date mentioned on the contract, and if no other players arrive, then he should win the semi by default. Somebody reports this threat to Joe. Joe has a word. Henry Nugget goes quiet.

Everything's possible, the saying goes, as long as you have a chip and a chair. The valiant production company arranges an emergency semi-final at 7 o'clock in the morning, booking helicopters to fly the players down to London for the funeral and back immediately afterwards for an all-night final on their return.

♠

There is no mention of Hemish's gambling during the funeral service. His relatives concentrate on Hemish's childhood, his professional success in the City, his devotion as a son and brother. Indian prayers are spoken and haunting songs sung. It takes place at Hoop Lane, just round the corner from my family home in Cricklewood.

I wonder what Hemish's colleagues and cousins make of the fifty men who are standing at the back of the funeral hall in black suits, dark glasses and extravagant jewelled watches. Each of those mysterious mourners is thinking not of the City whizz-kid, devoted son and practising Hindu, but the hero who brought a 2001 World Series bracelet home to Britain. Twenty players travelled back from Cardiff, a couple of dozen more have come from the Vic. The sprawling, dysfunctional family has snapped together like a fresh deck of cards.

After the service, Joe goes over to offer our condolences to Hemish's mother. The rest of us stay back, on our own side of the car park, keeping a respectful distance. The more superstitious among the gamblers say that Hemish sensed the clock was ticking and made sure to win a world title before he threw in his cards. He had just been winning and winning and winning: he won *Late Night Poker*, he won the bracelet, he was getting the lot in the cash games. He was even beating the roulette! It was a multi-gaming streak of form like we had never seen, ended suddenly by death.

Others are shaking their heads over the riddle of his illness, and blaming the air conditioning. Then we hug each other, the finalists return to the helicopter and the rest of the gamblers repair to the Vic, to toast Hemish and play poker.

♠

We went to the Vic after John Diamond's funeral, too. Back in March. Matthew, Giles, Patrick and me, straight from the wake. It seemed the suitable thing to do. Our friendship with John was so often conducted round the blackjack shoe and the poker table, why switch lanes now? And the casino is where you go on dark days. The dress code wasn't a problem because we were all in black suits anyway, like four Joe Pescis in a gambling movie. Sort of.

John himself was a wild gambler, always ready to double or bluff. The most shocking thing about his death was that he had been so incredibly *alive*. Although he had cancer, his departure was no less startling than Hemish's. With a terminal illness, you expect it and expect it and expect it . . . and then you cannot believe it has happened. Can't believe he got ill. Can't believe it was cancer. Can't believe he died. We went to the Vic in search of life, John's life, any life.

On this tribute trip, Matthew Norman (pretty wired on gambling himself, he built a garden shed purely for the purpose of playing online poker in it) kept creeping up behind me and whispering, 'Put £200 on red . . . it's what he would have wanted . . .'

'Hang on,' I said, too late, after all the money was gone, 'it's not what he would have wanted. It's just what he would have *done*.'

♠

The Vic is sad and quiet for days. Meanwhile, the big overnight deciding match unfolds desolately in Cardiff. Nobody feels much like playing or watching or discussing poker, but they feel more like playing or watching or discussing poker than they feel like doing anything else.

Joe comes third in the final. The winner is Padraig Parkinson, a smart, sharp, witty, hard-drinking Irish pro who nearly won the 1999 World Series. Padraig never played *Late Night Poker* in its early runs because, like his countryman Donnacha O'Dea, he disliked the idea of his game being watched by thousands of anonymous potential opponents. What's secret is secret. But the river has flowed on, television has started to seem normal, money has been added to the prize pool, and Padraig has turned up to win the tournament on his first attempt.

But he picked a strange one to win. I wonder what the viewers will make of this final when it is broadcast: no laughs or banter, each player in a black suit, all of them silent.

♠

Three days later, aeroplanes fly into the Twin Towers. It is a Tuesday.

For most of September 11th 2001, it seems like the world is going to end. All day, everywhere, people are staring at the television as if it were a horror film come to life. Soon, surely, the planes will hit London and Paris and Tokyo, and Will Smith will not be there to save us. We phone loved ones and summon them to our houses; we truly believe that we are all going to die. Then, around 7 p.m., a group of us look at our watches and think, 'Time for a bit of six-card hi-lo.'

The game is at The Sweep's house in Vauxhall tonight. Traffic is quiet. Everyone else is nesting, hiding, hugging. For the first hour of the game, we have the TV on in the corner. Then we switch it off. It was slowing down the action.

―❦―

A9 OFFSUIT

My heart swells to see familiar faces on the rail. My old Vic cohorts are coming upstairs from their cash games to see how I'm getting on. The Sweep and J.Q. from the Tuesday game are there. Neil and Rory are making encouraging faces. Michael Arnold will be doing the same, I'm sure, when he's quite finished shuffling about in his seat, looking for a cushion, squinting for a waitress, jabbing someone in the foot with his walking stick as he tries to hang it up. Other regular opponents are waving, winking, shouting advice. I love them for coming upstairs to funk for me. They'll have left their chips on the cash table, obviously; they keep checking their watches to be back in time for the hourly charge. They want to be supportive, but not at the risk of getting picked up from the game.

Jules Kuusik has just been knocked out from the big blind. That means there's no small blind on the next hand: just my big blind and I find A♣ 9♥. When Emad Tahtouh makes it 60,000 to go, it's an obvious re-raise for me. Emad was bound to raise there with anything at all. Michael Muldoon is away from the table – gone to the bathroom or something – and Chad Brown has already folded. There's no small blind to be defended. An aggressive player like Emad doesn't need much to raise it up. My A9 is about 90% likely to be good.

And yet . . . there are other considerations. This is deep-stack poker. I should re-raise just because I've probably got the best hand, and he should fold just because he's probably got the worst hand. But he probably won't fold. Emad would like the chance to play a big pot with me, especially when I'm out of position, and he can afford to. If he makes the call, it won't help me to narrow down his range.

And I'm still hung up on avoiding these weak aces. Even though, five-handed, A9 becomes a medium to strong ace, I can imagine getting tangled in a knot with it. With enough chips to play a flop, I'd much prefer to re-raise Emad with a stronger hand that I'll still feel sure is winning after cards, or a weaker hand that I'll know for certain I'm bluffing with. It's these middle situations that have got me in trouble in the past.

And I'm superstitious. I don't like it that Michael Muldoon is away from the table. I like things to be in order. I don't like playing the first hand after a misdeal. I don't like playing a big pot when a folder has accidentally exposed a card. I will always take my bets off the dice table for the first roll after a die has been on the floor. The absence of one of the players, five-handed, feels like something is amiss and ill-omened. That *is not a spot in which I want to play a hand that makes me uncertain. I have a logic for this tournament: I will raise when I know I want action or when I know that I don't, but not when I'm unsure.*

I throw the A9 away. I feel comfortable, why mess with a working plan? Still, I have to be careful. There are only so many good cards in the deck, only so many that I'll find, and I can't let Emad bully me off too many of them.

12

A BOAT BENEATH A SUNNY SKY

*'The remembrance of our friends is often associated
with games we have played together, sometimes even
when we have played only a single game and have
never met again.'*

– Edward Falkener, 1892

On and on and on, rolls the nimble Chinese wizard. It's like
there's no seven on the dice. Bang – snake eyes. Bang – boxcars.
Bang – little Joe. Who's betting the hard ways? Bang – the point.
Our chips are multiplying like rabbits along the rail. Me, The
Sweep, J.Q., Neil Channing and Michel Abécassis, the French
pro, all getting rich on the old guy's spectacular display. What an
arm!

It's 2 a.m. in the Golden Nugget, and we've been drinking
for a long time. J.Q. must have had nineteen White Russians. As
usual, he's unaffected. He'd be quite capable of downing twelve
more and then driving a 15-ton truck along a tightrope. But I
can't think of any circumstances under which this might be
required. The Sweep tells me to stop giggling and get my bets
on. I scatter chips onto the layout, muttering numbers.

Even The Sweep has had a cocktail, and he never drinks.
Twenty minutes into this incredible roll, I think I'll switch from
vodka to champagne. I can afford it. We can all afford it. I'm
clutching the table for balance, but that's the beauty of dice. I
don't have to think straight. I don't have to do anything except
throw chips and shout numbers. The old Chinese guy (Asian,
they would call him here in America) is doing the work for us,
and we're just betting on his action. We're getting rich. This is

one of the moments you dream about in gambling: fast, perfect, shimmering-golden, endless in victory. We cannot lose. We will never lose again. We will never be lonely, we will never get ill and we will never die. Our chip towers are rising and rising and rising. Dice are beautiful. Everything is beautiful. Everybody's beautiful.

♠

All old-school poker players love the rats and mice. It has been the downfall of many. The Sweep likes to quote our old friend The Clock, so named because he was in charge of the time-keeping on bank jobs, gazing mournfully across the casino floor and murmuring, 'These dice have ruined us . . .'

Willie Tann has freely admitted to dice disasters. This is one of the greatest tournament players to come out of London – he's been here for most of his seventy years so we can claim him as a Londoner, although technically he's Chinese, which I'm sure accounts at least in part for his habit. The Chinese crave dice. At the poker table Willie is shrewd and patient, analytical and thoughtful, crafty and cautious. Put him near a dice table and he leaks like a spinning sprinkler.

Many's the time that Willie has pulled off a big poker win, but failed to get his loot out the door for the dice tables purring like sirens en route. He should be a rich man, instead he is a Mock Turtle: master of Reeling, Writhing and Arithmetic, but ask how he is and you will always get a tired sigh and a tearful eye.

Willie is saved, time and again, by his sweetness and charm. With his gentle face, his mournful, kindly manner and his unquestionable poker skills, there will always be fellow players ready to lend him a bit of cash and get him back in the game. Others will eagerly buy a share of his action, knowing this to be a sound investment – and it is, but the investor would be wise to collect any winnings straight after the tournament, before poor Willie has had to pass across the gaming floor en route to the exit. His deepest comfort and joy lies in none of his poker results, but the fact that his son Jason has no interest in gambling. That is the one thought that always makes him smile. I don't spoil it by warning him, from my own experience, that Jason was always going to be careful; it's the next generation he should be worried about.

Willie once confessed to the author Des Wilson: 'People know I'm a gambler and I'm not proud of it. I've got a number of younger players who I'm teaching poker, who are gamblers. So I tell them about the mistakes I've made in life and I hope they listen to what I say and don't do what I did. I tell them it's no use doing what I've done. I'm ashamed of it. I try not to do it so much now. I've got few years left to live, and I'm determined to change my ways.'

Even as I read those words from my sick old friend, I simultaneously nodded at the wisdom of his advice and itched for the dice table. Luckily, dice is not a huge problem for me. Roulette used to be, and blackjack can still shake a mischievous tail, but I only ever play dice occasionally and in a group.

The group is key. You know that you have truly been bitten by the werewolf of gambling, just like drinking and smoking, when you find you are doing it alone. And you know that the wolf has chewed through to your liver when you're not just doing it alone, you're doing it *furtively*. I have gone to roulette tables at times of day when I knew I wouldn't bump into anybody. I have sat down at blackjack tables in the back, so as not to be disturbed. Dice – thank God – I have never played without a group of friends on either side.

Willie will arrive in Vegas and throw the first dice with his suitcase on the floor at his side.

♠

The beauty of this magical night in the Golden Nugget, just opposite Binion's Horseshoe where the 2003 WSOP is taking place, is that we all benefit from the spectacular dice roll. We're in it together. Not like poker, where we are out to take each other's money. Here there is no awkward dynamic of deceit at the table and friendship away from it. Here, only the house is the enemy. We are the good guys, the Troops Of The Righteous, fighting and winning. We can all cheer when it comes the hard way, all whoop when our hero hits the point, all share the spoils of victory.

On and on and on. We are immortal. If Sky Masterson thought he pulled off a miracle when he won a dozen gamblers' souls with a single dice roll, he should see this. The old Chinese man, whose name we don't even know, has been throwing the bones for 45 minutes without hitting a seven. But shh! No thinking about sevens. Definitely no saying 'seven' out loud. There are no losing sevens in our little spotted universe tonight.

The record for the longest-ever dice roll is held by the Hollywood stuntman Jack Davison, who threw for two straight hours on 12 August 1979. He began with a stake of $6, and finished up with $37,000. A couple of Christmases ago, Binion's unveiled a plaque to commemorate the occasion: Davison turned up in a black leather jacket, and a hat which had been given to him by John Wayne.

'There's something about playing craps which really energizes you,' he said at the ceremony. 'It just does something to you. It starts the adrenaline running through the body.'

Jack Davison was good news all round for Binion's. The more special ceremonies they can hold for Jack Davisons, the more Willie Tanns they can suck into the pit.

Being 'on a roll' in any gambling game can literally make your heart pump harder in your chest. Sometimes it happens at the blackjack table: bang, bang, bang, the cards fall right.

Sometimes the magic descends on roulette: number after number slots into place, and piles of chips are pushed your way. Casino managers send free drinks over, in the hope of keeping you at the table. Crowds gather, trying to share your luck. It is your night. As the hits continue, you take the bets uptown, betting more and more and more until you sense the rush starting to cool and the wheel, deck or dice changing mood. A night of this kind can keep you gambling for years, desperate to feel that beautiful rush again.

Our lucrative Chinese gryphon could break that record tonight. How can the roll still be going on? It's just insane. Number, point, number, point, number, point. After 55 minutes, we are joined by a mysterious gentleman in a suit. He is a senior casino manager who's been summoned out of bed to come down and keep an eye on the action. Make sure the house doesn't go broke. Cast a shrewd eye over the dice, check we haven't slipped our own pair into play. He smiles, he says hello, he congratulates us – but he's a cooler, sweating for a seven to come.

Eventually it does, of course, and we retire. J.Q., The Sweep and I, who all started with the minimum six-dollar bets, have won about four thousand each. Wow. This is the kind of money that people roll around in. Neil Channing, who bet bigger, must have won about $15,000, and Michel Abécassis got the *gâteau total*. The old Chinese man gathers his own winnings in his magical fingers and disappears back to Illyria. We know that we will never see him again.

♠

This might be the happiest that I have ever been. A gentler sun shines on Las Vegas this spring, and everything feels like a fairy tale. Even the poker has a sense of solidarity. Me, J.Q. and The Sweep, we travelled here together, we're all playing the same little tournaments and taking 5% of each other's action.

Straight off the plane, we went to play the Thursday comp at the Mirage, starting 4 a.m. UK time. Why not? We've passed over the magic walkway, through the looking glass, nobody can sleep on this side. The Sweep won the Mirage tournament that first night, got a trophy and gave us our shares. When I got back to my room I managed to doze off for a while, but woke up around 7 a.m. feeling excited. I forced myself to watch a film on cable; it would be offensive to call the others at that time of day.

Eventually I dialled The Sweep at 10 a.m. and he didn't even say hello. He snatched up the receiver, shouting 'I've been awake FOR HOURS.'

J.Q. and I have got rooms at the Nugget, along with the Hendon Mob and much of the British contingent. The Sweep is at Binion's across the road, in a manky room that was part of the old Mint. Keeping the exes down, feeling the history. And it's a damp old history.

We meet for breakfast in the Horseshoe every day around noon, which The Sweep likes to round off with a bar of weird chocolate from the casino store. Then cards cards cards at Binion's, the Bellagio, the Mirage, all afternoon and all night. We take breaks to muck around in Fremont Street, go on a fairground ride at the Luxor, eat chicken & tequila pizza at midnight or 9 a.m. or teatime.

We become obsessed with the I-C-Bears slot machine, stopping by a few times a day to feed in twenty bucks each and try to hit the ice bonus. Then I hit the armadillo bonus on the Texas Tea machine and feel a conflict of loyalty.

We develop a fear that Tristan, a player from London, is unlucky for us. He is a nice guy but he insists on wearing a green baseball cap. 'What an absolute Tilbury,' moans The Sweep when he sees the hat coming across the room. We spend a lot of time ducking behind the I-C-Bears machine, until that hat is safely away from the area.

We get free tickets to Celine Dion's 'spectacular' new show at Caesars Palace and can't help loving it. We watch *The Matrix 2* in a cinema downtown and I don't understand a single frame of it. We spend hours in the treasure chest of the Gambler's Bookstore, reading old tales of Big Julie and Jimmy the Greek. We get lost in Caesars Forum and find our way back to Poseidon's Fountain by following the stars in its mesmerizing, *Truman Show* sky. We send a postcard back to the card room at the Vic. We have the greatest dice roll we'll ever have.

This might be a city of whores, guns, drug addiction and sick gambling, but it feels like we're six years old and playing hopscotch in the garden all summer.

There is something almost unbearably happy about all of it. Pure pleasure, pure contentment, always curls around a small sad centre because you know there is nothing permanent. Even as you look at a river, it flows on to become something else. A shadow of cloud on the stream changes minute by minute. Even as you hold the water in your cupped palm, it trickles out.

♠

I am twelve years old, in Portobello Market with my father. He thinks it's time for me to start collecting something. So we are rummaging around the antique shops and the bric-a-brac stalls, looking at ornaments and knick-knacks and pictures and hats and stuffed animals and silver trinkets, deciding what I am going to start collecting.

It's a beautiful day. The air is soft and warm, smelling of jasmine and hot-dog stands. All the stall-holders are chatty and ready to haggle. I've got a toffee apple. In the back of a dusty little shop near the Ladbroke Grove end of the market, my father picks up a china boat. It has a funnel at each end, also made of china, and if you lift them out they are salt-and-pepper shakers. The boat is a creamy-pearly colour, with blue piping, and on the side is printed 'A Present From Southend On Sea'.

'How about that?' my father says.

I think it is the cleverest, prettiest thing I have ever seen. It is a lovely shiny object anyway, but it's also a salt-and-pepper set and it's *also* a boat!

'And it's a present from Southend On Sea,' my father says. 'You could collect china seaside souvenirs. You could look for ones that said Bournemouth and Weymouth and Margate and Clacton. That's about right for a collection: bit difficult to find, but not too difficult.'

We buy it for twelve pounds. 'Just enough to make it a significant purchase,' my father says, 'but not enough to cripple you.' The man from the shop wraps it up in newspaper and gives it to me. And as we walk back down the street, me gingerly clutching what at this point constitutes my entire collection, my father says, 'One day, when you're all grown up and I'm not here any more, you'll remember the sunny day we went to the market together and bought a boat.'

My throat feels tight because, as soon as he says it, I am already there. Standing on another street, without my father, trying to get back.

And yet I'm here, with him. So I try to soak up every aspect of the moment, to help me get back when I need to.

I feel the weight of the chunky parcel under my arm, and the warmth of the sun, and my father's hand in mine. I smell the flowers with their sharp undertang of cheap hot dog, and taste the slick of toffee on my teeth, and hear the chattering hagglers. I feel the joy of an adventurous Saturday with my father and no school, and I feel the sadness of looking back when it is all gone. When he is gone.

Is it *that* now, or *this* now? Am I in that London street, aged twelve, or remembering it from Las Vegas years later? Or reaching back towards both sunshiny places from another time entirely?

Doesn't matter. From there, from here, it feels exactly the same.

♠

I think nostalgia is a primal emotion, like fear and anger and (maybe) love. It just seems otherwise, because it has a long name and is tricky to define out loud. So you might mistake it for one of those fiddly, sophisticated feelings like schadenfreude or low self-esteem. But nostalgia is simple, basic, instinctive and it was always there. You can see it on the face of a zoo monkey that once lived in the wild. Or even one that never did. It still knows that it has lost something.

Ubi sunt qui ante nos fuerunt? That's what I learned at university, in exchange for a stand-up comedy career. *Where are those who went before us?* The wistful motif echoes through the Anglo-Saxon fragments that kicked off our English course – *Hwær cwom mearg? Hwær cwom mago?* And on through all the languages and all the ages, from *Où sont les neiges d'antan?* to *Sag mir wo die Blumen sind.*

One of our first impulses was to feel nostalgic even for times we had never seen. And you can feel nostalgic for something even while it is happening.

♠

Chris Moneymaker wins the main event! That's another kind of miracle entirely. Chris Moneymaker! Isn't that the guy who won his seat on the internet?

It has always been said of the World Series that it's not a truly open event. It certainly wasn't to begin with. The whole thing was dreamed up by the visionary casino-owner Benny Binion in 1970, when he invited seven of America's greatest card sharps (including Johnny Moss, Amarillo Slim, Sailor Roberts, Puggy

Pearson and Doyle Brunson) to play a series of matches in his downtown establishment. After these games, which Binion hoped would attract a mob of spectators to gamble on his dice tables and roulette wheels, he announced a vote to decide which player was best, and this man would be the official 'world champion'.

The electorate consisted of the players themselves. The result of the vote was an incredible seven-way tie.

'We're going to do it again,' said Benny Binion irritably. 'And this time you can't all vote for yourselves.'

After the reluctant second vote, the winner was declared to be Johnny Moss, the 'Grand Old Man' from Texas – though, in that first year, he was a stripling of sixty-three.

The following year, Binion held the tournament again, and this time the winner was decided by a knockout rather than a vote. The same guys got together, and played until only Moss was left at the table. Now he was a legitimate champion, although he'd only beaten a handful of close acquaintances to get the title.

The World Series has taken place in Binion's Horseshoe casino on Fremont Street every May since then. Johnny Moss went on to win nine World Series bracelets, playing his last WSOP in 1995 at the age of eighty-eight. Soon there were 40 players, then 60, and in 2003 there are 839. It has long since stopped being an invitational event – anybody can buy in – but it still hasn't been an open field because it's restricted to those who can put up the $10,000 entry fee.

For the last few years there have been satellites, to win seats into the main event for smaller entry fees, but it still takes a certain bankroll and confidence to fly out to Vegas and play them. The Sweep played one once. He got unlucky.

But this – this is something different. Chris Moneymaker, an accountant from Tennessee, won his seat in an *online* satellite! He played a match on the PokerStars website for only forty bucks, and snared a WSOP ticket without even having to leave the house. And then he came out here with the ticket and he's just won the main event, spinning that $40 into $2.5 million! Not only is he the first world champion to qualify on the internet, he's the first who really feels like a 'world champion' because the entry requirements are, suddenly, so much less restrictive. Truly, anyone can get here.

And his name, his real name, is Moneymaker? I swear to God, this year, someone is writing fairy tales. It gives me a strange tight feeling in my kidneys.

♠

I call my parents, who immediately demand to know why I haven't called before. I tell them it's because I'm having too much fun. I tell them (which is true) that I have been winning small amounts in the cash games, but I don't mention the dice because they'd only worry. I tell them about the Horseshoe breakfasts, and the fairground rides at the Luxor, and the Celine Dion concert, but I don't tell them that Devilfish crept up behind me in the card room at Binion's and growled 'I wanna taste your arse!' because I'm not sure they would understand that, from him, it was merely a social pleasantry. My father travelled in America in 1960, and I know that he popped over the Mexican border to have a few adventures. But he has never told me the story in every last detail, and I can return that favour now.

I tell them about Fremont Street and all the players wandering back and forth, saying hi to each other and going for meals at weird times of day. I tell them about the Venetian hotel, which is actually an improvement on the original Venice because all the crumbling ruins are built out of wipe-clean plastic. I tell them that I sailed round the whole place with Barny Boatman, after being offered the intriguing choice of 'indoor or outdoor gondola'. I assure them that the reason I'm up at 5 a.m. local time and talking very quickly is that I'm happy, not that I'm on drugs. I tell them they should understand how much I love them simply because I'll be coming home. Otherwise I would stay here for ever.

Somewhere in the adrenalized garble, I think I've lost them. But what my father takes away from all this is that I've gone to Las Vegas for a whole fortnight, only to play poker, and I haven't lost money. I'm a gambler. But I'm not going broke like Uncle Sid.

♠

On the cab journey back to the airport for the return trip, *Killing Me Softly* is playing on the cab radio. I'm listening to every phrase, feeling the scratch of The Sweep's jacket against my arm, smelling the aftersun on our skin (a fragrant bouquet of shea butter, coconut extract and propylene glycol), hearing the traffic and the music, sensing the awkwardness of J.Q. in the passenger seat as the driver makes conversation. Trying to inhale it all into a time capsule.

We play the slots in the departure lounge, but they don't have the great novelty machines like Texas Tea or I-C-Bears with their quirky bonuses. Just basic numeric jackpot stuff. I feel like I used to at the end of August, when the windows of W.H. Smith filled up with new geometry sets and it was time to go back to school.

The boys sleep on the plane. We land the next morning, take the Gatwick Express and say goodbye in the drizzle at Victoria.

♠

At the end of the Alice books, after she has travelled in Wonderland, socialized with cards and woken up, after she has passed through the looking glass, across the chess set and become a queen, there is a poem. It is an acrostic, spelling down through the lines the name of Alice Pleasance Liddell, who inspired the stories. When I am little, it's the first poem that ever makes me cry. It starts

> *A boat beneath a sunny sky,*
> *Lingering onward dreamily*
> *In an evening of July –*
>
> *Children three that nestle near,*
> *Eager eye and willing ear,*
> *Pleased a simple tale to hear –*
>
> *Long has paled that sunny sky:*
> *Echoes fade and memories die:*
> *Autumn frosts have slain July.*

As a child, I don't understand exactly what it is about. I can't read the significance of Alice reaching the final square and becoming a queen. But I feel the sadness in the poem, and, in this later now, I know why.

It's because everything is in the present tense, even though it cannot all be; either some of it has passed, or some of it hasn't happened yet. The sky is sunny, but it has paled. The boat is lingering, but it is gone. It's July, but it's autumn. This is a riddle, a paradox. Lewis Carroll must be either looking back into the past, feeling the sunshine and the drifting boat as if he were still there . . . or looking forward from the present, imagining a time when the sky and the boat and the summer will have vanished.

Which is it? Doesn't matter. Wherever he stands, he feels both at once. The current, the retrospective, the projected, all are written in the present tense because they are all, always, mixed up together. Because, even as something is happening, it is gone.

Ubi sunt qui ante nos fuerunt? Where is the boat? Where is the summer? Where are the children?

---

73 OFFSUIT

Jan Sjavic makes it 80,000 from the button – four big blinds, which is supposed to signal (truly or falsely) that this is a real hand and not a button steal. I'm not going to get involved with seven high, from the small blind. I am not looking to get tangled up unnecessarily with Jan. He is a very strong, talented long-time pro. He won this very tournament in 2001, before the EPT had been invented, when it was the European Championship. He cut his teeth in the underground card rooms of Oslo. He beats the high-limit cash games in Vegas. I have no reason to cheek him with a 73 move.

But at this stage, with just five of us left in contention for the title, the end in sight, the crowd getting noisier, every pot is key for me whether I am in it or not. When Chad Brown moves all-in from the big blind – raising the possibility of knocking out Sjavic, and bringing us down to four – I am paying extremely close attention.

Sjavic calls the all-in, and rolls over a pair of sixes. It's AQ for Chad Brown, a standard 'race'. But Chad has more chips, so it's only Jan who can be knocked out.

The flop comes . . . 3♦ 6♣ 7♠ . . . A set for Jan, Chad drawing nearly dead to a runner-runner straight . . . Q♠ 3♥. As it happens, I would have made a full house, but the canny Norwegian would have had a bigger one anyway. Thus, he doubles up. Damn.

PART THREE

13

THE MONEYMAKER MIRACLE

'The audience didn't tune in to see an incredible display of intellectual ability. They just wanted to watch the money.'
— *Martin Scorsese,* Quiz Show

Suddenly, everyone sees the potential of the internet. It can make world champions! They are signing up to PokerStars in their thousands. Not just for next year's WSOP satellites; they are playing exclusive online tournaments, cash games, free games, single-table, multi-table, heads-up.

Late Night Poker was the first scatter of gunpowder, internet technology fattened the pile, and Chris Moneymaker's win is the spark required for a global explosion.

New poker sites are launched every day. And their owners realize, post–Moneymaker, the value of putting a human face on their product. Endorsement. Memorability. Accountability. The poker language of flops, straights, deuces, cowboys and shipping the sherbert to Herbert is suddenly being diluted by phrases like 'target marketing' and 'brand awareness'.

Thus, the Hendon Mob get the sponsorship deal they dreamed of. It isn't with a drinks company or a car firm after all: the internet is the future. But, of course, it was always the future and the future is now.

The four boys agree to wear logos for the Prima Poker network, write online diaries, make promotional appearances and have their tournaments subsidized around the world. In January, they sign the first million-dollar contract in poker.

No longer do professional players struggle to describe them-selves as 'businessmen' or 'jewellers': they reveal their true lifestyle with pride, inspiring envy and fascination rather than pity. New live tournaments are being created across Europe and America. Poker is suddenly mainstream, played at dinner parties, written about in magazines and discussed at water-coolers.

Holdem is the only variant going. Even in the Vic, the Omaha and Seven Stud games are dying. The regulars are sniffing the wind of change and know that Holdem is what the youngsters want to play. If there are eggs around, we want them cracking up in our game.

I might have felt an autumnal shiver, as our cab drove back towards McCarran airport, but for poker it really is a new school term: the first term of Year Zero.

♠

Sportsmen, actors, pop stars and aristocrats are fighting for seats, as if it were a round of musical chairs at Elton John's birthday party.

When Channel 4 made *Celebrity Late Night Poker* with Amis and Alvarez and Gervais, three years ago, it took painstaking research to drum up six players, two of whom were mere authors and a third was no more than a journalist. But this is the autumn of Anno Moneymaker. Suddenly, there are enough famous poker enthusiasts to make an entire novelty TV series, with 42 players and a chunky £25,000 first prize. This is *Celebrity Poker Club*.

The studio is a tangle of bizarre juxtapositions. Britain's biggest soap star, Dirty Den, is ready to do battle with mutton-chopped racing pundit John McCririck. World snooker champion Mark Williams and royal stepson Tom Parker Bowles are preparing, in all seriousness, to take on ventriloquist Roger de Courcey. Slender Welsh *auteur* Jon Ronson is squaring up against giant black cricketer Gladstone Small. Actor Keith Allen, the hard man of Dickens adaptations, is looking unprecedentedly nervous as bespec-tacled inventor Sir Clive Sinclair enters the room.

I have met Keith Allen before. Every trendy private members' club in London is now trying to run a poker game, and I was invited to a tournament at the Groucho in Dean Street. Keith Allen advised all the people on his table to simply stop playing while everyone else in the room got knocked out, to guarantee themselves prize money. I told him I would consider that cheating. Keith Allen suggested that we 'take it outside'. Always irritated by any threat of bullying, I agreed immediately. Allen, perhaps realizing that he might look a bit of an idiot if he took me onto the doorstep of a trendy London club and punched me, changed his mind and sat back down.

Hello again, Keith.

♠

Lined up for an ordinary high-stakes British poker tournament, I would expect to see: professional poker players (25), used car dealers (7), people who 'buy and sell things' (30), taxi drivers (8), men 'in the security business' (9), visiting Germans, Irishmen, French or Dutchmen who do much the same things in their own countries (15), twentysomething lads with borderline cool haircuts, just discovering poker (16 and rising), women (3, including me).

So it is weird to see so many celebrities playing, but the juxtapositions of genre and status aren't surprising at all. That is how celebrity works. Fame is one big bubble where they all meet. That is how Freddie Trueman's daughter came to marry Raquel Welch's son. That is how the American boxer Mike Tyson came to date the Streatham-born model Naomi Campbell, argued with her at a cocktail party and was sternly told to 'Leave that girl alone!' by the elderly Oxford philosopher A.J. Ayer.

'Do you know who the fuck I am?' snarled Tyson. 'I'm the heavyweight champion of the world!'

'And I am the former Wykeham Professor of Logic,' replied

Ayer. 'We are both pre-eminent in our field; I suggest that we talk about this like rational men.'

Now that's what I call a cocktail party.

And if there is one thing that flattens categories even more than fame, it is gambling. Plenty of incongruous people have found common ground on the baize, famous or otherwise. Tom Parker Bowles and Roger de Courcey have less distance between them than many who have won and lost money together throughout history. Dukes and dustmen have always met at racecourses; the Vic is full of class- and category-bucking friendships. Gambling is an addiction, and addictions level all.

I'm not saying these particular punters are addicts. But £25,000 is on offer, with free entry, and any gambler can smell that kind of deal from several counties away.

♠

Mark Williams is so keen for action that he can't wait for his heat to begin. Stephen Hendry and Dennis Taylor feel the same way, so the three of them start hustling for an all-night warm-up game. They want an appropriate location – somewhere cool, smoky, macho and underground. A seedy dive of cigar fumes, cheap bourbon and pure male aggression. Luckily, Steve Davis's mum's house is only five minutes away. Round hurry the boys and play cards into the small hours. I hear Dennis Taylor cleans up.

Poker is flooded with snooker players at the moment. That makes sense. It rewards the same combination of determination and patience, competitive urgency and shrewd judgment, as the game that made them famous. And, just like snooker, poker offers a juicy punch of sporting adrenaline without any requirement to sweat.

The oddest thing happened in the 2003 Poker Million: a snooker player won it. Matchroom Sport tried to relaunch that old Isle of Man tournament in 2002, in a London hotel, but it was cancelled at the last minute after a legal wrangle and threats of a police raid. It was finally resurrected in the safety of a Maidstone TV studio a couple of months ago and, after a dramatic late-night heads-up battle, my ex-boyfriend Joe 'The Elegance' Beevers conceded defeat and the title to Jimmy 'Whirlwind' White.

The snooker pro got lucky, there's no doubt about it. The 6-4 of spades, not traditionally considered an all-in calling hand, is now known in card rooms with grudging amusement as 'the Jimmy White'. But he didn't play badly overall, he just put a little too much faith in superstition and it paid off for him.

Joe was slightly miffed about the money. The 'Poker Million' title was purely nominal this time and, despite the $10,000 buy-in, he only got $70,000 for second place. When the players asked Barry Hearn, the organizer, why there was no added money, he said, 'We're putting in a bunch of snooker players who don't know what they're doing – there's your added money.'

Then Steve Davis finished 5th for $30,000 and Jimmy White won it.

I am not sure which is more remarkable: that a celebrity has won a professional tournament, or that Joe told me three years ago he would make the final of the second Poker Million, and he did.

♠

Martin Amis arrives. He's late but, in his defence, he has cut short a lunch with Prince Philip at Buckingham Palace to make the game. That's a conversation I'd like to have witnessed. 'Sorry, Duke, the venison's great and your racist jokes are some of the funniest I've ever heard, but there's action going down in Cardiff . . .'

This tournament certainly isn't 'a trip into the strange' for these celebrities, because their lives are very strange already.

♠

Even in a celebrity televised game, men are an overwhelming majority. Women are starting to have a go on the internet, relishing the opportunity (just as they do in chat rooms) to role-play from behind the safety of a screen name: to be more confrontational, or more flirty, or more openly competitive, than we are socially conditioned to be 'in real life'. But the live game remains male.

I have sneaked into this celebrity line-up on the grounds of having a picture byline in the paper, along with a couple of female newsreaders and novelists. My invitation to an all-star tournament might be tokenistic, since I've got relatives who wouldn't recognize me on a bus, but I wasn't going to turn down a free shot at £25,000.

I certainly still qualify for amateur status. I have no ambitions to be a professional, because I couldn't handle the stress and risk of relying on the deck for 100% of my income. But I am playing several times a week and my entire social life seems to have switched to the Vic. If I have a free night, I no longer call a friend or relax with a TV dinner, I go to play cards. Now that I am starting to consider some of the players there as friends anyway, it seems daft to do anything else.

And I have started going out with one of the players from the Tuesday game. Another resolution broken. I thought that I was absolutely sworn off poker players, but suddenly it feels exactly right. Like it was meant to be. He is as commitment-wary as I am, as keen on space, as ready to ignore the passing of time, as comfortable being awake at four in the morning, as happy to spend a 'date night' playing cards.

He is smart and sweet, dry and quiet, funny and tense and calm. He never tells anyone anything. On one of his early Tuesdays, he refused to reveal his postcode when calling a cab because he found it a terrifying intrusion of privacy. He took the phone into the kitchen to whisper those precious details. He reads books about assassins and spies.

How did we ever become a couple? God knows. The devil

knows. Maybe Devilfish knows? But it is perfect. My lack of neediness suits him rather than piquing him; he's the first boyfriend who never forces the issue. Quite the opposite. If I want a bit of space, he wants Canada. And so, as masochistically drawn to perceived indifference as everyone always is (or, for once, not blinded by proximity), I am crazily in love. I have a fantasy where we get married and live in separate houses.

Everything I said about 'No more poker players' is forgotten because this path makes perfect sense; of course we should be together. After all, Sugar Cane said 'No more saxophone players' and it turned out her true love was just another saxophone player in disguise.

♠

Based on my greater experience, matched up against several celebrities who only discovered the game five minutes ago, Jesse May makes me 5/2 favourite to win my heat. But Jesse was always a terrible bookie.

I don't feel so confident. Sometimes it can actually be harder to beat confused or clueless players than people whose bets are made with a logic that you can unpick. I have been running a monthly Holdem competition at the Century Club in Soho, which began as a secret plan to befriend wealthy poker hobby-ists, get them to the Tuesday game and take their money, but that never worked out and now I seem to be lugging chips and cards down Shaftesbury Avenue every month as a favour to the owner.

J.Q., Trouts and The Sweep have been coming along to play the competitions and act as 'table captains', helping explain the rules to enthusiastic new players who are drunk or rich or famous and usually all three. None of the Tuesday boys has managed to win the competition yet. They invariably get their bluffs called by opponents who don't realize that queen high is no hand, or their strong hands out-drawn by opponents who don't know they shouldn't go all-in with just two cards to hit, and drive home swearing.

Tonight, I find myself sitting next to the retired footballer Mickey Thomas, who asks 'What are my options?' every time the action is on him. And I mean every time. Ninety minutes into the heat, the tournament director is still patiently explaining, 'You can call . . . or you can raise . . . or you can fold . . .'

Eventually, Mickey Thomas scoops the majority of my chips with a full house he didn't know he had. Meanwhile, I've got trips with an ace kicker, marvellous. The only reason Mickey doesn't get the lot is that when he asks, last to speak on the river, 'What are my options?' and is told 'You can bet . . . or you can check . . .', he decides, with his full house, to check.

He is trumped in the bumbly stakes only by Leslie Grantham, old Dirty Den from *EastEnders*. In a three-way coup with a couple of cricketers, Grantham calls a big bet on the turn with the nut flush draw. Fair enough. The river brings a third heart, giving him the nuts. First to speak, Grantham decides to fold, out of turn, for no bet at all.

♠

Martin Amis is in the bar of the Hilton, challenging all-comers to Scrabble for £50 a board. I love Scrabble as I love a newborn kitten, but this seems a bad proposition to me. Amis the phrase-maker, master of language, viscount of the vast vocab, must surely be a favourite against almost anyone.

Before his heat, I asked Amis why he likes poker. I have asked a lot of people this question over the years and the answer is usually 'Oh, you know, the thrill, the money.' Amis replied: 'People often compare politics to chess, but it's closer to poker because egos are involved. On a chessboard, the properties and powers of a bishop are permanently fixed. In poker, it's all wobbled through the prism of personality.'

I fancy he's got the edge over John McCririck at a language game.

So, shouldn't be green here. I'd love to tell my grandchildren I played Scrabble with Martin Amis, but no self-respecting gambler would take a 50/50 when they consider themselves 6/1. And I'll probably never have any grandchildren. Therefore, the move must be simply to *watch* the games, and bet on Amis to win.

It's all going pretty smoothly. But, as I have done in nearly every form of gambling at some time or another, I press up once too often. I'm now betting £500 and Amis is playing the TV presenter Grub Smith. We're in the end game. I'm standing behind my man. His rack is SSRIEEO. He has had the two Ss for a few turns now – waiting, presumably, as any good Scrabble player would, to craft them into a bingo. Or at least snare a triple letter score. Only a fool uses an S for an ordinary word. And here, his patience has paid off. SOIREES!

Amis shuffles the tiles back and forth on the rack. Can't he see it? I am obliged to remain silent, obviously. Amis drops a tile on the floor. He fumbles around and replaces it slowly in the rack, all fingers and thumbs.

Shit. The man has been swigging whisky for hours. He can make no sense of this rack. The tiles are just hieroglyphics, dancing in front of his eyes. He's got no chance of finding 'soirees'. In the end, it's a miracle that he manages to find 'sees'. I've done my money again.

♠

Meanwhile, the comedian Rory McGrath is claiming that he can name the capital of every state in America, and offering to prove this for £5 per state. But the only person here who might have a chance of competing against him is Jesse May, our Yankee commentator, and Jesse's too savvy to bet against a potential hustler;

he doesn't want cider spilling out of his ear onto his new purple velvet jacket.

Back at the studio, even the lunchbreaks are no rest from gambling, as the Marquess of Worcester insists on borrowing the TV company's poker chips in the hope of winning an extra few quid off Craig Charles from *Red Dwarf*. And win them he does; *noblesse oblige*. Jesus, these famous people *love* gambling. They are truly sick. I'm impressed.

♠

I ask Clive Sinclair, 'Do you remember the old Stakis basement?'

Sir Clive is one of the few who have been involved in the game for a while. The footballers and cricketers have all started playing recently, in sweaty locker rooms around the world. The snooker players have been sucked in via the Ladbrokes Poker website.

But Tom Parker Bowles, Ben Elliot and Zac Goldsmith have a regular private session on the top floor of Aspinalls in Mayfair – a sort of child school of the notorious old Jimmy Goldsmith/ John Aspinall/Lord Lucan poker game of the 1960s. Actor Dexter Fletcher was taught by his parents as a kid, and rediscovered a love of cards during the shooting of *Lock, Stock And Two Smoking Barrels*. Al Alvarez chose poker as an escape route when his first marriage was breaking up, and Keith Allen learned 'accidentally at the National Theatre'.

And Clive Sinclair has always been a fan of mind games.

'Of course,' he chortles, 'those hi-lo tournaments, Wednesday nights, was it? Thirty players, stale sandwiches and a £700 prize pool.'

We look across the room at the famous faces, buzzing and gambling on whatever they can think of, waiting to play their big televised £25,000 match. Clive admits he may have got in early with computers and electric transport, but he never saw this coming.

He whispers to me that the opponent he fears is Irish international footballer Tony Cascarino, who has retired from professional sport and is (they say) mopping up in private Omaha games at a country club in Hertfordshire. I cheer him up with the news that Cascarino is terrified to take on Channel Five newsreader Fiona Foster, as he believes that he can never beat a woman at cards.

Everyone has someone else in the line-up who inspires fear, or awe. The experience of moving in exalted circles is no help to Tom Parker Bowles when Al Alvarez enters the room. Tom is so excited to meet the author of *The Biggest Game In Town*, he is physically trembling.

To my surprise, I'm rather falling for the posh boys. Chippy as I am, I didn't expect to warm to such a noble bunch – particularly Zac Goldsmith, the tweed-jacketed millionaire who hopes to become a Tory MP. I imagined a lot of brainless laughter and bread-throwing, and I didn't think they'd give me the time of day.

But I soon realize that the loneliness of school, followed by the comfort of the Vic, has turned me into some kind of inverse snob. I start paying closer attention when I see Goldsmith's urgent love of poker and, once I'm listening, I can hear that he is softly-spoken but whip-smart, super-articulate and very kind. I suppose people are only unpleasant, really, when they're frightened of something. These boys are so pukka that nothing is a threat; they move with the grace of a benevolent universe behind them; they are friendly, gentle and interested.

I always knew that defensiveness makes people rude, because I have grown up with people being dismissive of my father to my face. They want to demonstrate that they don't think he is superior to them, just because they have read his writing or seen him on television. So, sometimes, someone will tell me,

'Alan Coren? I've never found him funny,' in a way that they would never tell a butcher's daughter, 'I reckon he sells crap meat.'

These boys are showing me that the truly confident have no need to belittle anyone. It just doesn't occur to them that deferring to Al Alvarez's poker experience, rather than dismissing it, might in any way demean them. It reminds me that Henry Higgins treats a duchess as if she were a flower girl, but Colonel Pickering treats a flower girl as if she were a duchess. It also reminds me that Freddie from the Vic is lovely to everyone. And he wins everyone's money.

They are all delighted with the daily lunch at the studio: stews, roasts, sponge puddings and custard, just like school. Tom Parker Bowles tells me about the time he ate dog in the Philippines. He explains patiently, as though I weren't the thousandth person to ask him what this was like:

'It was the smell that put me off. It smelt of damp dog. Do you remember that from childhood, when you've been out playing in the stream all day, the way the hound smells when he comes bounding through the house?'

Damp hounds in the stream? Bounding through the house? We really did have different childhoods. I remember the smell of cigarettes and petrol on the back seat of a Fiat 127 . . .

I say, 'I know exactly what you mean.'

♠

Back in London, there is much muttering at the Vic (a community which is rarely slow to mutter or quick to praise) about the cheek of these celebrities coming into the televised game. They can't play, it's clownish, it's a joke, who would be interested. But then most of them, especially the ones who rejected invitations to *Late Night Poker*, or never received them, scoff at televised poker anyway. They are always pulling apart this move or that, from last week's episode.

They are not entirely wrong. The subtlest poker skills come out in slow structures and cash formats; most importantly, the only true test is over the long term. Television offers fast, gambly No Limit tournaments because they are quick to film and easy to follow, not because they make the best showcase for technique.

But that's not why the players scoff. They scoff because it's what they do. As the scorpion said, this is Africa. Poker players are the bitterest, most resentful, most grudging, most jealous humans on the planet. They enjoy nothing more than schadenfreude. They hate nothing worse than someone else's success. They are happiest when describing a huge pot lost by a regular opponent. They don't care who won it. They just enjoy talking through the bets, in juicy detail, and concluding, 'He done two bags in the hand. Gone skint.' That delights them. And they are angriest and most miserable when standing up, tapping the table and saying, 'Nice hand.' Their only comfort after that is to see a rival lose a bigger pot in unluckier circumstances.

God, I love them.

Celebrity Poker Club is won by Clive Sinclair. So that is a victory for the Old School over the new trendsetters, and should make the traditional Vic players happy.

But, of course, it doesn't.

---

86 OFFSUIT

Emad Tahtouh raises to 60,000 under the gun. I now have the kind of hand I'd much rather re-raise him with than A9 – sounds weird, but at least I know where I stand. I want the fold. And if I get the call, I'll know I'm behind. I'll know if the flop is good for me or not. Without the uncertainty that accompanies a medium-strength hand, I'll be on top of the situation; can't get in too much trouble.

But while I psych myself up for the bluff, Michael Muldoon gets in first with a re-raise to 180,000.

Of course, if I stick in my entire 900,000 stack now, they would have to believe me for aces. It would be an incredibly gutsy play. But it's too kamikaze; I pass. Emad calls.

The flop comes 3♥ 2♥ 7♦. Emad checks. Muldoon bets 300,000. Emad moves all-in. Michael Muldoon passes in disgust. I later discover that Muldoon had been making a move with 89, and Emad was happy to put his whole stack on the line with A♥ J♥ – two overcards and a flush draw, so bound to be in strong racing shape even if he wasn't winning already (which he was). Good aggressive play from Emad: this is why I am dodging round the guy. But I can't keep doing it. If I want to have a chance in this tournament, I have to take on everybody.

Looking at those hands, it also seems likely that if I had made the huge pre-flop bluff of putting in the third raise over the top of Muldoon, it would have got through. Emad had a very decent hand with the AJ but it couldn't take that much heat, and Michael had nothing. Interesting.

14

4 a.m.

'. . . and I look outside to see what's going on, but
there's only New York going on.'

— Francis Dunnery

I'm in the Vic. The tenor of the game has changed; it gets good
at this time of night. Breaks up or gets good. A bunch of lads
have come in tipsy from a night out, and are playing for more
than they should. The game was going to break up an hour ago,
but there is a silent understanding between the regulars that an
opportunity has arisen and nobody's going anywhere. Drunken
City boys are exactly what the doctor ordered. Sleep can wait.
As soon as they fell through the door, loudly asking where to get
chips and how to sit down, Freddie took his coat off again.

♠

I'm driving home. It's going to be a gorgeous summer's day.
Normal people will be waking up in a few hours, pleased to see
sunshine. But I'm on a high from the profit, and loving the soft-
ness of the small hours, and taking a detour round Hampstead
Heath to see the ducks on the pond and the tired, happy cottagers
emerging from the trees. Everything is so beautiful. I'll be home
soon enough. I love going to bed in daylight.

♠

I'm in Vegas, at the cash desk, juggling two phones. This is a
nightmare. It's midday in London but nobody's answering at Lloyds

Bank, and the woman at the cash desk has picked up the house phone to call some kind of security clearance man who doesn't understand my accent.

I have no dollars left. I need to arrange an overdraft extension, now. It's embarrassing, it's shameful, but the woman at the cash desk has seen it all before.

The blackjack got a little out of hand. I went back upstairs twice to clear my safe of all remaining dollars. I opened the 'last three days' envelope, I opened the 'emergency cash' envelope, it's all been scraped away. I'm here till the weekend with nothing to live on. I've borrowed $2,000 off Neil and lost that as well. I feel suddenly very far away from home, stuck without funds. This has gone horribly wrong.

It all started misfiring after that hand where I split eights three times against a 6, ended up with five 18s, and it came 5,5,5 for the house. Horrible. Disgusting. The pain of that third five. I felt sick when it came down, thumping onto the table like an act of violence. Sometimes it really feels deliberate, like the deck is out to get you. You feel like you've been punched. You feel anger, resentment, hatred. And now I don't know how I'm going to pay the hotel bill. These casino people, so friendly when you sit down, won't be so friendly if I have to check out with an empty wallet.

But it's okay, because if I can just increase my overdraft, and get another few thousand over the counter, then I can play my way out of it. Simple as that. I'll play my way out of it.

♠

It's Christmas night in the Vic. Not December 25th, December 18th when we get our free Christmas dinner in the restaurant. We met in the pub first, where J.Q. beat D.Y. at chess and I lost £200 betting Neil that *Fairytale Of New York* on the stereo was the original and not a cover version. Stupid. Never bet on facts.

Then we came into the club, ate our free turkey and staggered over to the table to play some 'fun' poker. Stakes half as big as usual, and everyone drunk. We've all got a free cuddly toy that came with dinner. Nobody knows any children to give them to. Maybe the waitresses will take them? One of them must surely have a child.

This might be the best poker game ever. Everyone's giggling, humming and raising blind. Then it stops for five minutes, after someone asks which is the only London Underground station that contains none of the letters in the word 'mackerel'. That takes a while, drunk.

Jeff Duvall pulls up another couple of thousand. He's wearing a paper crown.

♠

I'm playing on PokerStars. This is probably my fifteenth Sit & Go of the night. Mr Big was playing a while ago, we were visiting each other's tables and writing messages in the chat box. At some point, I played a heads-up match with The Camel. A dumb decision, when he's platinum star on PokerStars and by no means the value, but I was so pleased to notice him online from his home in North Yorkshire. Haven't seen him in the flesh for ages.

They've both gone to bed now. At least I assume so; if you type their names into the search box, it says 'Player not found'. I should go to bed, too. It's 4 a.m. But just one more . . .

I have a problem with going to bed at night. Don't know why. I'm tired all afternoon, but completely alert after midnight, always ready to write emails, read books, surf around on Google, play on Stars, tidy up, anything but go to bed. Maybe it's to do with playing live poker three nights a week, sleeping all morning on those days and getting up early on others. I have a sort of permanent jet lag. But it isn't just that; in the middle of the night I feel excited to be alive, and I don't want to waste it sleeping.

Going to bed, such a happy fantasy at teatime when I have a column to write and I can't stop yawning, becomes, after midnight, something to be constantly postponed and avoided. It feels like I'd be missing something.

Knocked out of the Sit & Go in second place, for $800, I think about retiring for the night. I think how good it would be to have seven hours' sleep, to start the day fresh, to get things done. Then I think about playing another one. I feel suffused with relief, and click 'register'.

I remember when I was eight years old, finishing a marathon family game of Monopoly at 10 p.m., hours after bedtime, and saying, 'Can't we play another one?' My father was never going to say yes. It was late, and Monopoly takes ages, and we never played more than one game. But he did say yes, and my mother put the kettle on, and it was the happiest moment of my life.

♠

I'm in the Vic. I was going to leave at 1 a.m. – I was £5,000 in front, and I'm supposed to be up in the morning – but crafty old Gino talked me into staying another half hour. 'Come on, come on, we have fun!' he cackled, snatching the £10 table charge from my stack.

Then Devilfish turned up and sat in our game while he was waiting for the Omaha, and now it's too much fun and I can't leave. My +£5,000 has slipped down to +£3,000. That always happens, if you stay beyond the point you were going to leave. It'll be a miracle if I get up in profit at all.

Devilfish is on good form tonight. He tells Fadi (an enormous, muscular Iranian-American who's started playing here lately) that he's going to call him Rambo.

'But I'm taller than Rambo,' drawls Fadi, 'and bigger, and better at poker.'

They start debating whether to have a press-up competition, right here on the floor of the Vic.

Gino, who must be sixty, reveals that he does a hundred press-ups at home every morning.

'Yes,' says Devilfish, 'but without your boyfriend underneath you, it's different.'

This gets a big laugh, and there are jealous glances from the Omaha table. That's a line-up of absolute rocks, all strong opponents, playing in silence. Dave Winston, J.Q., Pineapple, George Rousseau, Simon 'Clint' Eastwood. God knows why Dave wants to go over there. It looks like the poker game from hell.

Devilfish and his girlfriend Jade have just got back from Vegas, and Jade says they shared a table with Mike Tyson in the Lights Bar.

'Some women find him very attractive,' observes Trevor Coles.

'Attractive?' I say. 'He's a convicted rapist!'

'Yes,' says Trevor, 'but not all women are as fussy as you.'

♠

I'm in Baden, Austria. As opposed to Baden-Baden in Germany. You can play poker in both places; many's the player who has missed a competition after going to the wrong one by mistake.

I'm doing well in the tournament, I've got good chips at the end of Day One. Maybe I've got the hang of competition poker once and for all?

This is an odd, scenic little town. Very cobbly. I'm too adrenalized to sleep after all that poker, so I'm wandering around it in the dark. I'm safe enough. Nobody gets attacked in a town where everything's cobbled. Unless it's in an Agatha Christie novel.

Some of the players are flying home tomorrow on Peter Gould's private jet. What a nonsense. It's only a two-hour flight, no shame in British Airways. Still, they love the luxe. I came here by train, on the Orient Express. People don't realize that the

Orient Express is a line, not a train. It's the old line from Paris to Istanbul via Strasbourg, Vienna, Budapest and Bucharest. Those beautiful old Nagelmackers carriages ran along it for decades, but they don't any more. The luxury 'Orient Express', or rather now the 'Venice–Simplon Orient Express', is a holiday package operating somewhere else entirely.

Taking the real Orient Express has a certain romance, peering out of the window at frozen little German stations in the middle of the night, seeing what kind of person would clamber on and off this ancient route these days. But it's not about fat cigars in glittery dining cars. It's a bunk bed, a poky toilet and a platter of cold meat if you're lucky. I got off at Vienna, and took a cab to Baden on the edge of the Wienerwald.

You can walk round the whole of this bijou spa town in about twenty minutes, so I do it twice. I think about my strategy for Day Two. I peer into the shop windows, to see if there's anything I can pick up later in the week as a going-home present. The selection is not wide. It'll have to be a marzipan church, a set of Mozart napkins or a staring, jewelled doll.

The air smells of sulphur and spicy fruit punch. I wonder if I would ever have come here, otherwise?

I'm driving home. It's a nasty November night, rain thumping onto the windscreen, trees blowing about. There's nobody else on the road at all. That was a bad session (−£1,500) and I'm disappointed, ashamed. I see a postman wandering miserably down the street in a cagoule.

Seems early for a postman. That's a job I could never do. I wonder how much he gets for walking down the street at 4 a.m. in the hounding rain? Still, at least he gets something. Guaranteed. Not like poker. They never tell him at the end of the shift, 'You despatched the letters badly today, so you have to give *us* £200.'

I'm an idiot. I should never have sat in the thousand game. I don't play properly there. And I should never have tried to outplay Freddie. I was greedy and impatient and stupid.

Freddie was looking good tonight. Getting the lot. He told me about how he used to run a fruit and veg stall on Petticoat Lane, and drove the produce around with a horse and cart. One night the horse, Mary, crashed into a car. She was fine, the car was dented. That would make a great opening image for a period drama set in the 1930s. Horse vs. car, a battle of old and new, like Phil Hellmuth trying to beat Tom 'Durrrr' Dwan.

Then Freddie flopped top two pair, and I flopped bottom two pair, and he cleaned me out. Again. At least I can tell myself it was inescapable. Usually with Freddie, he makes a massive bet, if I fold he shows the bluff and if I call he rolls over quads. He's a warlock, that man. But this one was just a cooler. And I had nothing on deposit at the Vic. I'll have to go to the bank tomorrow.

On the corner of Marylebone Road and Albany Street, I see a man sleeping on a bench. Wow, how can he sleep in this weather? I can hear the wind over the radio, and the radio's pretty loud. That man must be very drunk indeed. I wonder what sort of dreams he's having, with his body knowing that he's cold, but his mind blocking it out. I pull over, take the last £20 out of my wallet and tuck it under his arm, for him to find in the morning.

♠

Lots of Londoners have come to Brighton for the festival; the cash game (bar a couple of local regulars) feels like the Vic on holiday. Neil and I had fish and chips on the seafront and waved at passing gamblers. Neil is one of the nicest guys you'll ever meet in poker, and definitely the most loquacious. You know he doesn't have any dark corners because he'll tell you everything that enters his head, the moment it gets there. Bit like my brother. Sometimes Neil gets annoyed with me for 'keeping secrets' when we are supposed to be friends, but it is usually because I haven't been able to get a word in.

He is very sensitive. His rat-a-tat chat might give the impression of a thick skin but, like my brother, like Devilfish, like anyone who talks a big game, everything is fragile. So you must remember to be careful. You will feel like Alice, constantly offending the swimming mouse, sometimes because she is careless enough to discuss cats and dogs without thinking, but sometimes merely because the mouse mishears the word 'knot' for 'not'.

Neil is a very clever, canny gambler, but he's been unlucky. He built up a huge bankroll a few years ago and ploughed it into buying bookmaking pitches at racecourses, just before everybody started betting on the internet and the pitches slumped in value. He lost everything. This is where players disappear, do bad things, knock friends for money, end up in prison or abroad or wherever that dark place is where the Missing Players go.

But Neil's a stronger character than that. He stayed put and started again, small-stakes poker, small-stakes sports betting, and he's building it all back up. Not hampered by excessive pride or ego, so rare in a poker player. His nickname is BadBeat. He doesn't need to play the Big Man, and that's how you know he is one. His ambition is to pay back everyone he owes by his fortieth birthday: couple of years to go and he's nearly there. I know he'll do it. Over the fish and chips today, I was simultaneously considering dumping the mushy peas on his head and shouting, 'WHY DON'T YOU EVER LET ME SPEAK?', and reflecting that he is one of the very best people I know.

Like Baden, if it weren't for poker I might never have known Neil was there. And I'm very glad I do because, unlike Baden, Neil is all fruit punch and no sulphur.

So here we are at the cash tables with the rest of Vic-on-Sea. I came second in tonight's tournament – wasn't a big one, £2,800 for second place – but I can't go straight to bed so I'm spinning it up in a £100 game.

The guys are talking about a cricket result that worked out lucrative. They love cricket bets – all those options for buying and selling runs. Neil told me you can even bet on the outcome of the toss, and if there are enough superstitious people on Betfair you'll get odds. That's a no-brain move for any rational punter.

Now, for some reason, the conversation has turned to the question of how cricket would be affected if the world was flat rather than round.

'There'd be a lot less variation on the pitch,' observes one player thoughtfully.

'And we'd never play Australia,' says another. 'That would just be stupid. But we might still play Pakistan.'

♠

It's the early hours of Christmas Eve, the real one. I've won £1,785; shame I already bought my Christmas presents. I'm driving back through shimmering, frosty streets. Everything is sparkling and pretty and festive. There are tiny coloured lights in the trees. I've just exchanged hugs and kisses with my adopted Vic family, left them to do whatever they do over the holy days, and later I'll be going to spend the night and eat turkey and swap gifts with my proper family. Life is perfect.

My back wheels skid on a patch of ice. I recover the car, but there's a flash of blue light behind me.

'How much have you had to drink?' asks the policeman.

'I can see why you'd ask that,' I say, 'with it being Christmas Eve. But I haven't had a sip. I've been playing poker, and drinking cups of tea all night.'

The policeman makes some kind of sarcastic comment, but he's amused. He doesn't even test me.

It's okay, though. I wasn't bluffing.

♠

Devilfish is telling a story about a man in a poker game who pretended that Dave was a great friend of his. It was weird, Dave says. This guy was boasting about all sorts of things, his money, his sex life, and he was boasting about how long he and Devilfish went back, even though they'd only met a handful of times before and Devilfish was sitting right there at the table.

'So I announce that I'm writing a book,' says Devilfish, 'and I say, "You should really be on the cover, with your arm round me." The lad goes all perky and says, "Yeah, that'd be great." I tell him, "The title of the book is *Cunts I Know*."'

Everybody laughs. There's a pause. Then Trevor Coles says, 'Actually . . . that might sell.'

---

74 OFFSUIT

My favourite hand! Well, second favourite: I prefer 74 suited. Especially in clubs. I always play this aggressively in a cash game, raise pre-flop and bet every street until they crumble. Or I can get paid off if I actually hit something.

Listen, I'm not recommending it: 74 is a terrible hand. But I have a sentimental attachment to it. It was the favourite holding of Adrian Cheng, who played in that old school with my brother and his friends, back in the 1980s. He always raised with it, superstitiously. I didn't understand (raising, without an ace?!), but I thought it was funny. Since then, it has certainly proved a lucrative pair of blackjack doubling cards. So I have borrowed it for poker, in tribute to Adrian, who gave up gambling years ago, and it is now my mysteron hand, my joker. When I'm playing hard and betting every street in my Tuesday home game, the others know fine well that it's either a monster or it's the old 74.

Tournaments are different, of course. Unless the stacks are very deep, you don't have the chance to bet every street without going all-in.

Have to be a bit careful. I have been known to pass this hand in certain tournament spots — although it chokes me.

In this case, Jan Sjavic has made it 70,000 to go from the button. I'm in the small blind. I certainly can't flat call with 74, I'd have to introduce Jan Sjavic to Mr More — and Jan hasn't shown much evidence so far of raising with trash. He's probably got something. Superstition or otherwise, it would be daft to jam in an unnecessary wedge in this spot. I pass.

Chad Brown, in the big blind, thinks otherwise. He moves all-in. Chad is shorter-stacked than me, and needs to gamble. He may not find a better opportunity than this: just one opponent who might pass and (if he calls) might lose the pot anyway. No Holdem hand is ever that big a favourite over another, with five cards to come. But I don't personally think that Jan will pass.

He doesn't. The cards are rolled over: Q♠ 8♠ for Chad Brown; 9♠ 9♣ for Jan Sjavic. It's a shame for Chad that Jan has 'the blockers' to his possible straight . . . brings Chad down to about a 70/30 underdog. But hey. Any two cards can win.

The flop comes . . . T♣ 2♦ 6♥. No spades at all, so that kills the flush draw. Chad Brown is needing a queen pretty badly right now.

Turn . . . 8♥. River . . . J♠.

And Chad Brown is out! Tisket tasket, no trophy in the wicker basket for our American film-star visitor. We are down to four players, and the prize money just soared into six figures. There's a big jump after 5th place, Chad's exit means £110,000 for whoever goes out next. Maybe the old 74 was lucky for me after all.

15

DESPERADO

'Have a chocolate muffin,' Charlie says.

'I don't want a chocolate muffin.'

Charlie looks at me. 'You really must be in a bad way.'

I look back. Although we're in a crowded Brick Lane café, surrounded by a noisy mix of cockneys and Bangladeshis and trendy newcomers to East London, I'm wearing a pair of pyjamas with a coat over the top. My face is blotchy because I cried in the car all the way here. This is the quiet half hour before it starts again. When I've picked up my cardboard cup of tea, and he's got his sandwich, we'll go to his office over the road and he'll sit working on his computer and I'll curl up and cry on the other side of the room until it's time to go home. And the other people in his office will think, 'There's Charlie's weird friend again.' But I won't care. I am in a bad way, yes.

♠

Desperado is on my special mix tape for poker travel, along with *The Gambler* and *Better Not Look Down*. I used to be amused by the idea of myself as a lone cowgirl who didn't need love. I wasn't going to come down from no fences or open the gate. *Desperado* made a good, camp psych-up song as I drove across the country, sailed across the choppy Irish Sea or flew across the Atlantic, to make my romantic poker fortune. It used to give me a high, moving fast and playing that loud. Can't listen to it now. It sounds mocking. 'Freedom, oh freedom', well that's just some people talking. The sky won't snow and the sun won't shine, it's hard to tell the night time from the day. The lyrics come into my head in dreams and I've started taking pills to shut them up. They no longer make me laugh at the cartoon heroism of my own independence, they just make me think about him.

♠

I am a moron. I'm a total and complete Grade A fucking moron. I had to fall in love, and I had to fall in love with someone who didn't want to be fallen in love with. And just to make it perfect, absolutely to guarantee that the heartbreak would leak its black syrup into every tiny crevice of life, I had to fall in love with someone from the Tuesday game.

Of course I did. Of course I did. I understand how love works. How many people have thought they were in love with me, over the years? Maybe seven or eight. And they thought it because I was distant. It was easy: I never want to spend that much time together, I never talk about love, I never talk about marriage; instead of a ticking clock, I hear a faraway shuffling deck; instead of talking about children, I run off and play cards. If you have to fall in love with someone, fall in love with me! I won't cause you any trouble. And after a while, I will back off completely and you will be free again.

So the universe, in its infinite cruelty, has to send me this guy. Cool as a baker's hands, cool-tempered, cool-spirited, and more instinctively solitary than anyone I've ever known. So self-assured, yet so self-conscious, that he has more reserve than a Swiss bank. He once told me that it was snowing the day he was born.

Never the value at poker, a super-rock, gives nothing away, he plays his real cards and his metaphorical cards as tight and careful as each other. And he, this guy, he has to wander across a London card room one day, he has to say something wry, and The Sweep has to say, 'He seems all right. Let's ask him to the Tuesday game.' What was I, insane? It's not like he came here to gamble.

It was all so predictable. Suddenly I'm not the one making space. He does that job, so I take a couple of steps forward, and bang: I'm the one who wants to spend more time together, I'm the one who fails to hide it properly, he's the one who does the breaking up. Of course he is. I understand it so completely, I can't breathe.

Your heart is supposed to get broken for the first time when you're a teenager, young enough for it to meld back into shape almost immediately. It isn't supposed to bounce and beat merrily along for years before it gets its first proper kicking. I'm crippled. All I can do is put a coat over my night clothes, curl up in Charlie's office and cry.

And because he was part of everything, part of the Other Life, part of Tuesdays, I have nowhere to pretend. I don't get anything back that I'd been missing. It can't feel like it did before we met, because something appeared and disappeared that I can't forget. It was a strange sort of unexpected hope, for a life and a feeling that I didn't think I wanted, or didn't think I was capable of, but that suddenly became possible, but is gone again.

I took Ecstasy once. Everything went soft and hazy and colourful and musical and loving and gentle. Then, the next day, everything felt dark and heavy, pointless and bleak, drained of blood and life, so I never took it again. But now every day is like that day, that second day.

♠

Strangers are starting to write on the internet about finding me attractive. The discussion forums have boomed alongside the playing sites, but the female contingent in poker has not. So, just as I have been a sole target for flirting in casinos, I'm a bit of a sole target for online flirting on UK poker sites. They write that they want to sleep with me, or go out with me, or marry me. It's kind, it's funny, but it makes me feel worse. Lonelier. They would never think anything of the sort if they actually spent time with me.

I don't really understand the loneliness. I wasn't with him before – I wasn't with anybody – and I didn't feel lonely then. Where did it come from? Why have I become so weak? The unattached world seemed like such a beautiful, free adventure. And now it's all so cold and blank.

♠

Amarillo Slim has been done for sex offences. He was originally charged with three counts of indecency against his 12-year-old granddaughter. He plea-bargained it down to misdemeanour assault, something like 'inappropriate touching', and took a $4,000 fine.

On the websites, people are saying that if the man has the nerve to turn up for a game of poker after this, he should be beaten unconscious in the car park.

It's so sad, so horrible. When you're depressed, you start expecting everything to be grim; part of me thinks *of course* the old hero, the story-book road gambler, the 10-gallon-hatted character who met my father at the BBC, the legend I was so excited to meet at the Poker Million, the emblem of romance, should turn out to be a revolting old nonce. Let the gloss fizzle and strip from everything, leaving rusty old metal behind. I hope I never see him again. But still, I post on the websites, you can't start enthusing about mob violence against a man in his eighties. Not against anyone. But an octogenarian? You can't, you just can't, gang together and agree to break his legs. I say we should just leave him alone, in every sense. They say I'm a bleeding heart liberal and a soft touch.

♠

A couple of weeks later, a story comes out about a young player called Alex. He's a regular at the Gutshot, a new and not entirely legal poker club that's opened up in Clerkenwell to cater for the sudden wave of recreational young players who don't much fancy the Vic. I've been there: it's very New School. Light, bright, friendly, chatty, youthful. Great for the game. I prefer the Vic.

Anyway, so this Alex, whom I've met once or twice, turns out to have a peculiar and very disturbing website. Somebody posts a link to the site, full of race hate and anecdotes about gathering with fellow Holocaust revisionists in Tehran. There are many references to the Nazi-sympathizing 'historian' David Irving, whom Alex describes, oddly, as 'a Zionist agent'. Is David Irving just not anti-Semitic enough for Alex's taste?

There is also a story involving allegations about the sexuality of a prominent Holocaust denier and something about jerking off into a handkerchief with a swastika on it. The swastika detail is kind of hilarious. Does a Nazi have to be a Nazi *all the time*? Can't he jerk off into an ordinary handkerchief?

But the site is stomach-turning. It makes me wonder how on earth the guy can bear to play poker. The game is a mixed bag of classes and races, and if this little runt really believes that stuff about Jews, Asians and Chinese people, he must feel sick every time he goes into a card room.

I post on the forums that my approach to him would be exactly the same as to Amarillo Slim: if he comes into the Vic, I'd leave. If he sits in the game, I'd get up. I don't want to take his grubby money, and all I want to give him is a wide berth.

Others reply that a man's political leanings are his own concern, no business of his poker opponents. No obstacle to a decent game. They have no interest in ideological crime.

♠

There are plenty of criminals in the Vic. You learn not to ask too many questions. Sometimes the anecdotes at the table involve prison life. Sometimes a skilled thief like The Swan (RIP) is referred to in respectful tones. Often you'll hear a funny story like Tall Alan's tall tale of the singed banknotes in the cash game. Two of my favourite players are retired burglars.

Generally, you know who most of the crooks are, you don't know who the others are, and it isn't openly discussed. One exception is the 'bungling burglar' who was written up in the *Sun*. His name didn't appear, but the story described an unfortunate incident when he attempted to knock off a warehouse and got stuck in the goods lift.

Poor old Arj. He had, sensibly enough I suppose, decided to rob the place on a Friday night, giving him a clear two days before the break-in was discovered on Monday morning. But he hadn't legislated for getting trapped in the lift. He was stuck there all weekend, with the burglar alarm ringing in his ears. He was very relieved to be rescued and taken to prison.

Anyway, Arj carries around the *Sun* cutting to this day. He's proud to be in the paper. And it's a funny story. Nobody in here thinks less of him.

Amarillo Slim (though not Race Hate Alex, despite my own revulsion towards him) is unusual in crossing the card room's moral divide. The key is: mere crime, or full-on sin? Most crimes are forgiven, or quietly overlooked, in casino life. Theft and burglary are considered perfectly fine, as long as the target is an anonymous business or company. If the victim is a sympathetic individual, best not discussed. There's one likable fellow who embezzled a pension fund to pay gambling debts. It is never mentioned in front of him. People are squeamish about that particular incident, but they understand the motivation.

Violent crime is seen as broadly fine if the victim deserved it. If not, mum's the word. When an old friend of Willie Tann's clubbed an aggressive creditor to death with an ashtray, the main feeling in the Vic was that the defendant had been an idiot to take the ashtray with him from home, when any sensible person would have looked out for a weapon at the crime scene itself. Then it's just manslaughter.

The disapproval, the fury, the impossibility of forgiveness are reserved for those who welsh on bets and knock on debts. If a man has to share the room with a player who borrowed money and refused to pay it back – not through honest inability, but through dishonest manoeuvres, lies, 'forgetfulness' – then he will spit that player's name with bile and shiver with anger as he looks at the defaulting face. It might be only £100, it might be twenty years ago, but he still sees the slimy runt, the gutter drak, the sickening cockroach who squats at the poker table in oozing disregard of the outstanding sum.

This is a place of decency, of gentlemanly understanding and sympathetic help. If a man needs a gift of money in here, he can have a gift of money. If he needs a loan, he can have a loan for as many years as he will stand up and say honestly that he can't afford to pay it off yet. But if he is underhand, if he hides a win or pretends the loan never happened, he is a bastard and a cheat and the worst kind of unforgiven wretch.

♠

I am shocked by the eagerness of 'the poker community' to beat up an old man, however foully he's behaved, and depressed by their indifference to hate crime. But so what if we are at odds? Maybe it's best that way. Poker is supposed to be a lonely road. Poker is cruel. It's deceptive, aggressive, anti-social and expensive. Money is lost, pride is damaged, trickery prevails and individuality is all. Poker doesn't even have the partnership spirit of bridge, let alone the team spirit of football.

For victory there must be defeat, for wins there must be losses, for triumph there must be misery and disaster. There is need and greed and cheating and grudge-bearing and hatred and rudeness and threat.

Compared to the solidarity at the dice table, poker is sick and wrong. Every time I win, a fellow gambler has lost and I have taken his money. If he is a good man, he will smile and tap the table. If he's a bad man, he will bitch and whine. Either way, he's disappointed, he's upset, he's a little bit crushed. He isn't happy for me. He is angry with me and miserable with himself. Even if it's only a tiny pot, somewhere these feelings will snap and crackle.

Tournament poker is the cruellest. However big the field, out of dozens or hundreds of players, only one will feel good when it's over. The rest will be dejected, regretful or broken-hearted. Disillusionment for those who get knocked out and miss the money, disappointment for those who make the money and miss the final, frustration for those who make the final and miss the top spots, and you know who feels worst of all? The player who comes second. Mike Sexton calls it 'chasing rainbows'.

Or is cash poker the cruellest? At least a tournament has a set buy-in, a predetermined maximum loss. Cash games . . . on a bad night, when you can't win and you can't get up, suddenly you're wearing roller-skates on an icy mountain with eight other people pouring crude oil from the top. Down, down, down, past the shelves of empty marmalade and the bottles saying 'Drink Me'. It's helpless, it's shameful, you just want to get out of it and you can't. All those people you were laughing with earlier: now you hate them. Sitting there with your money. Strangers, thieves, bastards.

But home games, 'social games', can feel even worse. There

may be banter, laughs and pizza, but somebody will always get
screwed over; friendship can always be compromised by the embarrassment of financial defeat. Losses range from crippling to
annoying wherever they happen. Yes, it hurts to slide your money
across to some anonymous opponent in the casino – but if
anything, it can be harder amongst friends. Home games are
riddled with tricky dynamics of pride and rivalry. And it's
awkward for people to leave a 'social game' before the evening
is over, which can lead to players getting in over their heads and
everybody feeling bad. Is poker horrible? It is if you're doing
it right.

Somebody cheated in the Tuesday game once. Disgusting.
In a friendly home game. Most of us met in the Vic, and
some of us never see each other away from poker, but we are
friends nonetheless. You don't come here and cheat. But it
happened.

David Wood noticed first. He talked to the others and they
all watched P dealing off the bottom of the deck. Nobody mentioned it to me. Maybe they thought I'd be too upset. Suddenly,
one Tuesday night, out of nowhere, Robert challenged P and
they threw him out. He's never been back. I see him in the
Vic sometimes. He says hello, I say hello back, and I feel
uncomfortable.

♠

One night, I'm sitting in a cash game next to an old Chinese
man who keeps losing his sit-down stake, pacing and re-pacing
the same circuit from the cashpoint to the chip desk to the table
like a sick polar bear, because he doesn't want to admit defeat
and go home. He began the evening all chuckly and happy,
looking forward to a good night out. Now, he's quiet, desperate,
shoulders hunched, laughter gone.

I limp in to see a flop with K♣ 8♣. As I make the call, I

have a sudden flashback: I'm in a room in a house in Nevada, away from the Strip, sitting with a notebook. I'm young, I'm green, and Huck Seed is telling me about winning the World Series with 'king-eight suited' and I don't understand why he's playing such cards. And now, here I am playing them. Am I a more sophisticated player now? I didn't even *consider* passing this hand. I could make a flush, two pair, one pair . . . I've got two completely different straight draws . . . I could bluff, I could make moves . . . no, Christ knows, I might have been a better player then. At least I knew how to fold. Back then, I was scared of losing; that's no good. But, right now, I don't care if I win or lose, and that's worse.

So here I am with K8 and it comes down 3 8 8. Well, wey-hey, aren't I the greatest player of all time. I bet. The old Chinese guy raises. I re-raise, he goes all-in for his last £400. Could he have A8? Could he have 33? While I'm thinking about it, he looks at me mournfully and says: 'I'm losing thousands.'

But I have to call. He shows 87. No good. No good on the turn, no good on the river. He drags himself back to the desk, but now he finds his credit card is maxed out so he has to go home. And the fact is, I wish I'd folded. I am winning in the game. I don't need his contribution. And I don't need his plaintive, disappointed face fixed in my self-loathing mind; £400-worth of blood money.

♠

And yet, I can't be anywhere else. After a few weeks, Charlie has to move back to his own home and his own life; he can't sit on my sofa every night while I cry, and I can't sit crying in his office while he works. So, now, I'm taking a pill every morning and going to the Vic every night.

It's like going to bed when you have the flu. You're too hot, you're too cold, your head aches, your eyes hurt, even your skin is sore. You don't feel well or happy in bed. But you feel like death if you're anywhere else.

I remember when The Sweep was getting divorced, he was in the Vic every night. He said, 'I need the escapism. For some people it's drugs, or travelling, losing their problems in a different high. It's all fine, as long as you remember that when you get home, the problems are still there.'

Theoretically, you should avoid poker when you're already on emotional tilt. When The Cincinnati Kid is abandoned by his girlfriend, he quits the action to chase after her because the loneliness is affecting his game. He can't play properly until he sorts his head out. The book says, 'He had been a fool to let her go to her Mama's. There had been something underlying and nervous about the whole week. It was her.'

Sensible Cincinnati, protecting his bankroll by taking a break when he's upset. Winning over the absconded girlfriend first. But there are a million other griefs. You can't go chasing after a house that's burned down, or a dead friend, or a lost childhood, or a lover who doesn't want you back. So you sink into the hypnotic cycle of poker: shuffle, deal, call, raise, fold; shuffle, deal, raise, re-raise, call; shuffle, deal, call, call, call; shuffle, deal, fold. The kindly Valium of the deck.

And then you find two red jacks, and you raise, and you get two callers. And the flop comes with three small clubs on it, and the first caller checks, and the second caller bets, and you think *so hard, so hard* about whether your hand is good, about why he's betting, about why he called, about the other guy waiting behind, that sometimes you can squeeze out everything else.

♠

Here's a joke that Adam Heller told me.

Jim and Tom are best friends. They play gin rummy together every night for twenty years. One terrible day, Tom confesses that he's been having an affair with Jim's beloved wife. Both men are in tears. The wife is in pieces. She has fallen in love with Tom, but she also loves her husband. What is to be done?

Eventually, Tom has an idea. 'Let's put the whole business in the hands of fate and decide it with a game of gin rummy. The winner gets to be with her for ever. The loser promises never to see her again.'

'Good plan,' says Jim, blowing his nose and brightening up. 'And to make it interesting, let's play for 10p a point.'

♠

My old nemesis Christian reckons that poker acts as a thermometer, so you know when you're okay again. He's the boy who used to take all my living money when I was at university and commuting home to learn the game at a price I couldn't afford. A few years later, I bumped into him at a party and invited him to come along one Tuesday night.

Chris has sorted his life out and become a film producer. But I've learned how to play poker. I have my own group of regulars, my own home game, I've played on *Late Night Poker* and lasted nearly all the way to the first commercial break. Time to get even. When I invited him, I felt like one of those guests on American talk shows who used to be 20 stone, and confront their old school bullies to say 'Look At Me Now – I'm Only 19 Stone And I've Had My Hair Highlighted'.

Of course, Chris comes to the game and wins the lot. He barely loses a hand. Knowing him to be a Holdem expert, I deal five card stud with the down-card wild and any like it. He pairs his hole card and makes a royal flush.

We talk about playing poker at grim times. Chris says, 'When I got chucked, I played continuously for four months on the trot. I've never won so much in my life – I needed a wheelbarrow. It's very good therapy, and it also tells you when you're feeling better. After four months, I stood up from the table and said, "God, this is boring."'

That last bit isn't happening to me. Maybe that means I'm not getting better, or maybe it just means I've been sucked in. I can't walk away from the tranquillizing therapy of the cards and the distracting adrenaline of the money. And I want to be near the people, with their upside-down lives and their hidden failures.

♠

The funny thing is, even as I am isolated by the players' weird attitude to the Amarillo/Race Hate situation, and even as I am saddened by the cruelty of the game, I feel closer to them, and to it, at the same time. The simpler love I felt before, the gentle admiration of the poker family, was a 68% fantastical construction. It was Hollywood love, not the blood and guts of a real relationship.

I get it now. Feeling alienated, isolated, thinking dark thoughts even as you laugh at jokes, saying 'Nice hand' even as you feel crushed, being among them but not of them, that *is* being one of them. Sitting around a table with a bunch of people who feel as cut off as you are, at least some of the time; that is community. We are all imperfect in the Vic, and if we weren't, we wouldn't be here.

That is, ultimately, what we have in common. That's why, although I'm not a man, I'm not a cockney, I'm not Chinese, I'm not Greek — I'm not even very crafty — I feel like I fit right in. It's because we all have a reason to be here, a lot of the time, in the middle of the night, away from the normal world, playing this game that throbs like a mosquito bite on the soul. It's not just an addiction to the game, it's not just a way of making money. These days we could just stay at home and play online, after all. Internet poker slots beautifully into a happy domestic life. But we come to the Vic.

Maybe we have a reason to be here, and maybe it's just a reason *not to be somewhere else*. And maybe it's both. And maybe we all have different reasons from each other, and maybe each of us has different reasons for ourselves, and maybe these reasons are not always easy to explain – but there are reasons, and these reasons create an unspoken bond, and this is why I feel more comfortable here than I would in a room with a million girls who look like me and talk like me and come from where I come from. If it's a sickbed, at least it has a lot of patients in it. This card room at the Victoria Club in Marble Arch, a few steps from the juice bars and hookah pipes of the Edgware Road and the lunatics at Speaker's Corner, I need as much as I need my real family. And the more the players bicker and bitch and fall out, the more they remind me of the extended family that I never quite knew, only heard about and glimpsed at funerals. So maybe it's a call of the blood. Or maybe just a mental affinity. But I'm discovering a different kind of truth, now: the lonelier I feel in here, the more I feel at home.

Who knew the warren could get any deeper? Boys, boys, boys; meeting Joe was my tumble down the rabbit hole but, in this dark rejected spring, I can finally see the ladder disappearing.

♠

He still comes to the game on Tuesdays. Thank God. If friendship was lost, then all would be lost.

I understand why he doesn't want to be with me. I'm grateful that he ever thought he did, even for a little while. I don't, I can't, feel resentful about not being loved; how could I? But I can't stand not being able to love. I want to stroke his hair, bake him cakes and give him presents. And I despise myself for such a suffocating, smothering thought.

Not that I'd say it to his face, of course. He would be horrified and embarrassed. None of this is his fault. When I see him,

I am as airy as I can possibly be. I'm fine, I'm fine, I'm fine. I will behave that way for years and years, and one day it will become true.

∿

A9 OFFSUIT

Again! This is the first half-decent hand I've seen since the last A9. I'm not passing it again. There are only four of us now, making my hand even stronger. Also, Emad Tahtouh has not yet had the chance to raise.

So, I make it a standard 60,000 (three big blinds). Emad passes the button. Michael Muldoon passes from the small blind. But Jan Sjavic re-raises from the big blind, to 100,000. A minimum raise! Technically, I raised 40,000 and he is raising 40,000 more.

An alarm bell rings in my head. I really don't think Sjavic has been getting out of line in this tournament, and I haven't been the most active player at the table either. Does he need to re-raise me, out of position, without a big hand? He probably has a big hand. And the minimum bet, too. He wants me. Or he's supposed to.

However . . . It's terrible for my table image if I make my first raise in ages, and am then seen to throw it away for a re-raise. It could encourage the others to trample all over me. I can't just give up immediately. But I don't want to shovel the chips all-in when Jan Sjavic might, just might, have a monster.

I opt for making my own small, but not minimum, re-re-raise. That's enough to show that I wasn't on an empty steal – and enough to test how much Jan really loves his hand – while saving a few chips behind. Raising another 100,000 is showing strength and commitment to the pot, but giving myself a secret escape route.

Jan moves all-in.

Well, that answers that. He wasn't screwing around. He's really got a triceratops of a hand. There's no way I'm calling a five-bet, all-in, from Jan Sjavic, with A9. True, I have put in so many chips already that I am nearly obliged to call for value — but Jan knows that. He absolutely cannot be bluffing, semi-bluffing, or anything like it. He has AA or KK. There's a small chance of QQ, but I don't think so. His hand is so big that he's absolutely unafraid to jam in every last chip, before the flop, against a fairly tight player who has shown serious interest and is priced in to call.

I pass. Jan Sjavic has AA. The absolute lumbering nuts.

It's been a nasty skirmish, and taken me down to less than 400,000 in chips. That's just twenty big blinds. Trouble territory. Especially with aggressive old Emad lurking there on nearly 2,000,000. Now, my back's against the wall somewhat.

But I should be grateful. I am grateful. If Jan had just flat called my re-raise, and I'd hit something on the flop, then I would have been knocked out of this tournament. What fails completely to destroy makes strong: I may be battered, but I'm still alive.

16

IF YOU WANT IT . . .

. . . Here it is, come and get it.

I'm sitting in my local Italian restaurant, spaced out on citalo-pram, waiting for Nasty Nick. This is weird.

This is weird because I'm not in my pyjamas and I'm not in the Vic either. It's weird because it's my first social engagement since a doctor told me I had 'clinical depression' (which doesn't mean much, but people who are crying every day take comfort in the affirmation of a diagnosis), and it's with a pantomime villain from the TV that I've never met before. It's weird because I watched Nasty Nick shock Britain with his devious behaviour in the first series of *Big Brother*, which set the template for reality TV successes and failures for some time after and helped me win lots of money betting on it. The reality markets on Betfair are the best thing to have happened in sports betting for ages, especially for me because I know nothing about horses or football but a hell of a lot about soap operas. And it's weird because, when you're spaced out on citalopram, every-thing's weird anyway.

For *Celebrity Poker Club 2*, a few notorious 'bad boys' have been selected to add spice to the line-up: jailed stock trader Nick Leeson, disgraced game-show contestant Major Charles Ingram, and my lunch date, 'Nasty Nick' Bateman. Everybody wants to know how these three contestants, all famous in one way or another, rightly or wrongly, for cheating, will fare in a game where deceit is actively encouraged. But Nick is not too familiar with poker, so the production company have asked me to meet up with him and offer a few tips.

I would be excited to meet a major character from a TV genre which is so culturally hot and so lucrative for betting, except that excitement has been wiped off my emotional palette. The pills take the edge off everything. They blunt the nightmares, which is what they were supposed to do, but they blunt everything else as well. I just feel indifferent. Losing all the highs and lows, funny how the feeling goes away. My brother says I am acting like a zombie. But it's a relief, it's better than the alternative.

Nasty Nick arrives, to the immediate bustle and buzz of the waiters, and slips off his overcoat. My cloudy brain is in no state to judge anyone socially, but he seems fine, just like anybody else. And he grasps the rules of poker pretty quickly. It only takes a couple of hours to decide he's ready to face the challenges of a celebrity tournament.

We shake hands, say we'll see each other in Cardiff, and he passes me a package wrapped in brightly coloured paper. I open this unexpected thank-you present. It is the autobiography of a Moroccan princess. This seems quite an odd gift.

'She had a terrible life,' says Nick. 'It'll make you cry like a baby.'

I say: 'Oh, good. Thank you.'

♠

I'm in the first heat of the tournament, which is a big advantage. I'm nervous about being far from the Vic for a whole week; my best chance of playing properly is to attack the competition on Day One, before I get too homesick. Of all the bad states for playing poker tournaments – anger, fear, insobriety – the very worst is 'wanting to go home'.

And there is an unexpected extra edge for me in the first match: it is massively delayed. The dealers, Marina and Peter from the Concord card club, are fog-bound in Vienna. My opponents have plenty of time to grow nervous and bored, but I'm happy staring into space for a few hours. It's what I have been doing most days anyway.

When the dealers finally arrive, it is without their uniforms, which are still en route from Heathrow. We don't sit down to the game until midnight. This is a particular problem for one of my opponents, the TV psychiatrist Dr Raj Persaud, who is due to address a conference of nurses in London at 9 a.m. tomorrow.

'They're not even normal nurses,' he moans. 'They're wound-healers! It's an incredibly difficult and dedicated branch of nursing. If they thought I'd been up all night, smoking cigars and playing poker, they'd be rightly horrified.'

Even for those who don't have an early appointment in a different country, this is annoyingly late. They're tired. But the hour feels normal and natural to me. Midnight is when poker is played. I have been far more disadvantaged by televised matches that are played, for studio reasons, in the morning.

As the others start to yawn and yearn for their beds more than victory, I am just starting to wake up. One by one, they sleepwalk out of the game and soon enough I am heads-up with Dr Raj. This proves a surprisingly easy match-up because, despite all his scientific qualifications, he doesn't seem to have worked out that all the hand values change when there are only two players at the table. It is not about the cards at all, any more, but the attitude. He's passing hands like 77 and AQ, while I'm raising automatically with K4 or 89. My head still feels kind of drugged and heavy, though less than it does away from the table, but it doesn't matter. It means I feel no fear in moving my chips without a hand. I just raise and raise and raise from the button like a robot, which is exactly what you're supposed to do. Thus, at last, I win a televised tournament heat outright.

♠

The next morning, I watch the darts champion Eric Bristow win the second heat. In the corridor afterwards I say, 'Congratulations! See you in the final.'

'I don't give a fuck who's in the final,' he replies. 'I'm going to win.'

And he walks off.

♠

I am glad to see the following heat won by my favourite Eton charmer, Tom Parker Bowles.

♠

Of the bad boys – Nick Leeson, Charles Ingram and my protégé Nasty Nick – none of them finishes anywhere. Some of the observers are saying this proves that wiliness and deceit alone cannot win poker tournaments. But I play in the Vic, I know different.

Major Ingram's wife Diana (who was referred to as 'Lady Macbeth' during their preposterous trial for cheating on *Who Wants To Be A Millionaire?*) is also playing, but she gets nowhere either. All she does is disappoint the crew, who were desperate for Charles to cough 'Nut flush!' when she was considering an unwise call.

It falls to the Major to be this year's greenest poker player, making an error that trumps even Leslie Grantham's inexplicable fold of the nuts the year before. Ingram decides, most bravely, to run a huge bluff against Steve Davis, one of the strongest opponents in this field. Just like a professional, Major Charles bluffs before the flop, and again on the flop, and again on the turn. Fire, fire, fire. I like his style. I'd like it even more if he didn't, most *unlike* a professional, turn his cards face-up as soon as the river is dealt.

Tournament director Thomas Kremser is obliged to warn the

Major that the hand is not finished; there is further betting to
be done. Obediently, Charles turns his worthless cards face-down
again – and moves all-in. For Steve Davis, it is not a difficult
call.

I suspect immediately that Charles Ingram is innocent of all
charges in the *Who Wants To Be A Millionaire?* scandal. After this
Laurel & Hardy poker display, the scam of having someone
cough loudly at the sound of the correct answer seems a little
too sophisticated for him.

♠

The celebrity drug-smuggler Howard Marks is here, playing exactly
as you'd expect from a lifetime dope-smoker. He has to look back
at his hole cards every few seconds. He also does everything five
times slower than the normal human speed. In that heat, they
manage about three hands per hour.

In my own spaced-out state, I look at Howard as something
of a soulmate. During the breaks, we chat to each other at a
treacly pace, each of us drifting off mid-sentence without the
other noticing. But the funny thing is, whatever the drugs are
doing to my emotional range, I still play poker at the normal
speed and he doesn't. I find him frustratingly slow to watch. It's
as though the game is the only thing that counteracts my new
biological clock.

♠

The ventriloquist Roger de Courcey is back, and this time he's
brought Nookie Bear. He brings Nookie Bear in to his post-
match interview.

When Roger explains how difficult it is to see the flop across
such a big table, the bear goes cross-eyed. When Roger says, 'I
don't think I played aggressively enough,' the bear shouts, 'Too

aggressive, more like!' I truly think it is two sides of Roger's brain fighting it out.

My own mind has similar arguments with itself after tournaments. Perhaps I should invest in a puppet. That way, when I'm beating myself up for re-raising all-in with two jacks against obvious aces, my bear can shout, 'You did nothing wrong! He could have had a pair of tens!'

♠

Willie Thorne, the snooker player, makes the final. I decide to tell him the story I once heard about a guy who tried to blag a free room in a hotel near the Crucible by claiming to be Willie Thorne's agent. The hotel receptionist went away and spoke for some time into the house phone. The guy started to feel nervous. Maybe the hotel knew what Willie Thorne's agent looked like? It was next door to the Crucible; Thorne's entourage was probably in that hotel all the time. The receptionist must have known immediately that he was an impostor.

When she returned, she said, 'Please wait here, the manager would like a word.'

'Oh, God,' the guy thought, 'they've rumbled me. Shall I run for it?'

But he daren't leg it. He wondered what was going to happen. He thought, 'It can't be a crime to pretend to be someone's agent, can it? Then again, I asked for a free room. That's fraud. You get longer for fraud than for anything else, except murder. I'm done like a kipper here.'

But when the manager arrived, she was wreathed in grateful smiles. 'Thank goodness you've turned up,' she said. 'I assume you can now settle Mr Thorne's bar bill, which he appears to have left without paying.'

Halfway through this story, I wonder whether Willie Thorne is going to be offended. It must be the stupid anti-depressants, taking the edge off my sense of what is appropriate to talk about. But I press on anyway, and Thorne laughs for about half an hour. What a lovely man. My eyes are suddenly hot and sore like I'm going to cry. It's another of the strange side effects of this depression, or these pills: as soon as anyone is kind or lovable, I get tearful.

Now I want Willie Thorne to win. He seems so lovely, and he deserves first prize. That kind of thing matters far more to me, right now, than winning a tournament myself.

When the final begins, I am concentrating so hard on the cards that I barely notice who is getting up and walking away. I can hear myself joking and chatting, but I'm not listening, so I don't know what I'm saying. My opponents are just shadows, disappearing one by one from the table. Except for Willie Thorne, who has taken on some kind of angelic shape; when the two of us are left heads-up at the end, I feel at last like I am taking on a real person. I want him to feel the pleasure of victory. But I know what it would take to lose the match – turning weak and passive, calling and folding with mediocre hands – and I can't bear to do it. It's too close to how I actually used to play.

So I play properly, and win the £25,000 tournament, and burst into tears.

♠

When David Beckham cries, everybody sniggers. When Matthew Pinsent cries, everybody cheers. In the summer of 2004, they all seem to be at it.

This is a big sporting summer: a European Championship and an Olympics. When England crashes out of the football and Beckham is photographed crying, commentators put the boot in. He missed a penalty. It's all his fault. The drippy little shit.

Matthew Pinsent, though, is hailed and loved for his manly tears. He has won his fourth gold medal, at the Athens Olympics, in the men's coxless fours. Everyone is moved by the damp lashes of a winner – as long as he is a winner. We only care about the winners.

When I was at primary school, I was in Scott House. Captain Scott was the first national hero presented to me, the first icon. Our young minds were inspired, in classic English style, by the story of a man who set out with big ambitions, botched them, came last and died. Froze to death a failure. The lesson set before us, aged six, was: lose with dignity.

My old school house has now been renamed after Florence Nightingale. Nobody's impressed by the ambitious, stoic old captain any more. He's a loser. Already, in the new wave of poker excitement, the world is greedy for fresh young stars who look like they have never lost a pot. The idea of *Late Night Poker*, of shedding light on the quirky old characters of the game – the Surinder Sunars, the Mickey Wernicks, who have won and lost and won and lost and lived a lot and most of all survived – is making way for a different kind of heroism. Old warhorses no good, unbroken stallions required. The Hendon Mob, with their sponsorship deal, are already sloughing off their old Ealing Comedy style, no longer making rueful jokes about the hand-to-mouth poker existence but, instead, asked to justify the deal by jealous fellow players online, publishing lists of their extensive tournament successes. They must feel like they have to.

For me, winning and crying are just a coincidence. Everyone tells me how moved they are to see how much the victory means. But it means nothing. I am crying purely from the effort of not crying for the previous four hours while we recorded the tournament. I would have cried if I lost, cried if I won, cried if I hadn't bothered playing. I am all over the place. I'm a winner. I'm rich. I'm glad about the money, don't get me wrong, I needed some; but it's a faraway gladness, a distant sense of the practicalities made comfortable, a bankroll built. And for what? Just to keep moving. Lucky at cards, unlucky in love, ruined by knowing that the former doesn't neutralize the latter. In the old joke, Jim and Tom care more about winning the money than the wife. I wish I knew their secret, even as I stuff packets of £50 notes into my suitcase.

♠

Now there's a new problem. My ten-year college reunion dinner, which I promised to attend, is happening tonight. At 8 p.m. In Oxford. It's now half past nine, and I'm in Cardiff.

I hadn't imagined there was any chance I would make the final, never mind win it. I accepted the reunion dinner invitation months ago, not anticipating any kind of clash. As it is, I gargle down a polite bottle of champagne with my opponents and the crew, buy a few more bottles for them to drink without me, and spend £250 of my new-found wealth on a taxi from Wales to England.

Now it's after midnight. The college is dark and the dining hall closed for the night. But the alumni are exactly where I expected them to be: drunk on the floor of my old tutor's room, while he is hooting merrily and cracking open fresh bottles from behind his desk, as if the last ten years had never happened.

Realizing I've forgotten to eat all day, again, I drag a couple of them to their feet and over the road to the kebab van, where I take my biggest gamble of the day on a grey, glistening doner. We really could be eighteen again.

Except we're not. This scenario should be a cartoon fantasy: arriving at my old college reunion, admittedly unmarried and childless and without really a proper job, but freshly crowned as a poker champion, with a trophy and a suitcase bulging with cash. And arriving glamorously late, because I was busy trouncing a table of world-class sportsmen, netting the title and pocketing the money. Isn't that the way you go back to college reunions in dreams? The good dreams?

But what do I know about good dreams? I'm taking pills to stop me having nightmares. I just want to go back. Back to Christmas, so that I can act cooler and not screw up my relationship with an overdose of affection. Back to last summer, when it seemed miraculously possible to have love and poker at the same time. Back to springtime in Vegas, when we skipped around like kids on school holidays and I was the happiest I've ever been. Back to the days when I never expected to fall in love anyway, so it didn't matter. Back to my real college years, when I could afford to spend any number of nights throwing up dodgy kebabs because I had so many more in front of me; back to that happy time in the comedy club above the pub; back to that sunny day in Portobello market with my father, clutching his hand; back to the magical night when my parents said we could have one more game of Monopoly even though it was after bedtime; back to being a little child at family gatherings peopled by forgotten great-aunts and uncles, and back and back to the Anglo-Saxons and the Medieval Romans and *Ubi sunt qui ante nos fuerunt?* I have never wanted to go back in time before. It was always enough to look forwards and back in one busy continuous present. Now I'm aching to escape it. I feel old.

♠

A few weeks later, there's a poker festival at the Vic. The Sweep, J.Q. and I all make the final of the Pot Limit Omaha Hi-Lo event; I finish fourth for £2,128. Then I get my biggest-ever cash in a professional tournament: second in the Pot Limit Holdem for £14,910.

This is ridiculous. I can't stop winning.

A4 OFFSUIT

I can't win. I haven't picked up a chip in ages. Or a proper hand. If this were the first and last day of my life, it would say 'She had weak aces' on my gravestone.

This time, I'm in the small blind. Muldoon and Sjavic pass. I should probably move all-in. Or I could opt for a sort of stop-go: complete the blinds, then move in on the flop. Emad Tahtouh's in the big blind with a dominant chip lead and I've got the short stack; his pre-flop calling range will be broad, but after cards it's trickier for him unless he hits. So, I will call now and move on the flop.

But Emad raises all-in from the big blind. Well, of course he bloody does. Absolutely standard. He didn't just wake up this morning and decide to give poker a try for the first time in his life; there's no way he was going to let me see a cheap flop, or make a move on him after it came down, when he's got me covered by a million chips. More than a million. He'll do this with absolutely anything.

Unfortunately, I just don't have a calling hand. If I had A9 this time, I'd call instantly. But A4? Let's say Emad has a hand like 7♦ 5♦ – I'm not much better than 50/50. And if he does happen to have an ace or a pair, I'm sunk. Do I want to gamble for my tournament at these prices? It's not a scary gamble for Emad, he has too many chips. For me, it's life or death.

I should have just moved in myself, probably picked up the blinds, and if he has a big hand, then good luck to him. Instead, I've allowed this exploitation and I can't call. I throw the A4 away. I'm annoyed with myself. I played that all wrong. I got over-sophisticated, planning what I'd do on the flop, failing to factor in what Emad would do if I limped, when I should have just peeled back the ace and stuck my chips in immediately. That was not a good stop-go situation, I'm an idiot. I've come so far in this tournament; I grafted my way through the early stages, built my stack in the middle stages, and fought my way to the final through a combination of gutsy moves with nothing, smart marginal calls, and magical luck when I needed it. Now I'm letting the whole thing dribble through my fingers. Enough negative thinking and self-pity. Time to regroup.

17

HUNTING JAGUARS

*'I'd rather write a cheque for $32,000 now than
lose a really big amount . . .'*

— Henry Fonda

In 1960, Doyle Brunson is heading to Mexico for a jaguar hunt.
He takes a break in the Sierra Madre, where he climbs up and
down a mountain in less than two hours because Sailor Roberts
has bet him $2,500 that he can't. 'Hell,' says Doyle when he gets
down, 'I coulda done it in twenty minutes if the price was right.'

A few years before this, in the Fifties, young Doyle gets the
opportunity for a golf match against a local hustler in Fort Worth.
The guy wants to play for $3,000 per nine holes: $3,000 for the
front nine, $3,000 for the back nine. Doyle readily agrees. They
play the first nine holes; Doyle loses, and withdraws from the
match. The original $3,000, he explains, is all the money he had
in the world.

This is truly one of the Old School degenerates.

Doyle Brunson is born in 1933 to a Baptist family in West
Texas. He's a big lad and a great athlete, but he breaks his leg
in an accident at work, scuppering his basketball promise and
leaving him with a permanent limp. So he turns into a road
gambler, travelling the American South making illegal books,
betting on sports and fleecing opponents in lucrative private
poker games. He plays with gangsters and cattlemen, oil barons
and crooks. A lot of crooks. He forms a bookmaking partnership with Amarillo Slim and Sailor Roberts, fading the line across
the southwest. They call him Texas Dolly.

In 1970, he's there in the line-up for the first-ever World

Series of Poker, when all the would-be champions fit round a single baize table and the first prize is simply glory. In 1972, Doyle gets down to the last three but withdraws from the tournament, for fear that any publicity around the win would shame his elderly God-fearing parents. There is nothing respectable in being a gambler. But what do his parents' friends think he's been doing for money all these years?

Once Doyle has withdrawn from the 1972 tournament, it's won by his old buddy Amarillo Slim. Slim milks it like a prize heifer, going on talk shows, publishing a book, becoming the only famous poker player in the world. You've got to guess that Doyle finds this immensely annoying.

Then, in 1976, Texas Dolly has another good run in the World Series of Poker. Of course he does. Only 22 runners and they're all waiting for aces. The art of poker is patience and big cards, playing them hard when they come, that's what everybody does. Doyle is one of the first to figure out that if you find some little cards, maybe a 45 suited, or something really crazy like a T2, they can upset aces and kings like castor oil under a hospital trolley. That's what I learned in the North London private games with Joe, four years ago, but this was decades earlier. Doyle is the only one at the table who pushes with anything. You can say this for the guy: he's a gambler.

His strong, counter-intuitive style powers through the field and this time, maybe because his old buddy won the title and Doyle can't bear the one-upmanship, he stays in action, beating all 21 opponents to become the 1976 World Series of Poker champion. By now, the contestants are putting up $10,000 to play. But the payout structure is not complicated: Doyle takes the lot, $220,000.

Then, in 1977, Texas Dolly does it again. Back-to-back World Series titles. This time there are 34 runners. Still winner-takes-all: $340,000 for the Old School legend.

Then, in 1978, Doyle makes his biggest mistake. He writes up his poker theories in a book, *How I Made Over $1,000,000*

Playing Poker, and after that, everybody he meets is playing suited connectors and weird hands, bullying and pushing with draws and semi-bluffs, no longer waiting for aces, and sometimes maybe he regrets writing it.

♠

In 2004, I am watching the 71-year-old Doyle lever his 20-stone bulk through a crowd of hopefuls. There aren't 22 players this year. There aren't 34. And there aren't 839 like last year. This is the first World Series of Poker since the Moneymaker Miracle, and the field numbers 2,576. That makes a prize pool of more than $25 million. It's no longer winner-takes-all: even with $5 million for the top spot, at least five millionaires will be created. Whoever comes 9th in the final will win more than double what Doyle got for scooping the lot in '76. There are so many contenders that they can't all fit into Binion's Horseshoe, and are scheduled to play on alternate days.

They aren't gangsters and cattlemen, oil barons and crooks. They aren't Texans of the Old School, nor Californians on holiday. Their nicknames aren't 'Puggy', 'Dolly', 'Treetop' or 'The Greek'. They don't wear cowboy hats and rhinestone-studded boots. They aren't 71 and they aren't 20 stone. They are young, Scandinavian, blond, healthy, polite and good at maths. They are the pale, Nordic offspring of Huck Seed: this is the era he unwittingly pre-dated, with all his talk of game theory and lactic acid. I thought he was an anomaly who stumbled into poker by mistake, but now there are thousands of them. They wear tracksuits, Nike trainers and PokerStars T-shirts. They carry iPods, sunglasses and bottled water. Their nicknames are 'Grr197(Malmo)' or 'xxj21179'.

The internet army is here.

Doyle Brunson looks absolutely baffled.

♠

It's not helping me feel much younger either. We were the young ones, me and The Sweep and J.Q.; even D.Y., with his blazers and lace-up shoes and sensible haircut. We were the kids at the Vic. But we seem to have entered middle age overnight – apart from D.Y., who was probably born holding a chess set and a copy of the *Spectator*.

Once again, J.Q. and I have got rooms at the Golden Nugget while The Sweep is nursing his bankroll at the old Mint. This year, he says his room smells of shit. Oh, well. Maybe he can buy a handkerchief with the savings.

The Nugget card room is open for the first time in years. We play cash poker in there, watching the Big Game in the corner. They sit at a special roped-off table, playing the mixed rounds (Seven Stud, Triple Draw, Hi-Lo) at $4,000/$8,000 limit. We play $10/$20 limit. They're playing 400 times bigger. Still, $10/$20 feels pretty sizable to me.

Doyle Brunson is often in that corner, presiding over the Big Game. But the eyes aren't on him. Everybody's watching the young black kid in the nine seat. Draped there in a gangly shape, chin ducked, baseball cap on his head, is 28-year-old Phil Ivey from New Jersey. I've only just heard of him, though he's already won four bracelets, three of them in the same Series two years ago. But with the mushrooming of poker magazines, poker discussion sites, even poker radio shows, Phil Ivey's name has gained a sudden currency. Everybody has a crush on 'the Tiger Woods of poker'.

He looks like a sports star making a guest appearance on a celebrity table. His face seems too fresh for the late nights, his body too tall for the squashed seat, everything about him too alert, too young, too agile for the sedentary patience of the game. You'd swear he had ducked in for a couple of hours and would get bored, chuck it all in with no hand and wander off to do something else. But they say he is the best in the world.

So, I stare at him from the cheap seats. I am fascinated by his massages. He is being massaged all the time, round the clock.

There are three girls on task. One of them is doing his shoulders, the other two are doing his feet. Now they're rubbing his legs. Now the feet again. Now they all swap positions. Phil spins his chair round so one of them can get at his back. Another works on his scapula. Phil puts out his bets with a graceful, leisurely hand, no movement above the wrist, no disturbing ripple for the girl at his shoulder. This massage has been going on for about four hours. How much more relaxed does the guy need to be?

The kids love it. They stand on the rail, watching Phil Ivey getting massaged. They are desperate to be him. Occasionally, a security guard comes across to move them away. It's weird. Time was, poker players were the poor cousins in Vegas. It was hard to find a hotel-casino that would even give us floor space. The dice and roulette and blackjack punters would get free meals and courtesy limousines, complimentary suites and show tickets; poker players would get a distasteful look and a grudging point towards a few shabby tables in the back. Now, it's 'Move away, please. Keep behind the rope. Don't get too close. This is the Big Game.'

No disrespect to Doyle Brunson, I'm sure some of them recognize him, too. His book, now re-titled *Super System: A Course In Power Poker*, has found a whole new market in the young generation. The man's no fool. He has made a living in gambling, by hook and by crook and whatever it took, for more than fifty years. He'll find a way to cash in on this poker boom, don't worry about that – unlike his old road buddy, best friend and bookmaking partner Amarillo Slim, who was the first poker celebrity all those years ago. Now the boat's come in, Slim has no chance of unloading any cargo, due to that sickly business with the granddaughter. He is frozen out. Nobody wants to sponsor him, talk to him, play with him or get him promoting anything. This is a shiny new world, and his memory is being mopped off it. The would-be mob can take comfort: no doubt the loss of all that potential fame and revenue will pain Slim far more than any car-park kicking would have done.

Meanwhile, Texas Dolly gets rounds of applause when he

lumbers through the card room, or speeds through on his little mechanized golf cart. They recognize him. But they don't want to be him. They want to be young and rich and beautiful, hanging at the table in sports gear. They want to drive Ferraris and drink Cristal, they want to have gorgeous girls sitting behind them for no financial recompense, they want to be massaged for eight hours at a time. They want to be famous, respected and admired. They don't want dusty roads and secret adventures. The ones that recognize Doyle Brunson are impressed, but he's an old man with a weird history. They look at Phil Ivey and see their own bright futures.

Doyle is already losing a million in the Big Game, this year.

♠

D.Y. decides to get a massage. This is a remarkable decision for our favourite young fogey, who I would have assumed was too uptight to get the rub-down in public. But hey, we're on holiday. In a moment of astonishing hedonism, D.Y. actually removes his blazer.

When I first met D.Y., I disliked him enormously. I drew negative conclusions from his neatly brushed hair, his daily uniform of blazer and chinos, combined with his libertarian politics. But I disliked him mainly for his lack of tact. The first time we ever met, he bustled over to me in the bar of the Holland Casino during the Master Classics of Amsterdam and lisped, 'My friend Dominic and I often watch you on *Late Night Poker* and I mutht ask thith: when you have tho little grathp of the game, how can you afford to play?'

It took years for me to understand that D.Y. hadn't meant to be rude. He's just missing something in the armoury of traditional social etiquette. He is very smart, yet completely unfettered by diplomacy and utterly unable to imagine what others may be thinking. One shade the more, one ray the less, and he would be an autistic savant.

He doesn't follow the normal rules of conversation. One night in the Vic, I asked how he was and he replied, to the whole table, 'Not too well, I'm afraid – thuffering dreadfully from piles.'

I couldn't help laughing, out of sheer surprise at his honesty. Taking this to be the relieved merriment of empathy, D.Y. chirped, 'Do you thuffer from haemorrhoids, too?'

As soon as you accept that D.Y. lacks a masterful social polish, you are free to see how smart, lovable, hilarious and ultimately admirable he is. I now know what a blessing it is to have him around.

J.Q. and The Sweep are deeply amused to watch him getting a massage. The spectacle is vastly improved by the fact that the masseuse is married to one of the other players in this cash game, an ill-tempered local tournament director.

The director is in a foul mood because he is losing. He is not a gracious loser. He is aggressive and rude to the dealer. He keeps making what he believes to be brilliantly cutting put-downs of the other players, only to be met with silly replies and a lot of laughter from this bastard English group around him. Now he's having to watch his own wife give a soothing massage to one of them – the freaky one with the posh voice and the lisp. He can't bear it.

Meanwhile, D.Y., utterly unaware of the dark looks from the tense husband, is making appreciative noises as he gets massaged. It must be his first time. Every time he murmurs or smiles, the grumpy tournament director shakes his head furiously and throws in an irritable raise. They are like a pair of cartoon characters having a stand-off, except D.Y. doesn't know the stand-off is happening. He is in his own private world of delight. J.Q.'s shoulders are shaking. When D.Y. actually starts groaning with pleasure, The Sweep has to stand up and walk to the other side of the room. He is almost in tears.

♠

The Sweep and I had a fairly successful trip to Paris a few weeks ago, making money in the cash games at the Aviation Club. There are people who might advise against going to Paris with a broken heart, but I've never found it an especially romantic city anyway. It's grey, trafficky and expensive, with a few decent landmarks dotted around otherwise gloomy buildings and a lot of tetchy, unfriendly people. I can get all that in London. And I *love* London. So why go to Paris?

Only for the poker. The Aviation, on the Champs-Élysées, is a beautiful place to play and the games are famously good. The French are loose, crazy players. The Sweep heard my sob stories patiently and we had a lucrative trip. I only cried once in the card room.

But maybe it was a mistake to come to the World Series? Moments of laughter at the card table are islands in a much murkier river. Vegas was paradise for me, but the most glittery and exciting place in the world is quickly malformed into the loneliest, the emptiest and the cruellest. Desert is desert, whatever they build on it. With sad eyes, you see the sickness and the seediness. Instead of the wondrous palaces on the Strip, you see the homeless on the outskirts. Instead of the glorious winners, you see the miserable losers. Instead of the beautiful girls, you see the plastic strippers and ageing whores. Instead of friendly smiles, you see manipulative greed.

Mary Poppins, the magic nanny, has a medicine that tastes of strawberry, lime cordial or rum punch, depending on the drinker. So it is with Vegas, but one of the flavours is very bitter indeed. The taste of paradise, this year, is soured by my spirits.

♠

But how could I not come? In this fast-developing world of internet poker, the Prima network, sponsors of the Hendon Mob, have offered to put me in the main event. They'll pay my $10,000 buy-in money, as long as I mention them when writing up my 'first World Series experience' for the paper. So I said yes. I might be clinically depressed but I'm not insane.

The great mass of players are queuing for two or three hours on the dark, dank Binion's staircase, just to hand over the $10,000 entry fee or collect their seat assignments. The main bulk of the field have already won their seats on PokerStars for a few bucks, just like Chris Moneymaker did, and are queuing only to be given a table number. Those who are parting with the ten bags of sand shoot jealous glances at those who are not.

The competitors' names have always been posted outside the tournament room in a roll call of glory. But not this year, because there isn't enough space on the wall. They have come from South America, from Scandinavia, from France, from Germany, from the UK. They have even come from Hollywood. Tobey Maguire, Leonardo DiCaprio, James Woods and Ben Affleck are giving the boys a spin.

Poor old Maguire gets a rough ride. Fellow players and rail-birds shout, 'Whatcha gonna do, Spiderman?' whenever it's his turn to bet. Leonardo DiCaprio creeps shyly in and out under a cap and shades. But Ben Affleck is very popular. He fell in love with poker a few months ago and has been hanging around the Vegas scene; there's a story that one night in the Bellagio card room he deliberately folded the best hand for $13,000 because he felt his young opponent couldn't afford to lose. So everybody likes him. The amateurs think this move revealed a great and kindly character, and the professionals are delighted to welcome an opponent who'd be prepared to fold the nuts under any circumstances at all.

♠

However I'm feeling, I can't dodge the wave of romance that breaks over the act of sitting down in the World Series of Poker

main event. Here we are, jam-packed into Binion's, the rickety
old spot where the great tournament has always been played.
Somebody is going to collect $5 million and the greatest title
that will ever exist in poker. It's hot, it's tense. And it's hairy:
Surinder Sunar is getting a massage without his shirt on. Must
be like running your hands back and forth over an Afghan rug.

Masseuses slide between the crowds, plying their trade,
shouting their offers. Girls in tiny dresses, with huge Southern
beehives and Barbie lipstick, squeeze through the room crooning,
'Cigars, cigarettes? Cocktails? Chocolate, candy, gum?' It feels like
a souk, except, as Martin Amis once brilliantly said, 'If you could
choose only one adjective to describe Las Vegas, that adjective
should be "un-Islamic".'

I'm unlucky with the draw. Everyone says, with all these
internet qualifiers, there'll be loads of value in the Day One
action: kids who have fluked their way in, or never played a live
tournament, getting nervous and throwing chips away. Free money
on the starting tables! Meanwhile, on my immediate left, I've got
the 2001 world champion Carlos Mortensen. He is an aggressive,
active, skilled player and he's got position. As BadBeat would say,
'Marvellous.'

The cards are not helping. My recent run of form seems to
have dwindled to drought at exactly the wrong time. I have aces
cracked twice. Then I flop a straight, but the Norwegian internet
player on my right has flopped a higher straight. Still, I feel
satisfied that I managed to avoid going broke. People can be too
quick to get themselves knocked out of a deep-structure tournament; in the World Series, with its big chips and slow opening
levels, a decent player should be able to get unlucky early without
being eliminated. In fact, with a few better hands and a spot of
timely bluffing, I manage to convert my opening $10,000 to
$15,000 by the end of the day.

Hundreds of others are being knocked out around me. With
so many kids in the competition for $10 or $50, it runs like the

Grand National in wet weather. Favourites are tumbling on all sides. Several fall at once, you lose track of who's gone and who's still there. It's carnage. There's a ripple of laughter at 7 p.m. when the tournament director announces, 'Congratulations, you have all made it to the last 2,000 players.'

♠

Day Two is dull, standard, no hands and no room for manoeuvre. I inch along the tightrope as best I can, but I can't make real progress. Without the cards to trap or milk, I'm reduced to stealing blinds to stay alive. It's not enough. Eventually, during the last level of the day, one of my attempted blind-steals gets a caller and I go out in 609th place. But I'm not too crushed. It's my first shot at the world championship, in a massive field, and at least I finish in the top 25%. And I didn't have to pay for my ticket. Unfortunately, you can't eat value.

♠

So, now what? Last year I was just idyllically happy to be in Vegas: the cash games, the sunshine, the banter, the amusement parks, the chicken & tequila pizza. This year, I'm kind of desolate. I spend a lot of time lying on my bed in the Nugget, staring at the ceiling. I can't say I'm suicidal, since, as Thomas Lynch said, 'Who among us in our right minds hasn't several times in the course of a life yearned for the comforts of absence and non-being? But there is a subtle and important difference between those of us who'd rather not be alive tomorrow – incomplete homework, biopsy results, romantic reversals, pregnancy tests – and those of us who want to be dead tomorrow and the day after and forever.'

I lack what he calls 'the determination, the pure resolve, to do one's self such massive and irreparable damage', and I hope I will never go deaf to the voices that whisper the case for staying around to see what happens next. But yearning 'for the comforts of absence and non-being', I understand exactly what that means. The thought of waking up tomorrow, and the next day and the next, makes me feel tired and sad.

Around me, with my bitter spoonful of Poppins medicine, I can see the truly hopeless and the truly suicidal. Somebody jumped off the roof of Binion's just before the Series started.

The heat is shrivelling. The food is a heap of fattening, stunting junk. The hotel-casinos are oppressive mausoleums of greed. There is a guy here from the London poker scene, he's married but he's got overexcited about a girl he met in a shop at Caesars Forum and he's started giving her chunks of spending money. He thinks it's romantic. It isn't. Everybody here is a hooker of one sort or another. I can't even feel excited by the crowds and the explosion in poker, I'm looking at them and thinking: who are all these people, with no romance and no history, who've come gatecrashing here with their own stupid ideas of 'cool', and why can't they just leave us alone? I feel sick and miserable and I want to go home.

♠

Another player from London asks me out on a date. It happens sometimes, but he really seems to mean it. He has decided that I am absolutely the girl for him. I'm perfect. I'm nice and I'm beautiful and I play poker!

He's wrong, of course. I'm not nice at the moment, my head is full of dark thoughts. And I'm not beautiful, I'm overweight and I have a bumpy nose and mismatched English teeth. I play poker but that doesn't make me perfect, it just makes me someone he was likely to meet. He's a sick gambler, he hates to leave the table or the bookie's, so he can only choose from the girls he sees in those places. Me, Shirley Lewis and the waitresses. If I were him, I'd go for Beverley. She's great-looking and she makes a lovely cup of tea.

The whole set-up is heartbreaking. This guy is fantastic. He's bright and funny and cute, and most of all he's *nice*. He's loyal and kind and honest and sweet; he is one of the good guys. He is trying to offer a beautiful world. But it just wouldn't be fair, he deserves better than he knows. If I could stop him from realizing how many other women are out there, keep him away from the world beyond gambling, maybe he would think I was perfect for ever. But it would feel like a trick.

He thinks he wants me, my heart is breaking for someone else, and the someone else has his eyes on the horizon. It's a cooler. Three hands looking at a flop, all seeing something they like, but all drawing dead. Why are we so unlucky? Why can't at least one of us hit the river?

The only thing I really want and need is friendship. But he's been in poker for years, and he's popular, and he's a man: friendship is easily come by. He can ask anyone on the circuit if they fancy going for a meal, without it looking like a come-on. I can't. What he would consider rare and special, in poker, is a romance. For me, it would be real friendship without an agenda. We are both offering and asking for what we consider most meaningful, but we're working with completely different hand values.

He says it's okay. And I think we stay friends, we travel together, I always hope he'll be at the table when I play, and I take pleasure and pride in his poker successes and commiserate with his failures, and I trust him and love him and it is one of the most important friendships I have. But this is a broken-jigsaw world, where no two pieces seem to fit together, and I don't know if he ever, really, understands.

♠

We have a new world champion. It is Greg 'Fossilman' Raymer from Connecticut, a patent lawyer and respected player from the East Coast games, who won his seat (of course) online. Greg seems like a nice, decent man. But, in my grey world, I am disappointed by his post-match interview. There are no tales of road gambling, mountain climbing or gangster hold-ups on the road from Dallas. Just a careful explanation of patent law and some thanks to his wife. Asked why he uses fossils as card protectors, Greg replies, 'Because otherwise the dealer might accidentally take away my cards.'

♠

I'm sitting at the old snack bar in Binion's Horseshoe, drinking a dodgy cup of tea and eating a greasy sandwich, watching the Irish crew get drunk around the bar. Watching the elderly waitresses flirt and smile. Watching the more impoverished Vegas gamblers circling the cheapest wheels and machines.

It has just been announced that this will be the last World Series at Binion's.

Benny Binion died a few years ago and his children fell out. Jack Binion sold his inheritance and moved out of state. Ted Binion died of a drug overdose, though people say it was murder. Barbara Binion committed suicide back in 1977. The whole operation ended up in the hands of Becky Binion, who implemented all sorts of unpopular and controversial measures, culminating in a legal battle with the unions for non-payment of various staff entitlements. That battle was lost, payments were still not forthcoming and the casino was crippled: a couple of months ago, it was sold off to the Harrah's corporation.

Everything is falling apart. Harrah's have no interest in the old building or the Binion's brand, only the title 'World Series of Poker'. Next year, the tournament will leave Fremont Street and move uptown to the business wing of the big, ritzy Harrah's property at the Rio Hotel. A super-casino, compared to the little

shack where it has always been. And it will happen in the blis-
tering, traumatic heat of July, because suddenly poker players are
not Benny Binion's friends, treated to Vegas in beautiful springtime and made to feel special, but mugs who will fill up the Rio
in a baking, ash-dry month when nobody else wants to visit.

What will the tournament be like in a giant conference centre
uptown? Where will we stay? The Strip is a big place. How will
we bump into each other in the street and go for coffee?

♠

I can hear people clapping upstairs; someone significant must have
gone. A reporter from one of the new magazines tells me it is
Doyle Brunson, eliminated from the main event in 53rd place.
He moved all-in with a pair of tens and got knocked out by a
kid who was wearing an iPod, didn't hear the bet, announced
'raise' and was obliged to call Doyle's all-in with A7. Course the
ace fired out first card off the deck, no waiting, and the old man
had to ship it. One for the New School.

It's nice of them to clap. But the applause probably didn't last
long enough for him to get all the way to the door. It's a big
room and he's 71 years old.

How many will come next year? Four thousand? The online
satellites will be starting soon. The good people of Scandinavia
will be locking up the best deals on flights.

As I sit at the dark bar, nursing my tea, Texas Dolly hobbles
slowly past and out onto Fremont Street.

A BREAK

*No sooner do I think 'Regroup' than the blinds go up – as if by way
of a punishment for the weedy A4. But before the new round, we get
ten minutes' break. Good; I need a cigarette.*

Ever since they banned smoking from the card room, some of us have been at a terrible disadvantage. The new players like it. Of course they do, it suits the sporty clothes and the clean respectable image of the game. Plus they're not getting a faceful of some old geezer's B&H every two minutes. But I think it's harsh. I mean, this is a casino, a place for addicts. It's unsympathetic to send us out in the road. There should be no outsiders here.

Then again, I used to have so many smoking-related tells, maybe it helps me. Cigarette in advance if I intended to play the hand, cigarette as a reward after pulling off a successful bluff.

And it's good for me to have ten minutes outside the Vic, quiet time, to have a word with my head. I don't want to hobble out of contention in this tournament. I've got to fight to stay involved. I can't let the game run away without me.

After the break, I must be ready to move in with any hand at all.

18

HOME

'They are creatures of contradictions – they are fiercely greedy, lavishly generous, wary in many things, reckless of life, ready to take any advantage, yet possessed by a diseased sense of honour.'
– James Runciman (1893)

Peter is dealing. He's got better at it, actually. I'm relieved for him. You don't want to be a slow dealer, or a clumsy dealer, or a baffled dealer, in the Victoria card room. The players give you hell. They give you hell even if you're a good dealer. Many croupiers quit, or move out to the pit, because they just can't hack it in here. The sourness, the abuse, the throwing of cards.

But you have to understand, these players are very involved. Maybe it's the case money on the table. Bad enough to lose it because they get unlucky or misplay a hand. But to lose it because the dealer isn't concentrating, or because they get a bad ruling, well, now there is somebody to blame.

Peter is a gentle fellow, with his head in the clouds a lot of the time. He gets involved in conversations and forgets what he's doing. But I can't bear it when they shout at him, because he's such a soft and gentle character, he just thinks they're being mean. Thank goodness he seems to have stopped making mistakes.

Just as I'm thinking all this, there's a misdeal.

'Sorry, sorry,' says Peter, gathering in the cards. 'Even a professional makes mistakes. Think of Hitler.'

'*Hitler*?' I say. 'That's the name that comes into your head, when you think of a professional?'

'He was very professional,' says Peter, immediately forgetting to shuffle. 'But he made mistakes.'

'He made mistakes, did he?'

'Military mistakes,' says Peter.

Ah, yes, military mistakes. Ethically, he didn't put a foot wrong.

'Are you going to deal the fucking cards, or what?' says Stuart Nash.

Stuart doesn't normally swear in front of me. He's a suave, handsome sixtysomething with silver hair and an urbane manner. Urbane for the card room, anyway. Sometimes he comes in to play for a couple of hours in the early evening, then leaves to buy dinner for a beautiful woman in a restaurant somewhere else. That's very unusual here. Most players, even if they had a date, would never be able to tear themselves from the game.

He looks across immediately and apologizes. He is horrified, he had forgotten I was here. I make a face intended to convey a ladylike shock at the rude word, combined with immediate forgiveness and understanding.

God, I'm glad to be back. I love this place. They will bluff me, beat me, occasionally even fear me, just like any other player, yet I am 'a lady' so they mind their language. They want to bankrupt me, destroy me, but not offend me. There is nowhere else like it in the world.

'Hitler had very bad manners,' says Peter quietly. 'Though he was nice to his dog.'

'Peter, have you recently watched a documentary about Hitler?' I ask.

'There was one on TV last night,' says Peter eagerly.

Stuart rolls his eyes.

♠

Other times, they forget my gender entirely. We are assumed all boys together when it comes to the question of honesty with partners.

I remember when the last seat in a brilliant cash game was

snatched by a player who'd just been knocked out of the £100 tournament. He was calling for chips when his girlfriend phoned. He took the call and we heard him say, 'Yes, I'm still in the competition . . . No, it could run late . . . There's no need to wait up . . . Oh, about fifty of us left . . .' The eight players at the table, each of whom knew this script backwards, had the decency not to burst out laughing until he hung up.

I remember once walking up the stairs of the Vic to hear an Arabic fellow shouting into his mobile phone, 'I cannot talk now! I told you I am not supposed to use the phone in the hospital!'

He managed to click the off button just in time, before the Tannoy announced, 'New shoe of baccarat opening upstairs, new shoe of baccarat . . .'

We exchanged polite, understanding nods.

There is a certain Chinese player whose wife has no idea he has ever been to a casino at all. He tells her he is working late at the office. I warned him that his wife would find out, eventually, that he was not spending every night in the office and would suspect him of having an affair.

'Ohhhhh, much better,' he said, nodding vigorously. 'Other woman much better.'

♠

Michael Arnold beckons me over, imperiously, to his seat on an adjoining table. Michael is the grand duke of the Vic, indivisible from the card room. Everybody knows Michael. He is an imposing figure, around 75 years old, large and Moomin-shaped, haphazardly dressed and usually wielding a walking stick. He wears Eric Morecambe glasses. He snoozes between hands. He looks innocent, sleepy and elderly; he often leans over to new players and chortles, 'I'm just a businessman who enjoys a game of cards!', but his mind is as sharp as a tack.

Michael, whom I addressed politely as 'Mr Arnold' for the first five years I knew him, is such a staple of the card room that he has his own catchphrase. Whenever a player gets up for the night, a croupier is supposed to allocate the seat to a new incumbent. Michael never waits for staff to notice the space; he booms 'One seat here!' across the room. Other people do the same thing, now, attempting to mimic Michael's voice. Scandinavian players, female players, even Steve with the tracheotomy, all can shout 'One seat here!' in the style of Michael Arnold. Later, when he gets into a little legal trouble over a chunk of missing money, some wag posts on the internet: 'One jail cell here!'

I walk obediently over to Michael's chair, and he proffers a whiskery cheek. As I lean down to kiss its bristly surface, I think of Great-Grandpa Harry again. How funny, I used to be aware of *not* kissing Michael hello. There was all that time when I would line up for the greeting, remember my great-grandpa and giggle at the thought of how inappropriate it would be if I absent-mindedly gave Mr Arnold a kiss, like when you call the maths teacher 'Mum' in a dozy moment. And now I'm actually doing it. Officially.

How old was I when Harry died? Five or six? All I remember about him is that respectful opening approach. He never came to see us, we were just expected to turn up and pay court in Lordship Lane at regular intervals. I would tiptoe nervously towards his velour lounge chair, kiss his scratchy face, then sit down and keep quiet while the grown-ups talked. As my lips meet Michael's offered jowl, it feels the same.

Michael wants to know how Vegas went.

♠

When I arrived home from Gatwick, I put my suitcases on the floor and started rummaging through old boxes. Eventually, under some old tax returns and a *Thomson Local*, I found the

journal I kept when I went travelling after I left school. Yes.
That is how it was.

Tuesday 4th June 1991

*We had an idyllic morning by the pool, wondering why cocktail
waitresses were wandering around offering 'hot towels'. It's 98
degrees!*

*We were meant to leave today but I persuaded Nicky it
made much more sense to stay in Las Vegas, what with the
AMAZING hotel deal. We hardly even need a room anyway,
I'm always so high from playing that I can't sleep.*

*Very funny moment at the desk when I asked if we could
have an even better deal if we stayed longer than 2 nights. I got
sent to a casino host who asked how much I gambled in the
casino each night, and when I said fifty dollars he laughed in
my face. But we did get free tickets to the Righteous Brothers.*

*Anyway, he was really nice. Everyone here is nice. The dealers
have started shaking my hand when they go off shift, and saying
'If I don't see you, have a safe trip.' We've made friends with
Donald the pool attendant, who is having his wife's wedding veil
and flowers put in a glass case in their hallway. They like to get
up early and make each other breakfast, which at the moment is a
drink of Chocolate Ultra Slim Fast. He's a born again Christian.*

This is a lovely place and I'm really happy.

Friday 14th June

*Have finally left Vegas, very reluctantly. But I sneaked in a last
few hands of poker before we left and won a final $120 on
roulette, which is brilliant! Actual money to take on the road
back! Hugged all the dealers. But I'm really sad about going.
Everything seems so boring and grey after Las Vegas, and London
definitely will be! I wish home was a BIT more like Vegas. It*

is definitely the best place in the world and one day maybe I'll live there.

I closed my teenage journal and re-read what I wrote this year from Las Vegas, for a newspaper at home, about the government's new plan for British 'super-casinos':

Do you know what Britain doesn't need? Giant casinos. The imminent Gambling Bill, which paves the way for new super-casinos all over the country, is morally questionable, aesthetically odious and financially terrifying. The idea of these enormous monsters encroaching over the land, ushered in by eager members of our excitable government, is like some horrible B movie. For all the souls and money that will be swallowed, they might as well be giant man-eating spiders.

Why would we want Blackpool to become Las Vegas? Have you ever spent more than a week in Las Vegas? Slots, shows, sunshine – fine for a few days on a general West Coast tour. Give it any longer and your soul starts to die. This city is a vast glittering coffin for the human will. Every man is on the edge, every woman has dollar signs in her eyes, every relationship is a sham. The town is lonely and loveless, with no society and no truth. The croupiers are instructed to smile and chat, disguising the fact that they are simply cogs in the giant machine which is working against you. When their shifts finish they take off their name badges, sit down at the next table and quietly, miserably, lose their salaries back again.

Hotel room windows don't open in Vegas. That's because too many people would jump.

Then I had a word with myself, slept for eight hours, and went to the Vic.

♠

For the rest of the year, I will be in here every night. Except on Tuesdays, of course. Sometimes, whether I'm winning or losing, happy or sad, I feel a rush of love for everyone in the Vic, whoever they are. Even Peter Singleton.

I love Tall Alan, who told me last night, 'Ginger Brian is a miserable sod. He went to McDonald's the other day and they wouldn't serve him. It was happy hour.'

I love bitter Irish Frank, who lost a pot to John Duthie last week and hissed, 'When you're outside selling the *Big Issue*, I'm gonna walk straight past. Before that pot, I was going to buy two copies.'

I love John Duthie.

I love the gamblers around us, sitting miserably at the fruit machines, who don't even have the sense to swap over to this game where they might have a chance of getting good at it and winning. I love the winners who dance and cheer, as though that were the end of the story. I love the Arabic men who sit out on the terrace smoking hookah pipes, like caterpillars on top of mushrooms.

I love the fact that so many people are called Dave, it's like a comedy sketch. Dave is a trier's name. It isn't a rich man's name. Last month, there was a casino promotion to win a car, and they brought in a Marilyn Monroe lookalike to draw the winning ticket from the barrel. The whole building went silent as she read slowly, in a breathy Marilyn voice, 'And the winner is . . . *Mo-hamm-ed* . . .' and she didn't even have to start on the surname before the poker players muttered 'Must be a fix,' while cheers erupted round the roulette wheels because they knew it was one of them.

I love it when we do get a player in here with a difficult foreign name and Jeff stumbles trying to read out a succession of Js and Ks into the microphone, while half the card room chuckles 'Easy for you to say.'

I love it that the casino lights keep tripping the switch in the fuse box so we get a series of power cuts, and whenever the room goes dark Dave Binstock starts singing Happy Birthday.

I love Freddie Carle, who never raises his voice at the table and who, when he's in a particularly good mood, will sing his own version of the Frank Sinatra classic, *I Done It My Way* . . .

I love The Sweep, who was once at the table during a debate about whether poker helps to stave off Alzheimer's. 'I want Alzheimer's,' shouted The Sweep. 'Otherwise I'll be remembering those bad beats for ever.'

With few exceptions, I love anyone who plays poker, who spends their life in the card room, who is hiding from something and chasing something, who knows there may be a better life elsewhere but is a little too frightened to look for it, who lets the invisible clock tick down as they play hand after hand after hand.

♠

'I'll have a little stab at it,' says James, betting the pot.

'A little stab?' barks The Sweep. He's tetchy because he thinks he might have Asian bird flu. 'A "little stab" would be a quarter of the pot. That's an absolute crushing grab.'

This Tuesday, we have been talking about which of the players would make the best prime minister.

'Not James,' says Ashley. 'He folded top set, that's no good in a prime minister. Italian defence secretary, maybe . . .'

'I'd make a good prime minister,' says Val. He probably would.

'The best prime minister is whoever hurries up and deals the next hand,' snaps The Sweep.

'James has got a stack of chips hidden behind his teacup,' I point out. 'He's definitely furtive enough to be a politician.'

'He's got it all worked out,' says Ashley. 'Those chips are in his wife's name.'

♠

I remember once sitting next to an elderly Dutchman, during the Master Classics in Amsterdam. On one particular hand, the aged fellow was motionless for three minutes until the dealer pointed out that it was his turn to act.

'I'm so sorry,' said the old man. 'I was dreaming again.'

'Dreaming about aces?' I asked.

'No,' said the old Dutchman. 'I was dreaming about when I was young.'

⚜

Q♠ 6♠

So, blinds up. I need to find some heart now, some determination. Blinds are 15,000-30,000 and my stack is only about 350,000.

You might not think, after all the talk of weak aces, that I'd want to play Q6. And I don't. But when your chips creep down towards ten big blinds (or, conversely, if you're a big enough chip leader to afford more gambling), you have to start trying to nick every chip available. In my position, I can't afford to get much lower or my opponents will be priced in to call any bet I make. Then I'd be relying on finding the best hand, and the best hand staying that way over five cards. That's like relying on a perfect bank holiday. Doesn't happen. Even if you do wake up to the blazing sunshine of two aces, a swarm of wasps will come down on the flop to ruin your picnic.

Jan Sjavic passes under the gun. I move all-in, hoping that Emad and Michael will find nothing to call me with from the blinds.

They don't. They both fold. I pick up the 45,000 in the middle, immediately increasing my stack by 13%. More importantly, I've started playing again.

I'm rewarded with a proper hand: A♥ 10♥. I move in again. The wisest advice I ever read about poker was, 'Mixing it up does not mean doing different things with the same hand. It means doing the same thing with different hands.' So, if I'm going to move in with Q6, I am going to move in with AT.

Michael Muldoon calls from the small blind. His stack is slightly lower than mine – he has 390,000 – so he is the all-in player. But I will be reduced to shrapnel if I lose this pot.

When he rolls over 7♠ 7♦, I feel calm. Sevens is a lucky hand, but it is going to be lucky for me. I am going to win this race.

The ace is the first card off the deck. The flop comes A♦ 8♦ 5♣. But the turn is Q♦, giving Michael the flush draw. I close my eyes.

When I open them, the beautiful A♣ is on the river.

Michael Muldoon is out.

And there are just three of us left.

PART FOUR

19

BANG!

Immolated in his very seat

Toby Young has just exploded. A tiny cloud of smoke hangs over his empty chair.

There is an awkward silence. Matthew Norman, Jon Ronson and Caitlin Moran are delighted to see him go, but the method has shocked them a little. Eventually, Ronson says: 'That's a brutal way to die.'

I love all this. Cartoon cards, cartoon flops, players disappearing in a puff of smoke when they're knocked out of a tournament. There is even a virtual drinks menu, where you can click for a cartoon daiquiri or margarita to appear at the table next to your name. It's just like playing Donkey Kong or Super Mario as a kid, except you can do it for money. Even better.

The money for this one goes to charity. In my new capacity as 'creative consultant' for the Paradise website, I have invited a snaggle of newspaper columnists to play an online one-table tournament, to introduce them to the brand. The brand! I am the mistress of marketing speak.

They are battling for the glory of their respective publications, and £1,000 for the charity of the winner's choice. Just as I did in that original nervous outing on *Late Night Poker*, they have all forgotten to concentrate on winning, in their terror of being the first one knocked out. There is massive relief when Toby Young (playing for the *Mail on Sunday*) takes that 'embarrassing' spot, although nobody expected to see the man immolated in his very seat. They type sympathetic remarks in the chat box to disguise their glee.

In the days preceding this match, bristling emails have flown back and forth between the players. Jon Ronson (*Guardian*) and Carol Sarler (*Daily Express*) roared that they would take down Matthew Norman (*Sunday Telegraph*). Caitlin Moran (*The Times*) warned: 'I don't want to scare or unsettle any of you unnecessarily, but you should know that I'm sitting astride a chair in a Stetson, I've just knocked back two whiskies, and I have a gun.'

That's my girl. Although the new image of poker as clean, sporty, youthful and mathematic has spread across Scandinavia and now beckons all ambitious young men between about 15 and 30, it clearly hasn't yet saturated the outside world. To Caitlin, poker still spells guns and booze and big hats. I like her attitude. I want her to win.

♠

As John Diamond once pointed out, poker is like parking a car: people invest it with a pride disproportionate to the act itself, nobody wants to be bad at it. They fear that a clumsy failure to get it right will reflect on their entire character, even if they are trying for the first time and might never go near it again.

The exception is Phil Hogan (*Observer*) who, true to the hapless persona of his brilliant weekly column, has failed to grasp the principle of one-upmanship. His pre-match email read simply, 'I not only don't have the slightest clue what I'm doing, but am also the least technically equipped, until about five seconds before we start when a man is coming round with a computer that can get the right channel. I confidently predict I'll be back at my day job, if I still have one, within ten minutes.'

Now, the verbal sparring is taking off in the chat box. They're all ordering martinis from the virtual cocktail menu, because journalists can never say no to a free drink, even in cartoon form.

♠

For me, at the moment, it's all about the freerolls. And the opportunities. The poker websites, bedded down in post-Moneymaker success, are throwing money around everywhere. Players are being sponsored all over the place. Paradise Poker has hired Freud Communications for profile-raising and the model Caprice for personal appearances and promotional work. Other sites are sponsoring whole TV programmes. Party Poker has put its name on a recent tournament for Channel Five, Pacific Poker is making a series for Challenge TV and Ladbrokes Poker has got one on Sky. I've got a job doing the commentary with Jesse May on the new series of *Celebrity Poker Club* and another commentating on a preposterous series called *Casino Casino*, which requires me to provide analytical voiceovers for blackjack and roulette games ('Ooh, he's bet number 32! What a choice! And now he's going for number 23, I can't believe it!'). I am also writing columns for a couple of the new magazines which have popped up overnight, *The Player* and *Poker Player*.

I am invited onto a national news programme to talk about poker. A man from Gamblers Anonymous is also there, broadcast in shadow, complaining about the Government's super-casino plans. I wasn't expecting that. I realize the idea is to set us up against each other. I will be Sky Masterson to his Salvation Army. He will plead for my soul and I will beckon him to Havana. Instead, I explain that poker is a game of skill and I hate the idea of super-casinos and massive slot jackpots as much as he does. Everyone is very disappointed.

Then I remember the time that Jac Arama was running a cash game somewhere on the south coast and found himself short of runners when a big fish was due. In desperation, Jac looked up

the nearest GA meeting and hurried down there. He walked up
to the front, asked if anyone fancied a game of poker, and seven
gamblers got up and walked out with him.

I decide not to bring that up.

♠

PokerStars, the biggest site, which provided the platform for Chris
Moneymaker to win his title and kick off all this madness, is
sponsoring the entire European Poker Tour. This is the brainchild
of John Duthie, the soft-spoken TV director who won the old
Poker Million on the Isle of Man. He believes there is room
for a series of tournaments all over Europe to compete with
the World Poker Tour (which happens only in America) and
cater for all the brilliant young players coming up on the
'wrong' side of the Atlantic. It is a classy, clever, patriotic idea.
And it is clever of PokerStars, too, to invest their promotional
budget in a live tournament series, the grass roots of the game.
All very elegant.

But never mind elegance for the moment. There is an old
saying in poker, to describe the feeling of being card-dead in a
lively action game: 'It's raining soup, and I'm standing out here
with a fork.' I am determined, in this soupy current rainstorm,
to get my teaspoonful.

Why not? Poker strategy requires any player to spot the
coups where profit can be made. Taking a free seat in a televised
tournament, or giving creative advice to a website, is no different
from calling in a multi-way pot with 6♥ 7♥. It is an opportunity.
It has potential.

You have to know your own strengths and weaknesses. There's
no point calling with 6♥ 7♥, if you will be too scared to semi-
bluff when you hit a draw. You should only keep the pot small
if you know you have an edge after cards. You need to understand whether you have a tight image or a loose image, so as to

know when to bluff and when to value-bet. Similarly, I have an idea where I stand in this poker explosion.

I am happy enough to call myself a player now. I know I'm a winning player, because my ledger of profit and loss for the year can tell me that. I'm still mainly a cash player, but have won a tournament. It was only a celebrity tournament, but that is my extra edge. I am a more memorable face than many who play better or have more experience than I do, because I am female and I do a bit of television. I might not be respected by the greatest players, but new players and recreational players can look at me and see a kindred spirit who has got lucky, tried hard and won some money.

A few jealous rivals in the card room, when they hear I've been invited to another TV tournament, tell me that being a woman in poker is 'an unfair advantage'. Please. I've had ten years of jokes about my tits, wandering hands on my leg, dismissive put-downs, blatant sexism, compromised friendships, inevitable heartbreak and scary walks down dark streets in lonely cities with cash in a vulnerable handbag. You want to take all that, for one free shot at the Victor Cup?

♠

Since I am getting into a few tournaments without having to pay, I give J.Q. and The Sweep 5% each of anything I win. We always swap 5% when we are playing the same tournaments, but these are bigger events or televised events that the boys don't have a chance to play. I have also got a column in one of the poker magazines for my friend Neil. Ridiculously, I write the 'High Roller' gossip column and he writes the 'Low Roller', even though he plays for much bigger stakes than I do. But it's cute to have our byline pictures next to each other and good for Neil to have a small income from writing not gambling: symbolic but solid. He's pleased, so I'm pleased. If you get lucky, you have to give something back. Sorting out a column for Neil, giving a share to the Tuesday boys, is my little gift to the poker gods. They are always watching, waiting to see if you deserve aces or deuces. These are tiny entrails in a petri dish, to keep them sweet.

♠

In a fast one-table tournament, luck can be as important as skill. The favourites to win my invitational journalists' event are Matthew Norman and Jon Ronson, who have been playing keenly for a while. But it is won by Carol Sarler, who learned the rules three days ago.

I am delighted for Carol, she seems truly proud and pleased. Norman and Ronson are gutted, but that's tournaments for you. I got crippled in the first *Celebrity Poker Club* by a footballer who barely knew which way his chair was supposed to face.

♠

A while later, Jon Ronson writes a blog about donating money to a dogs' charity after his son sees an appeal on television. Jon gives the money grudgingly, he says, and tells the following story.

'I once played in a charity poker game. The winner was to get £1,000 to donate to a charity of their choice. My £1,000 was to go to sick children. Midway through the game, I went all-in with a pair of tens. The *Daily Express* columnist Carol Sarler called. She had aces. I was knocked out. When I think back on that game, I imagine myself – a big, generous smile on my face – approaching sick children, my arms full of wonderful gifts. The sick children allow themselves small, hopeful smiles. And then, from nowhere, I am tripped to the ground by a cackling Carol Sarler, who snatches the gifts and scuttles off to give them to already overfed dogs. I suppose it is unfair to imagine Carol Sarler

– who I don't know – like this, but haven't dog charities got so much money they don't know what to do with it?'

I love Jon. What a natural player. There is something about him that has always struck me as perfect for poker anyway, something about the way his career is built on having a weedy exterior yet balls of steel, like Dustin Hoffman in *Marathon Man*. This is a winning combination for many poker pros all over the world.

And now this blog. Its grudging spirit is nothing to do with dogs or children, and everything to do with the bitterness of getting unlucky on a cold deck. It is gnawing at his soul. Five years from now, he will still remember the tens against the aces. He is no different from Riverboat Ray, the guy from the Islington game who remembers ancient Omaha hands and forgets the name of his granddaughter. Haven't seen Ray for a while. But Jon Ronson is just the same, letting that nasty fall of the cards colour his life for months afterwards. He is truly one of us.

Carol Sarler writes in the *Daily Mail*: 'I played poker once, in some so-called celebrity tournament and won it, to the tune of four figures for my favourite charity. You cannot imagine the excitement. In fact, so acute was the heart-thumping that then and there I recognized it for the seduction it was and haven't looked at a playing card since.'

I do not understand her so well.

♠

The Victor Cup is a new tournament organized by the Victor Chandler bookmaking company, which has launched an online poker arm like everyone else. Now they have agreed to sponsor a televised match to be broadcast on Sky Sports, Paris Première in France, Supersport in Greece and M-Net International in South Africa. It is organized in conjunction with London Clubs, to be held in their lavish Ambassadeurs casino: more sideways TV advertising. My free seat is based on an agreement to wear the Victor Chandler logo and write it all up for London Clubs' magazine.

But something weird has happened. A last-minute legal glitch prevents the tournament happening at Les Ambassadeurs, just like the one that stopped the second Poker Million from taking place in a London hotel. I have no idea why you wouldn't be allowed to hold a poker tournament in a licensed gaming club but our gambling laws are old, vague and needy of reform. Despite all the talk of super-casinos, the law is still stuck in an irrelevant cobwebby world of cutpurses and cribbage.

So a TV studio in Teddington has been converted into a 'lavish casino' for the night. It is all immensely camp. Gilt tables are laid with velvet cloths. Glass chandeliers have been hung from the ceiling. Beautiful Swedish hostesses have been hired to glide around with drink trays. All this has been cobbled together in one afternoon, using spray-painted cardboard and Plasticine. It's already smarter than the Vic.

I keep forgetting that I am in a TV studio not a casino. All the sights and sounds are just as normal, the clack of the chips, the swish of the cards, the clinking of glasses, the cheers of players surviving a nail-biting coup.

Actually, that's new. People weren't cheering a year ago, were they? The etiquette was always, get it quietly. Celebrating a win – even smiling if a pot went your way – was very bad form. Now they cheer, even when they are knocking somebody out. It is the natural effect of television, which likes emotion on the face of a winner, and of the internet, where players can cheer as loudly as they like because there is nobody to hear. But I don't like it in a live tournament. You are cheering somebody else's loss. Rubbing in someone else's defeat. Laughing as a fellow traveller watches his precious money disappear.

There's a hand on my shoulder. It is Victor Chandler himself, who has just been knocked out of his own tournament.

'Come on!' he urges softly in my ear. 'We want a woman in the final!'

Of course they do. Women are making headlines on the World Poker Tour in America; new poker fans can now include, among their heroes, names like Annie, Kathy, Cindy and Jennifer. It would be good for Victor Chandler, good for traffic, good for television, good for business, to have a female finalist. And good for me, too. Final-table prize money ranges from £5,000 to £250,000.

But I must win my table outright to make the final. We start ten-handed and I make it down to heads-up against the Irish player Paul Leckey. I'm playing good, aggressive heads-up poker, raising every time from the button. Pushing it. Playing back. I feel in control.

Then I raise with an A7 and Leckey calls. The flop comes A 2 J. He checks. I move all-in. He has a set of twos. He is Carol Sarler to my Jon Ronson. Damn damn damn damn damn. Knocking out eight opponents before conceding defeat to one is the best possible result without actually winning. In other words, the worst possible result. Sorry, Victor.

♠

I am playing so much poker now, I'm forgetting to have a social life. I haven't had a night out with Charlie for ages. So he's coming to meet me at the Vic tonight; we're going to walk down to the Odeon at Marble Arch and see a film. I'll probably go back to the Vic afterwards. This is pretty screwed up. At some point, I should make some effort to find a new boyfriend. But I just don't want one. I am still in love. I am still heartbroken. It was a bad fracture, a slow mend, and it still twinges on rainy days.

The film is called *13 Going On 30*. It's about a bolshie teenage girl who wishes she was older and wakes up transformed into an adult. Her older self is a cruel, amoral, lonely, bitchy slut.

She meets up with her childhood sweetheart, similarly shot seventeen years into the future, but she is now too horrid to win his heart. Much though the child inside the woman's body struggles to redeem herself by being a kind, loyal and charming grown-up, it is to no avail and the childhood sweetheart marries someone else.

Luckily, just enough 'wishing dust' remains for our heroine to return to her teenage years and choose different priorities: nixing the cheerleaders and hanging out with the fat kids, that sort of thing. Then she grows up beautifully and marries Prince Charming after all.

Marvellous. It is a great lesson for 13-year-olds. Play nicely, be kind to everyone and you will reap rewards in adulthood. But what does it say to the rest of us? There isn't any wishing dust. We can't return to our childhoods and do everything differently. So it is too late. There is no point trying to be a good person now. Nobody wants to marry us and marriage is the only happy ending – live with it. Enjoy the film. Don't forget to buy popcorn. And a noose.

Of course, the movie makes a false distinction between 13 and 30. If they think people grow up, they need to come into the Vic for a couple of nights. Or drop by my house on a Tuesday.

Last week, The Sweep got impatient because a hand of Leaners & Club Honours Six Card Replace took more than thirty seconds to play out.

'This game takes too long, I'm bored,' he muttered, wandering out of the room towards the loo. 'I'm going for a bath.'

Three players immediately replied, as is standard, 'More cheese with your whine?'

I find it odd, looking like a grown-up and sometimes being treated like one. I am allowed to have a mortgage and a driving licence. My friends are allowed to have children. How can they trust us with these responsibilities? We are just kids ourselves.

Sitting around a baize table, playing games and eating sweets and giggling at stupid running jokes is the only place we are not pretending.

What if I had some wishing dust and could start all over again? How could I change it so I wouldn't get my heart broken, so I would build a more significant life, fit more in, achieve higher things? At what point would I need to start the change?

I say goodnight to Charlie and go back to the Vic.

♠

I'm playing online and listening to a radio show where a man called Professor Richard Wiseman is publicizing 'The Luck Project', which will 'scientifically explore why some people live charmed lives'.

Scientifically? That sounds dangerous. Start believing in that stuff and you are making a god out of luck, which is what the sickest slot addicts do.

Lucky things happen, unlucky things happen. I started to get a little nervous of flying, years ago, and I knew I had to nip it in the bud. You can't play top-level poker if you're scared to travel. So I enrolled on a fear-of-flying course and it was fantastic. The instructor told us all about how aeroplanes worked, undoing the terrifying riddle of the giant metal weight in the sky, and he told us why the word 'terminal' and the screaming engine noise on take-off spark our subliminal and conscious fears of danger and death. He told us about the statistics of aeroplane disaster, as everyone always does, but in such minute detail that we could truly understand how safe flying is. I came away cured. Two months later, he died in a plane crash.

I have been terrified of flying ever since, but I know that it is just a superstition. His death was a coincidence, not a message. I am not so important that God would kill people off to warn me against flying.

I slide the cursor up to 'all-in', and win a pot with seven high. That's making your own luck.

Poker players are obsessed with the idea of some jammy bastard in the card room who is 'always blessed' while they themselves are the most ill-fated sod in the universe. And yet the whole point of the game is that chance is there to be controlled. That's where poker is different from roulette or the Lottery. The skill of this game is to maximize your return when you have lucky cards, minimize your loss when you run bad, and bluff with enough judgment and timing to make the hands irrelevant anyway. You command your own destiny when you choose your game, when you consider each decision, when you realize (to bank a profit or cut a loss) it is time to stop for the night.

At the card table and off it, luck is a bucking mechanical bull, but you can learn to keep your bum in the seat. As soon as you start putting your faith in the bull, rather than the bum, you are sunk.

♠

The new European Poker Tour comes to London. The card room is shivering with excitement: a whole new tournament! Except it isn't a new tournament, really. We always had the European Championships in the Vic at this time of year, and the two events have now been combined. So whoever wins this will be both the European Champion and the EPT London Champion.

I am in, thanks to a kindly sponsor picking up my £3,000 entry fee. But I have an utterly unremarkable day at the table, a series of nasty coups and irritating out-draws, knocked out by midnight.

Why do I always have to get so unlucky? It's not fair. It's like I'm cursed.

♠

In the bar, I watch a couple of teenagers ask Devilfish for his autograph.

It has been a strange journey. Professional poker players were the most furtive, anonymous people on earth. And then they were joined by celebrities. And now they *are* celebrities.

Ten years ago, I abandoned stand-up comedy because the underground went overground, there was too much attention, too much cool, too much pressure.

So what now? Scrabble?

6♥ 7♥

I am feeling absolutely determined. One thing I know is that I am not raising to pass. If I fold, I fold; if I raise, I'm playing.

I have accumulated a decent stack, more room for manoeuvre, no longer stuck in one-move territory. When I make it 75,000 from the button with 67, I already know that if I am re-raised from the blinds I will push back all-in. And it will be for nearly a million chips. And they will not dare call me.

But Emad Tahtouh flat calls from the small blind. Jan Sjavic passes.

The flop comes 2♠ K♣ J♣. Emad checks. I have nothing. Whatever he's got, he is beating me. I don't care. I bet 90,000. Emad folds.

20

TOUCH OF CLASS

A man like you should be at Deauville, or Le Touquet.

The air is chilled like champagne. It smells of oysters and lemon. Coiffed women stroll by with coiffed dogs. The beach is flawless down to the sea, nothing on it but one small boy playing neatly in a sailor suit. Shop windows sparkle. The mixed cries of seagulls and wood pigeons are interrupted only by the occasional soft whump of Bentley wheel on cobble.

Ordinarily, you wouldn't want a seaside resort to be cold. But it feels right in Deauville. Hot weather would be vulgar. This is the correct temperature for strolling on the beach in a silk dress and furs.

It felt very chic, back in London, to pack for a seaside holiday and not take a swimsuit. I brought a chiffon headscarf, white gloves, an ankle-length Italian skirt, a zebra-striped day dress, a shiny black evening dress, a pair of suede trousers, a grey silk top, a pink blouse, high heels and a pair of knee-length boots (not Wellington).

This is not an English resort full of chip wrappers, fag butts and locked-up amusement arcades, smelling like a fat kid has just relieved himself after too many alcopops. It is not Bournemouth, where I went on holiday with my grandparents as a child and have spent many happy weekends since, watching old *Hi-de-Hi!* stars in end-of-the-pier farces. Nor is it St Tropez, which may have a few glamorous whisky-coloured French women knocking around, but is still in essence a community of peeling sunbathers buying lilos.

Deauville, the jewel of the Normandy coast, is not about fast food and sandcastles. It is about oysters, race courses, casinos and Dom Pérignon. A trip to Deauville is a journey back to the 1920s, when it was the resort *de choix* for discerning duchesses, glamorous gamblers, young debutantes and the odd caddish gigolo on the make.

Pick up a shell from the beach at Deauville and you do not hear the sea. You hear the rattle of beaded evening dresses, the purr of a Rolls-Royce engine, the clickety-clack of blackjack chips and the snap of a gold cigarette case. It crops up as a location in Ian Fleming's first James Bond story, *Casino Royale*, and, disguised as Merlinville, in *Murder On The Links*.

In another Christie special, *Evil Under The Sun*, a murder suspect is wary of Hercule Poirot because there seems no reason for the natty fellow to be holidaying in England.

'A man like you', mutters the villain suspiciously, 'should be at Deauville or Le Touquet.'

I brought all these books with me and read them en route, in the buffet car of the rattling train. I am feeling so Twenties-literary on these cobbled streets, I'm sorry not to have a moustache. I could have waxed it in the bathroom mirror and twirled it when I had a tough decision with a pair of nines.

♠

I think this new European Poker Tour will bring a touch of class to the game. Luton and Blackpool are so pre-Moneymaker. This is what it's all about: a €2,000 poker tournament tucked into the Deauville calendar between Calvados Week and the international film festival. Watching from my window in the Barrière Hotel, I can see Jeff Duvall strolling along the seafront boardwalk, which is painted with the names of Hollywood stars who have visited, from Joan Fontaine to Matt Damon.

Jeff looks quite at home. As do many of the players here, most of whom have won the trip on PokerStars. This is the hottest new trend in internet poker: satellites to win a whole package holiday in Europe, flight, hotel, tournament entry fee, the lot. Deauville is thronged with people who would never have come here otherwise. Yesterday there was a young Texan on my table who told me that he found the town's neat little flower beds, stone-cellared wine museum and 'wooden architecture' so romantic that he proposed to his girlfriend immediately. If he's lucky, he'll win another online satellite, net a trip to the Caribbean and that's the honeymoon sorted.

♠

John Duthie is reborn as European poker's Mr Big. Here is a man who makes his own luck. And then sabotages it. And then makes it again.

Today, he is the creator of the European Poker Tour. He glides beneath the chandeliers of the Deauville card room in a bespoke suit, gold-rimmed sunglasses and a glittery Breitling watch. The highest rollers in the world nod respectfully as he goes by.

Seven years ago, The Chimney Sweep bumped into him one night in Vegas looking pale and weak. Duthie had spent his last five bucks on a hot dog two days before, and eaten nothing since. He had done all his money and was waiting for somebody in England to wire him a bit of cash to get through the rest of the trip. He knew nobody to borrow from. He had no credit at the casino. So The Sweep bought him dinner.

A few days later, The Sweep was confused to see Duthie playing in a $25-$50 game. This was huge. Duthie played small stakes in the Vic. But the following week, he saw Duthie playing $2-$4 limit. And then he saw him playing $25-$50 again.

In 2000, John Duthie won the Poker Million on the Isle of Man. He was in the newspapers, he was on television. The first player to win £1,000,000 outside America. Knowing himself,

Duthie had the cleverest idea of all time: he put a chunk of the money away, for mortgages and children's education, in a bank account that he opened *jointly with his father-in-law.* Brilliant. If it had been a joint account with his wife, he might have phoned her from a casino one desperate night and begged her to co-sign a big withdrawal slip. But a call like that to his wife's *father*? Never.

Then he got a suit made and kept the rest for gambling. And he was playing $2-$4 again soon enough, don't worry about that.

He is capable of the most brilliant, flairy moves of any poker player in the world. And he is capable of the most suicidal plays. When he sees a roulette wheel or a baccarat table, he can crack up like a riverbed in drought.

But when I see Duthie, in the grip of fever, burning through whatever money he has in his pocket, I see an act of salvation. Mr Big has already survived the toughest childhood of anyone in poker. And he has survived depression, and he has survived alcoholism. When I hear another player, watching with that wide-eyed mix of admiration and horror as John obliterates a stack of purple chips, say 'He has no self-discipline,' I think about the fact that he has not touched an alcoholic drink in over twenty years. The way he sits around a restaurant table after a tournament, watching players gargling vodka or shouting for Cristal as though it tasted different from any other sparkling wine, and he sips his cappuccino and smiles and sometimes he makes funny, laconic smalltalk and sometimes he says nothing at all. And sometimes he slips away, to a private table in the back of the casino, signs a slip for $5,000 and loses it, bang, in three hands of blackjack. And he enjoys that pain.

Mr Big is other-worldly, he is a cat who walks by himself. Everybody knows him these days, and everybody loves him. He is one of the very few, perhaps the only one, about whom you will never hear another player say a bad word. But he has no clique, no gang. He is everyone's friend and a little apart from everyone. I think it's because, having quit drinking when it was supposed to kill him, this whole section of his life is a freeroll, tonally different from everyone else's. He is always gentle, always sweet-natured, unless he is told that he *must* do this or he *must* do that or he *must* go here or there at a certain time, and then you see a flash of something pass across his face. Look away, look back and he is gone.

On his game, Duthie is a genius, an absolute Mozart of the baize.

One night he is sitting in a $50-$100 No Limit Holdem game in Vegas and he raises to $650 with Q♠ 8♠. A fearsome local pro called Viffer calls on the button.

The flop comes A♦ 9♥ 2♣. Duthie checks. Viffer bets $1,600. Duthie raises $6,000 more, with no hand at all. No pair, no draw. Viffer calls.

The turn brings another ace. Duthie checks. Viffer moves all-in for $18,000. Duthie calls immediately. The river card is 3♥.

'Jack high,' announces Viffer miserably.

'Queen high,' replies Duthie, scraping in a pot of over $50,000.

This is the bravest, craziest, most counter-intuitive poker you will ever see. He can also sit quietly, in a small game or a big game, nurse his stack, value-bet his strong hands and get paid off by fools who think he is always bluffing.

Later tonight, or tomorrow, or next month or next year, he will lose all his money in a baccarat game or a poker game at whatever stakes he can muster, and then he will find a way to make more money, and lose it back and win it back and lose it back. All of us who gamble know what masochism is. We know that smart poker is about controlling the risk of pain, mad gambling is about abandoning yourself to it. For Mr Big, that is the strongest attraction. This is how he releases the darkness from his soul and trepans the whispering spirits from his brain.

♠

There's no joy for me in the Deauville EPT, but I'm happy enough just to be here. It is a kitsch little town, strangely alpine for a seaside resort. It's all funny little half-timbered ginger-bread houses with pointy roofs. The cobbled roads are painted in cute scallop shapes and bordered by black-and-white checker-board pavements. I can see so many flawless French characters from the window, it's like a European *Truman Show*. As if an invisible director were shouting, 'Cue the cycling man with the baguette. Send in the old lady with the coral lipstick and the poodle. Bring on the twin schoolchildren with matching satchels.'

And Jeff, the London poker pro, wandering among them.

♠

Last night, the players hit the nightclub. Most of them were complaining about bad beats and the price of sandwiches. Some of them brought hookers. I got drunk and danced round a pole to amuse Willie Tann. For once, the Mock Turtle looked genuinely happy.

Oh, well. We were classy for a day or two, back there.

♠

Back home, Jesse May and Rob Gardiner have asked me to host a chat show called *Bar Beat* that they are making for a new poker channel on cable TV. I am not convinced that anyone will watch this poker channel, nor even be able to find it, but I'm sleepless with excitement at the chance to invite my favourite Vic players into the studio, see how articulate they can be on camera, with a licence to ask them anything.

I start with Michael Arnold, but he takes some persuading.

We're doing an episode about 'the changing face of poker' and I'm desperate to hear from someone who's been on the London gambling circuit since the 1950s. Michael, aged seventy, is reluctant to appear because he doesn't want his mother-in-law to find out that he plays poker. It's hilarious. He plays almost every night of the week. How has he kept that secret from his mother-in-law for five decades?

Eventually, I convince Michael to come along, on the grounds that the 90-year-old mother-in-law is never going to tune in to the poker channel. She can barely find Channel Five. So he hobbles into the studio along with two youngsters (online Sit & Go genius Andy Ward and magazine journalist Phil Shaw) and fellow Vic veteran Trevor Coles. I love the way Trevor talks. He actually uses the phrase 'had up before the beak', to describe what happened when he ran an illegal cash game in the 1960s.

I knew he would be poetic on screen. I'll never forget him telling me, in the card room one night, how he loves to visit the Turkish baths in the East End before a poker game because 'It's lucky to nip in and schmeiss the frummers.' I had to ask for a translation. I learned that it means, as I surely should have guessed, washing an Orthodox Jew with a sponge on a stick.

I was expecting the young players to rave about the modern game, while the old guys yearned for the authenticity of poker's past. It turns out to be the other way around. The youngsters, Andy and Phil, talk about their fear that the romance is slipping away. But Michael Arnold, refusing to fall into the predictable role of nostalgic old-timer, insists that poker is better than ever. He thinks the game is fresher and more respectable, livelier and more fun. He says that he has just come from a game where four of the nine players were university students and he thinks this is 'absolutely wonderful'.

But he also warns that some of poker's new-found respectability is a façade. 'It's about money,' Michael says, 'and wherever there's money there will be corruption. It's the same with politics and power. We can't completely clean it up, and we shouldn't sweep it under the carpet. As long as politics and poker exist, as long as money and power exist, there will be dirty things going on.'

One day I will think back on these words that Michael spoke. If *Bar Beat* had ever reached a significant audience, they might have come back to haunt him.

♠

Why is a final always called a 'grand final'? That is usually a redundant adjective, especially in Walsall. But the EPT Grand Final, amid the palatial casinos and fortified private castles of a tax haven on the Riviera, has earned its name. Deauville was smart, but Monte Carlo makes it look like Clacton.

What a weird, quiet place this is. There are no poor people anywhere. I imagine that a truck must pull up every day at 5 a.m. and release an army of them to sweep, clean, paint, empty the bins and depart again before the millionaires wake up.

Sitting under a parasol in the main casino square, with my parents, I see Devilfish heading in our direction.

This was always the danger. It was a nice idea – my parents on holiday in the South of France, me playing a tournament in Monte Carlo, why wouldn't they drive down to have lunch? – but I knew it might mean exposing them to poker players. My nice parents. My elegant mother. My gentlemanly father, who worked so hard to leave the sick gamblers of Southgate behind and establish himself in the world.

And here comes Devilfish. The man who crept up behind me at the WSOP and said he wanted to 'taste my arse'. Who has done prison time for burglary. Who was banned from the studios at Sky TV for groping a researcher. Who had tears of affection

and pride in his eyes, the day he told me that his 6-year-old son
had recognized his voice on the phone and shouted, 'Dad, you
old cunt!'

'David,' I nervously say, 'these are my parents.'

And Devilfish shakes hands very politely, makes smalltalk,
continues on his way, and my parents are rather charmed.

How grown-up we are, these days. On our best behaviour in
the millionaires' playground. Televised poker players. Minor
celebrities. Devilfish has had a lot of practice, now, in shaking
people's hands and being polite.

And my father has now met three modern poker players:
Amarillo Slim, Devilfish and me.

He doesn't fear my gambling, any more, because he can see
that I have played poker for years and not gone broke. I have
shown him articles about me in poker magazines, and packets of
money I have won. He is a little bit concerned about the lifestyle.
It confuses his admiring yet gallant ideas about women. He loves
to see that I am good at the game and I win, but he worries that
nobody is looking after me. He admits, 'I like to imagine a child
of mine striding across a saloon, sitting down in a poker game,
and the grizzled gamblers shaking with fear. But it might be a
bit less odd if it weren't a daughter.'

♠

Later that night, I am playing in the main tournament room of
the EPT Grand Final – the Salle des Étoiles, Monte Carlo – and
something about the room looks familiar. I have seen them before,
those little stars on the ceiling. Those sweeping velvet curtains.
That terrace overlooking the Riviera.

Hang on a minute. This is where Danielle got married.

We were like sisters, Danielle and me. She was born a week
after I was, three doors down. We slept in adjacent prams. We
went to primary school together. In the summer we played in

each other's gardens, slept in each other's houses, walked down to Cricklewood Lane together to buy sweets.

Aged 16, Danielle started dating a friend of her brother's. At 25, she married him, her first and only serious boyfriend. They had the wedding in Monte Carlo, outdoors by the sea, and the reception in the Salle des Étoiles. My whole family came along for the wedding, and my dad paid for us all to stay in the Loews Hotel. I remember dancing with my father under that starry ceiling. I remember Danielle's grandma, and various other elderly relatives, shaking my hand and saying 'Please God by you,' meaning 'We hope you will soon be lucky enough to find your own husband,' and looking meaningfully at Danielle's unmarried brother.

I wonder what they would make of Plan B.

♠

The internet is gurgling over the most recent episode of *Bar Beat*. The theme of the show was 'table etiquette': what is and is not acceptable behaviour in a poker game. What is a barring offence? What can be ignored? What can be let off with a warning? What is absolutely fine? The guests were my portly, blazered friend D.Y., an expat American player called Ron Fanelli and an internet whizz with a dark past who goes by his online handle Miros.

We discussed rudeness, swearing, aggression, cheating, colluding and marking cards, misinformation, violence, borrowing money without paying it back. We discussed everything that poker players do and we argued about where the line is.

Now, the poker forums and the chat rooms and even the chat boxes of the websites are ablaze with indignation. The anger is summed up in an anonymous post on the Hendon Mob forum, the chat page of my old friends' website, which says: 'Victoria Coren has brought poker into disrepute. She is giving people the impression that the game is full of cheats and thieves, that it's all about deceitful and underhand behaviour. Then there was all the stuff about fighting and threatening words. This programme was disgusting. Poker is a respectable sport.'

I read this post and I read it again and I read it again. Respectable? Disgusting? Disrepute? For nearly two hundred years after its grimy birth on the eighteenth-century riverboats of the American South, poker was *nothing but* cheating and fighting and 'underhand behaviour'. On grey-green Louisiana waters and dusty Texan roads, in smoky back rooms and dodgy saloons, cards were marked and bent and scratched and dealt, and money was taken by stealth and gun. It paid for a lot of big hats, and a lot of new guns.

Of course the game is cleaner now, and neater and sweeter and far more respectable, but ghosts can't vanish overnight. And I was drawn to poker by this sordid romance, the dark history, the whispering corners, the poetic language of Damon Runyon and Herbert Yardley, the seedy glamour of its old proponents 'Amarillo Slim' Preston, Jack 'Treetop' Straus, Alvin 'Titanic' Thompson and the rest of that shady, oddly named, card-playing crew.

It doesn't work that way any more. Hundreds of thousands of people have found poker in recent months, and they have done it through television, not books. They admire well-spoken, highly paid, corporate-sponsored professional players, not dusty road gamblers with dodgy pasts. It is a big, bright, shiny, respectable sport. And they think I am bringing it into disrepute, they think I am lying about its nature, they think I am forcing dark stories in where they were not: me, the girl who turned up at the Vic with her college degree, sounding like Princess Margaret, terrified to enter the card room, taking days and weeks and months and years to make friends, at last, with the gangsters and burglars and old storytellers from spielers gone by.

Me? I have never done anything disreputable, except in dreams.

———❧———

A♦ J♣

Emad has raised the last four hands in a row and won all of them without contest. This time he is on the big blind, which is a shame. It means he doesn't have the chance to try and steal it when I have a big hand. Three-way, AJ is huge. But I must give Emad this chance, just as I did a couple of days ago when I trapped him into raising with nothing, but he out-drew me. He will not out-draw me this time. When Jan Sjavic passes, I will weakly complete the blinds and let Emad raise. And then I will bring down the hammer.

But Jan does not pass. He makes it 80,000 from the button. Jan is a far tighter player than Emad, but my hand is still strong and he too must be adjusting his range for the short-handed game. I re-raise to 250,000 and Emad folds.

Jan flat calls. I know at once he has a small pair. Anything worse, he would fold for my re-raise. Anything better, he would move all-in. This is one of those situations where, even though I must act first on the flop, I am in the better position. I will move in on any reasonable-looking flop, and it is very hard for Jan to call unless he has flopped his set. Which he won't.

The flop comes 9♠ 10♥ 10♣. I don't mind this flop at all. If I move all-in and Jan calls with his pair of fives – that is what I am putting him on, a pair of fives – I am in reasonable shape with two overcards to a paired board. I can hit a jack or an ace, the board could pair again, plus there is the glimmer of a backdoor straight draw. And I have Jan out-chipped so I will still have over 150,000 if I lose the pot. It's not much, but it is not nothing.

And he won't call anyway. I move in for about 770,000.

Jan starts to think.

*He thinks and thinks and thinks. He counts his chips: 608,000.
After a while, Emad calls for the clock.*

*Wow. That is a harsh thing to do when a man is considering his
tournament life, with only three players remaining and a £500,000 first
prize.*

*Jan now has ten seconds to make his decision. What's taking him
so long? Despite my outs, I am praying for him to pass.*

10 . . . 9 . . . 8 . . . 7 . . .

On the count of 4, Jan Sjavic makes the call. Damn it.

*When Jan rolls over a pair of threes, I am forced to admit it's a great
call. Still, I am better than 6/4 to win the pot anyway. This is not a
long shot.*

The railbirds are shouting for an ace. God bless them.

*The turn comes . . . J♥! My card! Jan is dead to a three. And the
river is 8♥.*

*Jan is out! I don't cheer. I play by the Old Rules, I tell him 'unlucky'
and quietly stack the chips. Inside, I am dancing.*

*We are heads-up. We are heads-up. Unlucky Jan. And unlucky
Emad, who says he passed 9T on that hand. No wonder he was impatient and calling for the clock. He must have been in pieces. What he
doesn't realize is that if Jan were not in the hand, I would have check-
raised him out before the flop. But what if he had checked behind? I
might be out.*

*There is a short break while the money is brought in. Bundles and
bundles of £50 notes are piled on the table. There are so many bundles,
it has no meaning. As an amount to take home, even the second prize
is beyond my understanding. It might as well be comfits and a thimble
at the end of a caucus race.*

*And there is the trophy, a block of carved glass towers with the date
engraved into it, waiting to sit on the mantelpiece of a player whose status
will change overnight. I can't bear to look at it. There are only two of
us left to fight for this great glass elevator.*

*Trying to reconnect with reality, I walk over to the rail to see Jeff
and Rory. Beloved Rory, who has a share of me in this tournament, only*

because he refused to take a hundred quid for it a few days ago. He had a share in the little tournament and rolled it over. He believed I could cash in the London EPT. He could have taken real, folding money but he backed me. With his kindness, he has earned a share in £285,000. Or £500,000. It will be £500,000 if I win. And I can win. I know how.

Jeff tells me I must be patient yet fearless. And I will be, I will be.

21

BEYOND THE BLUE HORIZON

– lies a trade fair.

The room is vast, bright, clean, buzzing with business talk, tinkling with cash registers, packed with fresh-faced young people buying keyrings and posters and T-shirts and novelty packs of cards. This is the annual championship of the most secretive and counter-cultural game on earth. Welcome to the Rio.

'What is this?' blinks Anthony Holden, the dishevelled author of *Big Deal*. 'What is it?'

'It is,' I tell him, 'a trade fair.'

Harrah's, new owners of the World Series of Poker, new hosts in the conference centre of their glossy, promised, uptown property, have decided to place a giant trade fair around the tournament room. Why not? There are 5,619 people here to play the main event, 20,000 more to observe it and play the smaller tournaments, all of them ready to spend, all of them looking for souvenirs. Who said online poker would kill the live game? Who said everyone would stay home and play on their computers, no dress code, no travel, no trouble? The opposite has happened. There are more players at home, more in clubs, more in casinos. The game is now played, live or online, by 1.5 million people in Britain alone. There have been poker storylines on *EastEnders*, *Coronation Street* and *The Archers*. When the Archers are playing poker, you know that something big has happened.

Poker sites which were set up as hopeful dotcom punts are being sold for eye-watering fortunes. Except Dave Welch's. Our old friend from Luton and *Late Night Poker* collected thousands of pounds from fellow gamblers to set up a poker site. Somehow, the site never launched. Somehow, the money never came back. It is said that some people got their money back, but only a certain kind of people. Dave says that he himself was tricked by a third party who has gone on the missing list. Somebody certainly made a few grand out of this. But it's a shame they never actually launched the site, they would have made millions. However this scheme developed, there was something very English about its scale.

Nothing English about the scale of this trade fair. Holden and I shove our way out through the gannet-circled stalls, walk about eighteen miles back to the main casino floor of the Rio and duck into some kind of Tex-Mex bar by the sports book. A 12-year-old waitress shouts hello. Holden, looking more pink and tousled than ever, croaks for wine.

♠

'You've got to admit,' I tell Holden, 'it's nice that they want us here.'

I am reading Michael Craig's book, *The Professor, The Banker, And The Suicide King*, and it reminds me of the old days when 'The stereotypical view of poker by casino management was that it was an unwelcome distraction or, at best, attracted tightfisted locals who dressed sloppy, complained a lot and wanted everything for free.'

The new crowd isn't sloppy. They have designer shades and top-of-the-range iPods. Most of them seem to have maths degrees. Even Oxford and Cambridge universities have launched poker societies in the last year. Maybe you can get a half-blue in it.

And they are wanted in Vegas, they are beckoned. Large, comfortable, no-smoking card rooms are being built to lure them in. The Wynn, a vast high-luxury complex which just opened on the Strip, has hired the Canadian pro Daniel Negreanu to act as 'poker host' and sit playing cards at a prominent front table in front of an admiring crowd. They say he's getting $2 million for it.

Not everybody is admiring. Erik 'The Salmon' Sagström, a Swedish computer whizz who wins $1 million a year online and rarely leaves his house, will always be a hero to some and a geek to others. The geek jury consists of non-players and the Old School. But to the kids here, he is an icon.

Daniel Negreanu is a big star in America now. So are Phil Hellmuth, Phil Ivey, Howard Lederer. They are recognized in the street, given front-row seats at baseball games, and begged to wear this or that brand of sunglasses. In Vegas, they can't move for excited crowds, autograph-hunters, people wanting their pictures taken. They are Elsie, Lacie and Tillie, living at the bottom of a treacle well. What do they draw? They draw treacle. What do they live on? They live on treacle.

Beautiful women hang around them. Any big pro can have his pick of models, if he wants. There are girls everywhere now, beautiful masseuses, interviewers, lady journalists and bloggers, and girls who simply turn up in the hope of meeting or dating famous players. It makes me feel sorry for old Huck Seed, who moaned to me all those years ago about women thinking he was 'some kind of bum'. He really mistimed that World Series win.

But Tony Holden, taking a grateful gulp of Merlot, is lost in memories of the creaking wood and dust of the Horseshoe, the smoke and secrecy, the drunken players stumbling across the garish carpet. All gone now, as if they were never there, blasted away like litter before a royal visit.

'I realize with a sinking heart', he says, 'that the game I have loved for nearly forty years as a romantic, seedy, maverick outpost of *la vie bohème* has become just another branch of corporate-logo American capitalism.'

Poker was always driven by money, always. But Holden is right, it seems to be driven with new purpose. These millions of people who have swarmed into our dark little basement and switched on all the lights, they are not gamblers but investors. They are running towards victory, not running away from something else. And, suddenly, there is more money – incomparably more money – to be made from running and raking and filming and sponsoring the game than there is from playing it. A capitalist hierarchy has appeared overnight and shuffled itself into place.

'But it's been good for us, right?' I remind Tony, as our waitress removes the plates of guacamole and the second drained bottle.

I have had my freerolls. And *Big Deal*, the book in which Holden set out to spend a year as a professional poker player, which has ticked quietly along in print for fifteen years, has rocketed back up the sales list. The publishers have persuaded Tony to try his experiment again, in the booming bustling world of twenty-first-century poker, and paid him a handsome advance to do it. It will be called, of course, *Bigger Deal*.

He admits: 'I'm glad in the selfish sense that there's more money and there's great material for the kind of writer I am. But otherwise, I much preferred things the way they were fifteen years ago. All the romance has gone, the relish in doing something slightly disreputable, the edgy bonhomie in back rooms. I'll enjoy it this time round, but not as much. There are as many ghastly people to be avoided as there are new friends to be made. They care more about TV than playing the game.'

♠

This year is the 100th birthday of Las Vegas itself. Like any spangly old tart, Vegas has grown more respectable with age, but she still has the energy to throw one big, shiny, banging birthday party. She's getting drunk, dressing up and kicking her heels till dawn. If you're picturing an old lady right now, picture Sylvester Stallone's collagen-stuffed mother. Or Dolly Parton, still bewigged and rhinestoned in her sixties, explaining that she yearned from her earliest childhood to dress like a hooker. That's the kind of old lady we're talking about.

This year, The Sweep and I are staying at the Gold Coast, five minutes' walk from the Rio. Which is, in this withering July heat, just about long enough to die from exposure.

This is not like it used to be, with everybody wandering back and forth across Fremont Street, bumping into each other and going for drinks. Players are all over town now, it's impossible to arrange to meet anyone.

But we head up to the Strip to play in the new Wynn card room and the old Mirage one, shop in Caesars Forum and play blackjack along the ersatz Bois de Boulogne in the Paris Hotel. The Paris hasn't been doing so well since the French refused to 'back up' America's invasion of Iraq, but it's still perfect for anyone who has ever looked at the original Eiffel Tower and thought, 'That is all very well, but why can't I swim round it?'

Some parts of Las Vegas have acquired a family feel. And that is not a bad thing. Mustn't get too romantic about gambling's past. In her early days, Vegas was a wild thing who ran with a bad crowd. She was born with the advent of the railroad through the Nevada desert, set up as a tent town for rail workers in May 1905. Gambling was banned in Nevada in 1910 but this was ignored by our little tearaway, until the State Legislature re-legalized it during the Great Depression to get its hands on tax revenue. There was a brief lull during the Second World War, but Vegas hit her forties with gusto. By 1946, Bugsy Siegel had opened the Flamingo and by 1947 he'd been shot dead in his girlfriend's living room. Lucrative new hotels, most of them Mob-controlled, were springing up everywhere.

And it wasn't glamorous, it really wasn't. Card-counters got their knees broken, casinos were burned down and black gamblers were not welcome. When Lena Horne was performing at the Flamingo, she wasn't allowed to enter the gaming area. It may have been 'the marriage town' because it had no waiting period for licences, but any black person who tried to marry a white sweetheart was arrested immediately.

It's too easy to get sentimental. I read *Big Julie Of Vegas* and think about how cool it must have been. But it must have been terrible, too. Better to have these modern mega-resorts sucking in profit for a national chain, much of it raised from raking poker games among eager young novices, than white-only gambling and money going out the back way in a gangster's bloody hands.

♠

It's too hot to go to the pool. Stupid July. That doesn't bother most of the modern players, who are in their rooms all day anyway, playing online. Nobody saw Roland de Wolfe for a week. Then he suddenly reappeared, looking furious. He had got up too quickly to let in the room service guy and trodden on his laptop.

If it weren't for that, we might not have seen him all Series.

♠

I'm looking at a website which sells a motivational CD called *Manifest Money*. Maybe this is what the Scandies are listening to on their iPods.

This CD promises to reveal 'the limiting beliefs that have been preventing you from having unlimited potential when it comes to abundance'. It's actually a four-part CD set costing $99 + postage. And there's a promotional offer: the first twenty-five people to buy the set will win a long weekend in Las Vegas. I wonder whether a company truly interested in helping you sort out your finances would offer a free holiday in the gambling capital of the world.

I am Googling 'money' and 'meditation' because I have brought with me a tape called *Create Unlimited Financial Abundance For Yourself* that I found at the Buddhist bookshop in Bethnal Green. It seemed a peculiar thing to be selling in a Buddhist shop. As far as I know, Buddha told his followers to let go of their craving for wealth. But maybe I misunderstood the teachings. Gold Buddha money-boxes are still the biggest-selling souvenirs in Vegas.

This tape is all about picturing yourself wealthy in order to make it happen. I am concentrating hard as Glenn Harrold, clinical hypnotherapist, drones, 'Imagine you are standing in front of your brand-new dream car, which you have just paid for upfront. It's a top-of-the-range model with a fantastic luxury interior. Comfortable seats. Electric windows. A CD player with . . .'

. . . and there is a proper long pause while Glenn thinks about it . . .

'. . . all the latest technology present in expensive new cars.'

This is brilliant. Can I be properly hypnotized if I am laughing? I bet Glenn drives a second-hand Fiat. I could almost hear his frame of reference stretching and snapping in that pause. I don't know much about cars either, so I'm moving on to the next section: picturing a big lavish house.

There is only one piece of actual advice on the tape, among the long descriptions of expensive things I am supposed to imagine myself having, and this is to 'Take other positive action.'

In that throwaway phrase lies the key. It's like those weight-loss pills that guarantee a smaller waist but say, in tiny print on a leaflet inside, 'You should also cut your food intake and exercise daily.' Do it without the pills: same result.

You can't rely on CDs and magic beans. You have to go out and make things happen. I call The Sweep, meet him at the cab rank, suffer mild heatstroke during the four-second wait for a taxi, and we head off to the poker room at the Bellagio.

♠

Joe Hachem wins the World Series. Greg 'Fossilman' Raymer got $5 million for winning it last year. Joe gets $7.5 million and, like Greg, a sponsorship deal with PokerStars.

It is a popular result. Joe Hachem is a likable, professional poker player from Melbourne. He was born in Lebanon in 1966 and has come to Vegas with a huge crew of fellow Lebanese-Australians. The Sweep and I have been playing in cash games with a friendly chap called Emad Tahtouh, who has a share with Hachem and must be gurgling with delight at this outcome.

He was a chiropractor, Joe Hachem, until he had to retire after an illness. He went into mortgage-broking for a while, but for the last few years he has been making most of his money playing poker. People are pleased to see a professional win. It's funny, everyone loves the underdog and we should want to see an unknown kid from the internet scoop the money, but the triumph of a pro can be used as proof that skill will out, even in a gambly tournament like this one.

Andy Black from Ireland finishes 5th and gets $1,750,000. Coincidentally enough, Andy is a Buddhist. Maybe he manifested the abundance? This is a popular result, too. All the British and Irish players know and like Andy. He is a modest, unassuming, Buddhist kind of guy. This won't change him.

♠

Willie Tann wins the last bracelet! This year, several $1,500 tournaments are running after the main event, to satisfy the hunger of 20,000 new poker players. And Willie nabs the final one, with a prize of $188,000. Neil and I escort him off the premises, as it would constitute actual cruelty to leave Willie alone near dice tables with that kind of money.

I'm so delighted for Willie. It is fantastic to see The Legend garner a bracelet, which will be there for ever as a tribute to his poker skills. Sadly, it would be unwise to bet that the $188k will be there even a fortnight from now.

♠

I'm worried about Roland de Wolfe. He needs to get out more.

Roland is only a few years younger than me but I feel protective about him. Maybe it's because he grew up near me and went to school with my cousin. Maybe it's because he wanted to be a journalist and could have been a good one. He's bright and articulate and funny.

He left Birmingham University with a degree in 'Media, Culture and Society', whatever that means. He didn't work very hard. He tells me, 'Everything I have achieved has been through brains and charm alone. I haven't achieved much.'

He had a job for six months on one of the new poker magazines *Inside Edge* but, at the age of 24, has just given it up to 'turn pro'. This is based on winning a £150 tournament at the Gutshot.

I tell him it's a bad idea, when he still has so many options. The beauty of online poker is that you can play in small chunks whenever you want – or a whole day at the weekend – but he's too young to be doing it all week for ten hours a day. He needs to try various jobs, find out if he can crack it as a writer. He needs to get out and see the world, make friends, meet girls. He needs to move out of his parents' house and get his own place. He's a good-looking boy but he's getting chubby and pale. He came all the way to Vegas to sit in his hotel room playing online? He needs fresh air. I feel like I'm giving advice to a grandson.

Roland says that gambling is in his blood, like mine. He says he remembers playing poker on the bus to school, aged 12, with two friends: one of them now works for Ladbrokes and the other is a hedge-fund trader. So all three of them grew up into professional gamblers. I point out that the other two get a guaranteed annual wage, for gambling with other people's money.

But Roland can't face office life. He has ADHD, OCD and an attention span of about three seconds away from the poker table. And he hates getting up in the morning. He says, 'It's not that I'm suited to being a poker player, but I'm very ill-suited to being anything else.'

I tut at Roland, this mop-haired local boy with a world of choice, and tell him to get a part-time job. I tell him he needs some regular money coming in, experience of the job market, savings to fall back on, because poker is a long hard graft.

Three weeks later, Roland wins the WPT in Paris for €480,000. Within a year he is one of the most famous poker players in the world.

♠

The dream has got bigger for everyone. The professionals have stopped dreaming merely of freedom and now dream of celebrity. Amateurs no longer just want something fun to do with their mates on a Friday night, they want to win seats in major international tournaments, play like the pros, make their fortunes.

My goal is still just to turn a profit. To survive, like Mickey Wernick. It has to be, doesn't it? If you want to spend your life playing a game, having fun, staying up late and travelling the world, you can't hope for more than to stay afloat while you're doing it.

At the end of the year, my ledger reads

VIC CASH GAMES: +£9,860
TOURNAMENTS: −£6,325
ONLINE: −$263
OVERALL: +£3,335

The overall sum is not very impressive, maybe. Not to the crowd, if they could see it. I doubt it would dazzle Roland. But I am staring at the ledger with pride and delight and amazement. I made a profit on the year, for the third year running! I am making money playing poker! And that is without cashing in a single tournament for the whole of 2005. Mind you, that statistic is also the embarrassing bit. Time to start cashing in competitions again. My 2004 ledger was **+£50,000**.

Back in the summer, I sat with Mike Sexton in that soulless Rio tournament room, watching Willie winning his bracelet, talking about tournaments. Mike is a player from the old days, friend of long-dead Stuey Ungar, who has been skint a few times but now gets the lot as host and shareholder of the World Poker Tour. Mike warned, 'Everybody wants to play tournaments and be on TV, and win that pot of gold at the end of the rainbow with their friends and family watching. Fail to do that and you have the mental stress and anguish of feeling like a loser. If you don't have the right personality, you'll end up in the loony bin.'

But there is no escaping the dream now. The 'shabby' long-time players wanted people to understand the thrill and beauty of poker, this mesmerizing knot of a game that I have spent nearly fifteen years trying to unpick. We wanted it to be on television. We wanted sponsorship. We wanted security for poker's future. And now we feel . . .

It is as though your favourite band has landed a huge recording contract, guaranteeing them years of success with all the resources they want. As a fan, you are excited and optimistic, proud to share their music and relieved they can afford to stick around. But you are not entirely certain, all the time, that you didn't secretly love them a little more on those crackly old recordings knocked up years ago in the lead singer's garage. Before the drummer kicked smack and found Jesus. When they were bad boys, and nobody cared but you.

Q♣ 10♣

I know how I will try to win this tournament. Emad is a very aggressive player. I must turn that aggression against him, like a superhero reflecting an opponent's powerful death-ray right back into the villain's own eyes. I must let him feel confident. I must let him believe he can bully me.

That is the plan, anyway. But when I find QT suited on the first hand of heads-up and Emad flat calls from the button, I cannot bear to check. I must surely have the best hand. So I raise to 70,000. Emad calls.

The flop comes 5♦ 8♦ 10♣. Top pair! I bet out 100,000 and will call any raise. But Emad just calls.

The turn is 2♣. I bet 300,000. Emad calls again. What does he have? A flush draw? A weaker ten? A brilliantly disguised overpair?

The river is 9♦. Horrible. That is just about the worst card it could be. The flush has come. It also makes several straights. And if Emad has a ten in his own hand, he could easily have a nine with it.

I really hate this nine of diamonds. Truly, the curse of Scotland. And of London.

I check. I feel sure I must have gone behind, if I wasn't behind already.

Emad bets 600,000.

But here's the thing. He announces the bet out loud, in a firm and serious voice. There is something interesting about it. I am not sure what. So I take my time and I think.

I sip my tea. Emad waits. He does not call for the clock. He does not do anything.

And now I know what it is. Hours ago, on this final table, I folded a key hand against Emad and I flirted with him until he showed me his cards. And he had three queens. And when he had three queens, he did not announce his bet in a firm and serious voice. He seemed flustered and nervous. He chattered while I made the decision. And now he is silent.

I look over at Jeff Duvall, smiling from the rail.

Be patient and fearless, Jeff said.

This is the very first hand of heads-up. There has been no chance for patience. But maybe this is a moment to be fearless. Maybe it is time to go with my read and trust my gut.

I call the 600,000.

Emad shows J8. A pair of eights. No good! I have just won a big chip lead.

Why did he bet, when he had showdown value with a pair?

He bet because he knew I had a ten, and he thought I would pass a ten. Just like Barny, yesterday, knew I had a king and thought I would pass a king.

Well, I am not here to pass the best hand. I am not here, any more, to be grateful for making the final or excited about second place. I am determined, for the first time in four days, perhaps the first time in my life, to win the tournament.

22

ARAUCARIA

— never to know exactly when

I am in the £100 game at the Vic, comfortably in front, when the phone rings and I can see my brother's name on the screen.

You are not supposed to answer the phone in a game. I never do. And yet I know, somehow, at this moment, although my brother and I speak often, that I must take this particular call. I know it the way you know sometimes at the roulette table that you must bet a certain number. It is that same sudden certain feeling of fate, but this is a bad feeling. So I get up and walk slowly away from the table to pick up the phone and I don't say 'Hello,' I say, 'What's happened?'

♠

Freddie comes up to me at the cash desk where I am numbly counting out chips, and he says, 'What's happened?'

I tell him that I don't quite know what has happened, but my parents are on holiday in France and my father has been taken away in an ambulance. And my mother is alone in a waiting room in a French hospital. Fred gives me a solid, gentle hug and I look into his crinkled eyes and he tells me it will be all right.

♠

The cab stops outside my house and I run in, although there is no reason to run because the next plane does not leave London for Nice until six o'clock in the morning, to get a change of clothes and a toothbrush and all the cash I have locked up in my desk. And I close the door and go back up the steps and out to the cab where Giles is waiting, and then I go back in the house, very quickly, and take Jesse May's *Shut Up And Deal* off the bookshelf.

And I shut the door again and go back up the steps and out to the cab and we carry on to Heathrow, and wait.

♠

> *bitterness and denial aren't*
> *realistic ways*
> *to deal*
> *with something that happens again and again*
> *never to know exactly when*
> *but that the only stop is not to play.*
> *but to play*
> *that's the thing.*
> *shut up and deal.*
>
> — *Jesse May*

♠

They are long days.

♠

There is a routine. Wake up, phone the hospital, find out if he is still alive. Then wait until 12 o'clock when we are allowed to visit. Drive the forty minutes to Nice. Wait, feeling sick, for the doctor. Hear today's news. They cannot stop the infection. They have stopped the infection but they can't stop the bleeding. They have stopped the bleeding but he is still in a coma and they don't know why.

Yesterday I had basic school French. Today I am talking about kidney failure, heart failure, tracheotomies, septicaemia, MRSA, intensive care, depth of unconsciousness. I am glad we are having these conversations in a foreign language. It separates things.

♠

I am not ready for my father to die. That is what I tell God. I have been frightened of this moment for my entire life and I hoped I would be ready when it happened, but I am not. I think I am a 'strong' person but I cannot bear this to be now. He must not die, because I cannot have that happen. But he is going to die. Everybody thinks so. I have never been so scared or so sad.

♠

My brother phones his girlfriend in London every day, several times a day. Part of the weirdness, the loneliness, the fear, is being distant from everything normal. He yearns for her. I yearn for the Vic.

I need to play poker. I am aching with desire to get lost in the game. There is no internet connection here. There is no card room. I need to look at cards, to face bets, to think about maths. I need to hide there. I can't cope with full consciousness of what is happening. I have finished *Shut Up And Deal* and started it again.

♠

I believe in God. I have always believed in God. I tried not to, but I do. To some people that is as crazy as believing that green is unlucky, that a seven will come if you say its name near a dice table, that the air conditioning killed Hemish. It is as impossible to explain faith to someone who does not feel it, as it is to explain being in love to someone who is not. It is not the rules of poker or the workings of an aeroplane engine. It is the part of you that wants to win at poker, or wants to fly. I tell God, every day, that I am not ready for this.

♠

We get English newspapers from the shop in the village and try to finish the cryptic crosswords. There is something comforting about this new addition to the routine. It soothes my brain to concentrate on untangling the riddles. I have become superstitious about pushing through to solve every clue, feeling good omens if we triumph over the mysteries. Araucaria will not defeat us. His name sounds like another medical condition. But it is just a puzzle.

I have never felt closer to my brother. However all this turns out, I will miss these hours, sitting close together on the sofa, passing the pen back and forth, trying to finish the crossword.

Now we are having a break before addressing the last two clues and I am reading a news story about John Daly, the golfer, who has admitted in his autobiography that he has gambled away £33 million.

Part of me is impressed. The traditional gambler's response is 'Truly sick,' a mixture of horror, empathy and admiration. Admiration at the sheer scale of stubbornness, madness, self-destructiveness that could cause such a leak. Maybe alcoholics feel something similar when they hear that a colleague has been drinking paraffin.

I read this story hard, trying to slip through the bare facts, concise as crossword clues, and into the detail. I am with Daly as he drives through the desert from San Francisco to Las Vegas after losing to Tiger Woods in a tournament, the second-prize cheque for £425,000 burning a hole in his pocket. I know he doesn't feel like he's won £425,000, he feels like he's lost £750,000. Like Barny getting £30k in the World Series and heading for the dice table feeling like he'd lost a million.

I feel the impatience in Daly's stomach on that hot drive across California. He needs to be out of that car, off that road, urgently thumbing his money into the slots. The paper says that he got into town and lost the whole £425,000 in half an hour. The only surprise for me is that he made it as far as Vegas, rather than stopping at Whiskey Pete's on the border.

A few days before I left London, I misplayed a poker hand and lost £200. Only £200. But I needed to punish myself so I played a pig-headed session of blackjack and lost £1,400. The next morning, I spoke to Mr Big, who told me that he had gone on tilt himself and lost £10,000. We talked about what we could each have done with the money, the countries we could have seen, the food we could have eaten. I had the phone tucked between my ear and my shoulder because I was buttering some toast, running the knife round the groove of the tub to eke out the last of the butter. Full respect shown for a £1 purchase.

Was that two weeks ago? It feels like two years.

♠

My brother flies home for 24 hours. He needs to fetch clothes, pay bills and spend a night with his girlfriend. When he comes back, I fly home for 24 hours. I have no luggage. I go straight to the Vic.

Everybody asks about my father but I can't talk about it. I don't know why, but I can't. I see Freddie, whose hug I have been feeling for three weeks now, but I can't talk to him about it. I see Neil, who is one of only four people I have phoned from France, but I can't talk to him about it.

I take £750 from my deposit slip and sit down in the £100 game.The cards are large and bright.The chips are perfect mirrored discs. The shuffle sounds loud like an engine.

The boys are talking about a mysterious Premiership footballer who has got into poker and made tabloid headlines because he 'lost £37,000 on the turn of a card'. Outside this building, the nation is asking, 'Who is the footballer?' In here, they are asking, 'What was the card?'

Fred makes it £15 to go. I call. I feel like I am breathing for the first time in twenty-one days.

♠

My father is starting to wake up! His eyes are open, beautiful and blue as £25 chips. His body stopped failing but he stayed asleep for another ten days and nobody knew why. Now they are frightened of brain damage. He is out of intensive care, on the ward, and we see him at last.

He is starting to talk, but he is talking about cards. He asks, 'Where is the queen of clubs?' And he says, 'I think I can make four hearts.'

It's funny. Everything is funny because I can hug him and kiss him. But the doctors are worried by this card talk. They tell us it is probably the morphine. But we know they are frightened about his brain.

I am not frightened any more. When he asks if the diamond king will fall under his ace, I tell him that it will. When he asks about the queen of clubs, I remind him that it is in his own hand. I understand why my father's mind has gone to bridge, the game he has played for forty years. He just wants to control this baffling situation, that's all. He wants it ordered into thirteen clean tricks, fifty-two structured cards, four sorted suits, 40 neat points. And he wants to be reassured that the finesse will work, that the contract will be made, that he holds the master card.

I could talk to him like this for ever.

♠

'I've got a pain in my toe,' says The Sweep. 'I think it might be the start of a heart attack.'

'James,' I say, 'can you stop throwing sweet wrappers on the floor?'

'Or maybe,' The Sweep adds nervously, 'it's a stroke.'

It is so annoying when James throws sweet wrappers on the floor. It is annoying when he boils the kettle without enough water in it. It's annoying when he tries to pull the shutters up and breaks them. It's annoying when he knocks his wine glass onto the carpet, that's why I make him drink out of a tumbler.

It is annoying when Ashley laughs at me for misplaying a hand of hi-lo, when Val says 'Green me' instead of 'Can I have some change?', when I ask the boys what they think of my new table lamp or new haircut and The Sweep always says it's terrible.

It's annoying when they forget to say thank you for dinner, when they deal me out because I'm fetching their drinks, when they bicker about who's going to sit where.

But today I love all of it, everything. We have all come home. My father is well enough to have flown back to a London hospital by air ambulance. There are no 'visiting hours' and I can sit there with him all afternoon. He is not talking about cards any more. He is talking about how much he hates doing the exercises, how bored he is waiting for *Countdown* to come on, how dispiriting the series of patch-up operations is and how cleverly he thinks – he truly thinks – he is hiding his cigarettes from the nurses. He is all weak and tired and sore when they come to get him for physio, not quite up to it today, but once the door is shut he can spring onto the balcony for a crafty fag like an Olympic athlete. An Olympic athlete who smokes. He actually keeps a secret ashtray in his bedside drawer. He thinks it's secret, anyway.

And it is Tuesday, just like normal. I came back from the hospital an hour ago and put on the pasta. And now the boys are arguing and littering and making stupid jokes and my father is five minutes away, getting better.

♠

I know he will not be here for long. I know he has come back to say goodbye. We have all wandered into *It's A Wonderful Life* or *A Matter Of Life And Death*. The angels have met my father, irascible and restless and asking difficult questions about the queen of clubs; they have peered down to see some sort of wreckage; and they have said, 'Ah, send him back for a last scene.'

He does not have an illness any more. He is cured. But I know there will not be twenty years, or ten years, or five. I know it like you know, sometimes, on the roulette, that you must bet a certain number.

But this is neither a winning feeling, like the roulette, nor a bad feeling like my brother's phone call. It is a gentle feeling. From the ends of my toes to the top of my untreated roots, there is nothing in me but gratitude for everything in the world.

I have to lose my father. And although there is no reason, now, for him to die, I know it is going to be soon. Of something else.

But I will be ready. I will be so ready. I will be grateful that he came back to us even for five minutes, grateful that I am here to miss him because that is how things are supposed to work, and grateful that he was ever here at all.

You are meant to lose your father. It is happening to someone every day, every hour, every minute probably. So you have to be ready, and you have to be grateful. And I am. He is here now. This is the luckiest hand that was ever dealt.

♠

bitterness and denial aren't
realistic ways
to deal
with something that happens again and again
never to know exactly when

9♦ 7♠

I am thinking about my brother. He is at home, watching this final play out on the internet. Until today, I don't think he knew you could follow poker tournaments on the internet. I wonder if he cheered when we got heads-up. I wonder if he is remembering the days when he taught me the game. None of this would be happening without him.

And now I have picked up the Hugo! That's what this hand is called. I love it in a cash game. But, even though I have the button, I fold. My strategy was, still is, to let Emad destroy himself with his own aggression, and it will be good for his confidence if I fold the button. I want to give the impression of playing weakly, especially after that last big call. I fold.

23

THE MILL HILL MOB

A rat race reclaims its rebels.

A smell of griddling sausages rises over the tiled roofs and carriage drives of Mill Hill, floating away over the trimmed choisya and clean fishponds. Toto, we're not in Hendon any more.

Mr and Mrs Elegance are having a barbecue. Joe Beevers married Claire at last year's World Series, outdoors on a balcony overlooking the fountains at the Bellagio, and they have just become the parents of twin girls. So they have said goodbye to the flat above the bank and moved to this smart house in the more distant suburbs, where Joe can look at his apple trees over the top of his computer.

He met Claire when she was working as PA to a recreational poker player with an office job, and she is good news for all of us. Joe's life is freshened and lightened for being shared with someone who doesn't play the game, and in releasing Joe to find his proper partner, I was rewarded with a smart, sweet, funny girl to hang around with in Vegas, drinking cocktails and helping me to work out which of the other ladies at the bar are prostitutes. Usually all of them.

Joe is crazily in love with Claire, and comically proud to be a father, but I think I might be even happier they met than he is.

Ram Vaswani married Jackie at the previous year's WSOP and they have also moved, with their young daughter Hollie, to blossomy Mill Hill. Ross Boatman is now a father of three: Alabama is growing up and her new brothers, Buster and Rocky, are learning that key phrase, 'Daddy gone away, play poker, make money, buy presents.' He and Stephanie have opted for a house and garden in Holloway.

Vegas is looming again but it's all different now for the Hendon Mob. Instead of scrabbling a bankroll together and shoving a pair of pants in a holdall, Ross is spending his days trying to rent a family house in Nevada and sort out a passport for baby Rocky. Joe is trying to arrange childcare for the twins when they arrive.

Of the four chancers I knew six years ago, only Barny is still a storybook player of the romantic old school. He and his girl-friend still live in the Archway flat, have not yet had children and Barny is free to jet off early for Vegas and be there for what is now a staggering two months of tournaments.

But even Barny is not just a gambler any more. Like every modern poker player, he is a businessman.

♠

It all worked out for the boys. Their website, thehendonmob.com, is the most successful non-gaming poker site in Britain. They performed well on *Late Night Poker*, making many televised finals, and Barny became the series commentator. They signed the first million-dollar sponsorship deal ever made in poker, and have just moved to an American site which has asked the boys to be its first European 'faces'. With the flexibility afforded by sponsorship, each of them has now increased his lifetime tournament winnings to over $1,000,000. I'm shaking my head and remembering Barny, back in the Isle of Man, racing around selling shares as he tried to scrape together the tournament entry fee.

They might have been Delboy figures back then, gazing out of windows and promising 'This time next year, we'll be million-aires' – but they were right.

Ross has been a celebrity before, because of *London's Burning*, but people no longer shout, 'Where's the fire?' when he walks past. They shout, 'Raise!'

'We all get recognized a lot,' says Joe, 'but only in certain places. It happens at football matches, cricket matches, and obviously at poker events, and it happens in restaurants and bars.'

'Basically,' Ross points out, 'it happens in the places we go to.'

They all laugh. Ram says, 'We haven't tested if it would happen at operas.'

Joe still writes to Hemish's family, every year, to assure them he is not forgotten.

♠

In Vegas last summer, I started to worry about the Hendon Mob. Every morning, they got up early, dressed in their logo'd attire and sat down to play all day. They did this every day for seven weeks. They didn't drink and they didn't gamble on blackjack or dice. Joe did not fall asleep at the Pai Gow table. It was all terribly serious.

Between tournaments they manage their website and they go to meetings and they talk to their lawyers and they file their company accounts. I think Joe and Barny are probably working harder now than they ever have in their lives. Four full-time staff have been employed to help run the office and administer the website. Their latest wheeze is 'Pokermob', a service for downloading poker-themed ringtones and wallpaper for mobile phones.

It's all a very curious development for a game that was meant to be an antidote to corporate life. The rat race reclaims its rebels.

Even Ram, who is one of the sickest gamblers you'll ever be lucky enough to meet, is making business plans for the future, as any professional sportsman might. He has bought the snooker club where he used to hang out as a teenager and is doing it up for relaunch as a combined snooker and poker hall.

Then again, he also has a new addiction to high-stakes golf, the latest Vegas retro craze, where thousands of dollars are bet on a single hole. That can't end well.

♠

Like Barny, I'm still free from domestic responsibility. I have no idea whether I haven't got round to starting a family because I play poker all the time, or whether I play poker all the time because I haven't got round to starting a family. But I do and I haven't.

Still, I have started writing a weekly poker column in the *Guardian*, a proper broadsheet newspaper, and that feels very grown-up.

'Are we not children ourselves any more?' I ask the boys over the blackened hamburgers. 'Wasn't that the idea, to live like kids for ever? But *naughty* kids, up after bedtime in a dark secret world? You're all so sensible now.'

'I want my family in Vegas,' says Ross, 'but part of me misses the old loner thing, before poker got so big. Buttoning up your coat on a frosty night, getting behind the wheel and setting off for some mysterious location that nobody knew about. Smoke-filled rooms full of seedy characters, chit-chat and banter. It was a cowboy scenario, living life on the toss of a coin. These days I get up and make the kids' breakfast, take them to school, come back, have a bath and go to the office.'

Maybe that happens to anybody when they have children. But poker has changed along with the Hendon boys. On the forum of their site, a bunch of young guys are currently discussing the requirements for starting out as a professional player. They are posting about hourly rates, percentage of stake to bankroll, relative investments in tournaments against cash. One of them asks: 'Could any existing pros advise me on what my employment status should be? I know that I don't need to pay tax on my winnings, but am keen to make the appropriate NI contributions.'

I don't think The Cincinnati Kid ever asked that question.

♠

People aren't always nice on that Hendon Mob forum. They used to be. It was a little community of players and we all chatted amongst ourselves about good games, bad beats, cheap air fares and controversial episodes of *Late Night Poker*. But poker was still a secretive game, and a man's bankroll was his own business. Now, there is a vast community of TV viewers and internet browsers poring over the players' results, volunteering harsh opinions. The Mob had a bad run at last year's WSOP and the criticism was barbed.

Barny says, 'All sports fans reckon they've bought the right to tell the pros they don't know what they're doing. If you go to the football, there's always a 20-stone bloke behind you, watching a 21-year-old at peak fitness who can do things this guy can't do in his wildest dreams, yelling "You donkey!" It can be uncomfortable having a light shining on you, especially when you do badly and everyone's pointing. But what's going on in your head is still private.'

It's more than that, though. If people are seen as famous, some other people are going to dislike them. There was always financial jealousy and bitterness in poker, but it was muttered behind backs. The anonymity of the internet gives people a way of putting their most vitriolic comments in front of the players' faces.

People used to write me cute flirtatious messages on the Hendon Mob forum because I was the only girl who posted there. I still am. But now, when one person writes that he thinks I'm pretty, another comes back to say that I'm ugly or fat. There was a sinister remark a couple of weeks ago from someone, using a fake name obviously, about sitting next to me at the Vic and noticing that I had 'hairy arms'. I don't think I have very hairy arms. But I've started looking at strangers on the table, wondering what they are thinking and if they are going to write about me tonight. And I have started wearing long sleeves.

One guy posted to say I don't deserve to be sponsored into any more events because I've never won a proper professional tournament and I am a terrible player. Another poster came in gallantly to say that was a mean thing to write. A third gave his opinion that 'She is fair game because she is a celebrity, like Posh Spice.'

I don't know quite what qualifies as hairy, when it comes to arms. But I know that I am definitely not a celebrity like Posh Spice.

♠

I wonder whether all this is killing the personality that the Hendon Mob once wanted to put across. The original idea was all about self-deprecating British humour. The guys played down how good they were. They played up the bumbling hopefulness of the game, the borrowing of money to get into tournaments, the impoverished Delboy dreams of greatness. With sponsors to impress and carping railbirds to placate, is there any room for humorous modesty? Can it still be an Ealing Comedy?

'Unfortunately,' Barny chuckles, 'an enormous amount of that spirit still exists. However much money you've got, you can still lose it all in one day, on one bet.'

Ram stops mid-bite of his hamburger. 'Why is everyone looking at me?'

'When it comes to the wheeling and dealing around poker,' Barny goes on, 'we've cleverly managed to avoid getting properly rich through any of it. We've got our fingers in a lot of pies, but we don't seem to own any pie factories.'

Barny says he's still comfortable with a self-deprecating

image. He says, 'In America, players talk up how great they are, how much better than the next guy, and I find it a bit crass. Professional poker is different from medicine or writing or anything socially useful, because it's all about beating other people. You don't hear doctors saying, "I cure far more colds than the guy with the practice down the road." Personally, I'm happy to be at the top of my game, I don't feel disadvantaged against any player at any table, but I don't need to scream and shout about it.'

With everything taken into account, I wonder if poker life is any easier for the Hendon boys of Mill Hill. They aren't living hand to mouth any more. But with the public criticism, the pressure to get results, the corporate nature of the job, the loss of those lonely and romantic frosty nights, isn't it just a different kind of pressure?

'When I was a kid,' says Ram, 'I didn't even know about poker. I just wanted to be the world champion of something. Poker came along at the right time, it exploded at the right time, and we're all good at it. We're loving life. Are you kidding? It's the best thing that ever happened.'

♠

BadBeat pours another cup of tea and Mr Big butters a scone. I bite into a cucumber sandwich and turn up the volume on Wimbledon. It is 112 degrees.

If Grandpa Sam were here, he would say, 'It'd take a lot of this to kill ya.' But Grandpa Sam would never have been here, relaxing in a private cabana by the swimming pool at Wynn Las Vegas with a television for watching tennis, a room service button to order English tea, and special machines to spray a cooling mist over us as we lie on our padded loungers like fat billionaires.

Of course, none of us has any money. The Wynn has given

me a room discount and a free cabana because I've lost so much playing blackjack. BadBeat has played dozens of tournaments and cashed once, for $2,200, which doesn't begin to cover his over-heads. As for Mr Big, he tells us, 'Four days ago I put $112,000 in my box at the Bellagio. I opened it today and a moth flew out.'

Now well established as the CEO of the successful European Poker Tour, recognized all over Vegas as well as in Europe, John is assumed by everyone to be a multi-millionaire. He has almost convinced even me, lolling there in his Vilebrequin shorts and jewelled watch, eating his jammy scone, until I remember that I'm paying for this cabana with blackjack losses and Mr Big has been on terrible form.

This is how bad he's running: under severe pressure, he finally managed to get himself into an $8,000 pot in the $10-$20 NLH game with the nuts. He bet the river and his Vietnamese opponent shouted, 'I call!' Unfortunately, he had such a strong accent that John thought he'd said 'I fold,' and mucked his own hand. He asked for a ruling but, since the Vietnamese guy still had his cards and John didn't, Mr Big lost the pot. If you can't win with the nuts on the river, you're going home skint.

I ask John if he's been playing any punto banco. He says, 'Yeah, a bit of punto. And a bit of blackjack. And a bit of Pai Gow. And the slots . . .'

My own luck isn't going much better. My main event began with a cab driver who couldn't find the Rio, even though we could see its giant shiny tower on the horizon. So I knew it wasn't going to be a good day.

I flopped two pair and my opponent rivered a higher two pair. I raised with two black aces, got five callers, check-raised stubbornly on a flop of Q♥ J♥ 8♥, got three callers and had to check-pass the turn. I made a large raise with A♦ Q♦ and was rewarded with a risible flop of 4♠ 5♠ 6♠, as if someone was having a laugh at my expense. My final hand involved a moron who chose to call a pre-flop limp-re-raise all-in with AJ and cracked my AK easier than buttering toast.

You would need the very opposite kind of luck to win the World Series main event. This year, there are 8,700 runners and the event stretches on for thirteen days. You need miracles to get through. It plays like a croquet match with flamingos for mallets, hedgehogs for balls and players being beheaded on the whims of a mad queen. Johnny Chan, Johnny Moss, Doyle Brunson, Stu Ungar – they won this title more than once. Nobody will ever win it twice again. It is a madness.

I felt bruised and battered when I went out, of course I did. After that kind of luck, you always feel like you've been assaulted. But out here, now, I can't care. Tournaments are just daydreams, I'm with two friends I love, and my father is well again.

♠

This time, I am remembering to make it a holiday. It doesn't help to keep telling yourself that life is short but, as my father would say, 'It doesn't hoyt.' He pronounces it like that because it is an old punchline, though I can't remember the joke. Gamblers are the last people who need advising to 'live in the moment', since our lives can suffer from an inability to do anything else, but I am trying at least to make the moment good.

So I am going swimming, eating with friends, thinking ruefully rather than bleakly about unrequited love.

I've seen a couple of shows. The first starred Marcel Lüske, who insisted on performing numbers from his forthcoming album on a small stage at the Hard Rock Café. I was knocked out of the main event just in time to catch him singing *If You Don't Know Me By Now* in a heavy Dutch accent to a bemused crowd. He sounded like a poker player, but he looked magnificent.

The second show, nearly as entertaining, was Elton John at

Caesars Palace. This was a sparkling extravaganza designed by David LaChapelle, with a big-screen backdrop showing films of Pamela Anderson pole-dancing, Justin Timberlake dressed as Elton John circa 1975 at a party full of drag artists, and a violent naked ballet 'inspired by *A Streetcar Named Desire*'. The Sweep said that we should ask for our money back on the grounds that it wasn't camp enough.

And I'm considering going to see George Wallace. I don't know who George Wallace is, but today I saw an advert on the side of a cab, with the slogan GEORGE WALLACE AT 10 PM. NEITHER TOO EARLY NOR TOO LATE. And I feel so sorry for George, if that's the best reason his employers can think of for people to see his show, that I think I'll go along.

I have been to a few of the trendy new nightclubs, which all have names like Tryst and Tao and Ghost. They all, unfortunately, play thumping house music to appeal to the new crowd who have come 'to party' in Vegas in the footsteps of Paris Hilton. I made an enemy out of the DJ at the Ghost Bar when I passed him a note asking if he had any Jackson Five. He threw it back as though I'd asked if he had chlamydia. So I scrawled, 'This cool stuff is all well and good, but do you know what everybody wants, deep down, on a dance floor? Everyone in the world? *1970s disco.*' He gave me a sneer and turned the volume up.

If I were a visionary, or any kind of businesswoman, I would buy a property on the Strip and open a traditional Vegas 1970s disco lounge. It would make a killing. Maybe I should write to George Clooney about it.

Meanwhile, a Californian TV agent called Jamie Gold wins this biggest-ever World Series and collects $12,000,000.

Well, he doesn't exactly collect it. There is talk about him having been given the seat as a freebie in return for supplying celebrity players, and an agreement with his business partner to go 50/50 on any winnings, which is now being disputed. The partner says Gold is reneging on the deal. Lawyers get involved.

A judge places a restraining order on the money. People are saying how appalling it is that the new, bright, shiny World Series of Poker is being tainted with this kind of grubby to-do. But half the players in town are amused and delighted to see the title go to someone who may yet turn out to be an absolute underhand Old School drak.

♠

Vegas is getting sleazy again. I go to a party hosted by three players from the Midlands, where all the waitresses are topless. Apparently, you can order a drink from them or tip bigger and order something else. I opt for the drink. I am about to sit down on a large inflatable sofa by the pool when Marc Goodwin tells me this house is a popular orgy venue and has just been used as the location for a porn film. I decide to remain standing.

Then Michael Greco, a soap star who is starting to slide across the divide between 'celebrity hobbyist' and 'serious player', meets with an awkward incident. He has a good session in the $5-$10 Pot Limit Omaha at the Wynn and goes upstairs early with $2,500. Michael is sharing a room, as is common practice among players to keep the expenses down, and his roommate has brought back a hooker to share the other bed. The usual etiquette in these circumstances is for the second player to return to the gaming floor while business is conducted, but Michael doesn't want to risk the temptation of gambling with the winnings so he gets into his own bed regardless. 'I slept through the whole thing,' he claims. You'd think that sort of noise might wake a person – but no, because when the two boys get up in the morning, the lady has gone and so has the $2,500 that Michael left on his bedside table.

Two years ago, both these situations would have driven me to despair. This year, they just make me laugh and, in the second case, wish good luck to the hooker. These things happen in Vegas.

And I am all happiness because my father is back with us in the world, so the Poppins medicine tastes of cherry tart, custard, pineapple, roast turkey, toffee and hot buttered toast.

♠

The Lizard drops in for a bite of dinner and a nibble of black-jack, but the Wynn won't take his Bellagio cranberries. They reject $25,000 of potential action on the grounds that The Lizard isn't carrying his ID.

Giant egos are so common in poker, newly inflated by media attention, that it is startling to see somebody who hasn't got one. The Lizard does not tell the casino host that they should recognize him, that he has many millions in the bank, that he is one of the most respected players in this town, that he is the kind of person they usually fall over themselves to plead and flatter and bribe into their establishment. He does not point out that they are changing up chips for another unknown gambler in designer shoes and a Rolex, and that The Lizard is wearing jeans and an ordinary watch because he likes to, not because he couldn't afford those badges of status if he wanted them. He does not say a word. He smiles, says it is no problem, borrows a couple of hundred bucks from me and gambles with that.

A few months ago, The Lizard turned up at the Vic for a hi-lo tournament. He asked what was happening in the rugby, as he had 'a small interest'.

A new player, who did not know The Lizard, asked which way he had bet and immediately harangued him for the choice. He said that he himself had bet £50 the other way and it was 'a no-brainer'. He talked about the players, the history, the weather, carefully explaining the ins and outs of rugby statistics and how to profit from them.

In the surrounding seats sat Ashley, Adam Heller and The Sweep, wondering whether to say anything. But it was too much fun to watch. They were also busy wondering how they could get their own bets on, now they knew which way The Lizard was jumping, for his wisdom is prized from Vegas to Melbourne, from Brighton to Macau.

The Lizard listened politely, and he thanked the man for his advice, and he did not argue his own case, and he did not mention that he is the most successful sports gambler in the world.

Last night, I sat on this same blackjack table with Roland. Roland is still pretty new to the scene and enjoys the perks. Spinning it up for a few thousand, he summoned the host and asked for a private table at Tryst.

'I'm sorry, sir,' said the host, 'but that is not possible.'

'What do you mean it's not possible?' said Roland crossly. 'I'm one of your biggest punters. I'm asking for a table.'

'I'm afraid I cannot get you a table at Tryst tonight, sir,' replied the host. 'Would you like to book ahead for tomorrow?'

'I don't want to go tomorrow,' said Roland. 'I want to go now. Call your supervisor.'

'I will call him, sir,' nodded the host, 'but he will not be able to help you with a table tonight either.'

'Is this a fucking joke?' snapped Roland. 'Look at the amount I'm gambling here. I said I want a table tonight and your supervisor will get me one.'

'I am afraid he will not,' said the host, pleasure twinkling through his sorrowful tone like the tiny flash of gold in a prospector's pan, 'because Tryst is closed on a Monday.'

♠

This World Series marks the end of my association with Paradise Poker. Their site is going in a new direction, adding links from the poker to online blackjack and roulette. I could never endorse those things, and they want a whole different sort of campaign.

So I decide to take a deep breath and have a chat with

PokerStars. Last year I felt they were too serious for me, but I feel ready now.

I understand, looking at the stick the Hendon Mob have got, that sponsored players will get some ribbing and criticism however good they are. I am happier now, so I am happier about the poker revolution and ready to join in more whole-heartedly. And my tournament game is good, it is much sharper and more focused and determined than it used to be. I am no longer scared off by the class of PokerStars, I no longer dismiss myself as a novelty, so I ask them if they'd like to put me in a couple of tournaments.

They say they would be interested. But they do not want a loose arrangement where I wear their logo in a few events. If I sign with PokerStars, they tell me, it would be an exclusive agreement. I would wear their logo in every tournament I play. I would take no free buy-ins from anyone else. I would be required to play a certain amount of the time. Instead of a journalist who plays a bit of poker, I would be a professional poker player who does a bit of journalism.

My confidence may have grown, but this sounds nerve-wracking. That kind of agreement would get a lot of attention. I believe I can win, but – suspecting nobody else does – I wouldn't want to make too big a deal out of it.

So I say, 'Why don't you put me in the London EPT, and we'll see how it goes?'

7♣ 3♦

This is no hand whatsoever. Emad raises to 90,000 from the button. I fold.

24

BETTER NOT LOOK DOWN

*'Why, they're only a pack of cards, after all. I needn't
be afraid of them!'*

– Lewis Carroll

Vic festivals are always my favourite times of year. The big UK
players, who long since gave up grinding in our live cash games
to concentrate on international tournaments and the internet, still
turn up for these quarterly poker miniseries. The room is packed,
the bar is buzzing, the money flows, the waitresses run back and
forth with cups of dark-orange tea, Jeff Leigh presides over his
dozens of visiting dealers and hundreds of visiting players with
stern, sarcastic efficiency. As the contestants line up to take their
shots at the competition prize pool, Freddie waits at the cash
tables with a friendly nod for the unlucky knockouts and a sack
to take his winnings home. He is like Alice's crocodile,

> *How cheerfully he seems to grin,*
> *How neatly spread his claws,*
> *And welcome little fishes in*
> *With gently smiling jaws!*

This room hasn't really changed much since the poker explosion.
We get a bit more passing trade, the regulars have learned to be
slightly friendlier, Holdem gets a lot more action than Omaha;
otherwise, day-to-day Vic life grinds on as usual. The September
festival, culminating in the European Championship, was always
buzzy. But now that the European Championship is also the
London EPT, the big British names like Devilfish, Ben Roberts,

Dave Colclough, Julian Gardner, Roland de Wolfe and the Hendon Mob are bolstered by American and Scandinavian stars who have decided it's worth dropping by. Even Phil Ivey is here. Phil Ivey, the superstar who drapes over the Big Game table in Vegas with his gorgeous massage team, is right here in the Vic, stuck under a draughty air conditioning vent, wondering why Beverley has brought him the wrong sandwich, just like the rest of us.

Ivey never used to play in Europe, but he just had a spin in the Barcelona EPT and finished second for $470,000, so he has moved on to London. Even if I weren't already skipping happily around in a general state of delight in the world, it would still give me the deepest pleasure to see Phil Ivey and Pedro in the same room at last.

The divide is not so big. Phil Ivey might have hit the big time at a young age, he might drive a Mercedes McLaren and play golf for $100,000 a hole, Pedro might once have been homeless and still collects his dinner from under a gooseberry bush, but they both stay up late at night, hoping for aces. And if I wanted one of them to play with my bankroll and keep it safe, I'd give it to Pedro.

♠

This week is going well. I made the final of the £300 No Limit Holdem and finished eighth for £1,000. I'm very touched when Rory Liffey, with whom I swapped a share, says that he doesn't want to take his portion of the win and would rather roll it over for a tiny percentage in the main event. It's sweet of Rory, as though he really believes I have a chance in this main event, and it boosts my confidence.

On Day One of the big tournament, I feel strangely proud of pinning on the PokerStars colours. Many famous players are here in the same logo, including last year's world champion Joe Hachem, along with dozens of qualifiers who won their seats on

the site. With Paradise, I was always the only one. Novelty logo
for a novelty player. Now, although these well-known faces and
lucky or brilliant qualifiers are still my opponents for the duration
of the tournament, I feel, shyly, like a member of a proper team.
It's another boost, like Rory rolling over the share.

The superstars are mixed in with classic Vic faces like Mike
Ellis and Neil Channing, plus the expected local visitors like the
Hendon boys, Donnacha O'Dea, Davood Mehrmand.

A lot of people dislike Davood, the travelling Persian-German
pro, because his table talk can be a headache and a nightmare.
People think he's nuts. He is certainly unusual, as you'll know if
you have ever heard the story of Ken Lennard, the knife and the
fire extinguisher.

But I think of Davood as a comical Mad Hatter character, I
like him. He is always nice to me. I wouldn't necessarily want to
sit next to him without ear muffs, but he's funny and appealing
in small doses. Today, he is full of plans to launch an online poker
site in Afghanistan. Hard to see any flaws in that scheme.

The first day goes like any other tournament. Play pretty
solid. Sneak into a few pots with unexpected hands, when the
blinds aren't too costly. Otherwise keep it fairly tight because you
can't win the tournament in these early levels, you can only lose
it. But then exploit my tight image with a couple of timely bluffs,
to build the stack.

There is a very struggly phase in the afternoon, when I lose
a couple of nasty pots and go down to 5,000. But I feel a bravery
and a determination that I have never felt before. I start moving
in with no hand when I sense an opportunity to pick up the
pot. And I mean *really* no hand – not 6♣ 7♣ or suited wheel
cards, as I learned long ago to use for semi-bluffing, but real trash:
J3, K4, Q8. I have known for years that there are tournament
phases where it's not about the cards, only the situations. But
today, after all this time, I am actually *feeling* it.

It occurs to me that a bet from an opponent is like a heckle when you're standing on a comedy stage. It is a mini-attack. Some days, you don't know how to defend yourself against it. Some days, the attack is so good that you have to let the heckler win. But today, I feel like I did on that hot August night at the Fringe Club fifteen years ago. I am not going to be pushed around. I am in control of the situation. I am ready to craft my comebacks. I stand my ground, push when I sense the time is right, and force my stack up to 35,000 by the end of the day.

♠

A hundred and three of us return for Day Two, from a starting field of four hundred. My table is a little startling: Phil Ivey is in seat one and Tom Parker Bowles is in seat six. Frank Pini is the short stack in seat five. So we have an old Vic regular, an international super-pro and a royal. This is 21st century poker.

And where do I fit in? God knows. I've stopped wondering.

The opening levels of Day Two move fast, as they always do, since there are players who nurse tiny stacks at the end of Day One just to say they survived overnight. Then they all knock themselves out in the morning. Within 90 minutes, we are down to 80 players.

Phil Ivey gets unlucky when he finds AK and moves in to discover that 'Texas Johnny' Hewston is lurking behind with a pair of kings.

John Hewston is not from Texas. He has been described as 'a UK poker player, and for many years the hide-and-seek champion of Birmingham'. I won't speculate on what people mean by that.

Emad Tahtouh, Joe Hachem's friend that I met in Vegas, moves to the table in Phil Ivey's place, with a short stack. We play a pot which pleases and displeases me at the same time. I find AQ in middle position when Emad has the big blind. I would normally make a large raise, but I realize that if I make a small and weak-looking raise, Emad has the perfect stack for coming over the top and trying to bully me out. So I make a nervous, ladylike, 2.5x big blind bet. Sure enough, Emad moves in immediately. I call, to his horror. He has nine high. But he hits the flop and wins the pot. Annoying; he should have gone out there. But I am not as distressed as usual by the bad luck. I feel unruffled, unrufflable. I played the pot well. Everything is fine.

I am making the right decisions today. With better chips, I no longer have to move in with nothing, so I am concentrating on making smart calls and well-timed raises. By the dinner break, I am up to 70,000.

I'm delighted to find that Ross and Barny Boatman are still in the tournament, as is Neil with 30,000. Neil and I have swapped a share, as we usually do. I'd love to finish this tournament heads-up with him. But, in the real world, I'd love to just make the money. There are 55 of us left, 32 will cash, and the chip leader is American film star turned poker pro Chad Brown with 241,000.

First player out after dinner is the young Norwegian internet hero Johnny Lodden, who was chip leader at the end of Day One. As he walks away, disgruntled, Pedro tries to sell him a miniature fan.

At 10 p.m., I run into my first nightmare. Jonas Molander, a clever and active Scandinavian kid, raises to 12,000 and I move all-in for 70,000 with a pair of eights. Jonas calls immediately: he has aces.

Still, strangely, I don't feel bad and I don't feel scared. If I go out here, I will have gone making a strong play which would work in most situations. It wasn't an error. It was just unlucky that he had a real hand this time.

And maybe I will get lucky. Sometimes you have to. 75% of the people in this tournament are playing good poker, and the ones who make the final will be those who got lucky in the right moments. If I can get unlucky with AQ against nine high, maybe I can get lucky with 88 against AA. It happens.

And it happens. Bang, eight on the table. I'm still alive.

♠

At 11 p.m., we are on the bubble: 33 of us left, and 32 places get paid. Donnacha O'Dea moves in with 99, finds an opponent with KK, doesn't get as lucky as I did and we are all in the money, guaranteed at least £4,000.

After the bubble, everything speeds up again. Those who clung on for the money, like those who clung on to make Day Two, get themselves knocked out in a quick scramble. But I barely notice. I have that feeling, like I had in the final of *Celebrity Poker Club*, that the other players are just shadowy ciphers around me, disappearing one by one.

That changes suddenly at midnight, when I find myself in a pot with Barny Boatman. Barny is not a shadow or a cipher. He is an old friend, a loved and trusted cohort, a very real human. We have moved to the TV feature table and here he is on my left.

Everybody passes round to me in the cut-off and I find K♦ J♠. With blinds at 3,000-6,000, I make it 16,000 to go. Barny flat calls from the button. The blinds pass.

Flop comes 9♠ 10♥ K♥.

Top pair! It would be obvious to bet. But, hmmm . . . it is a dangerous flop. These are the kinds of middling cards that callers often have, plus there is a flush draw and possible straight. Barny called from the button. He is a creative player. He could have anything. If I bet out and he raises, I cannot pass and would have to play a vast pot on a very vulnerable board. I want to control the size of the action. And if Barny has nothing to do with this flop, I must give him a chance to bluff, not a chance to fold. So I check. Barny bets 17,000 and I call.

The turn is 4♥.

The flush has come. I check again and Barny checks behind. Interesting. This could mean that he has nothing, chanced it on the flop and has given up. But it is not like Barny to give up; I rule out that possibility. He must have something. He could have made the flush and is now tricking me. He could have a pair or two and is nervous of my having the flush. Or he could have picked up a flush draw and wants a card for free. He definitely has something. But what? I need more information.

The river is 8♠.

There is 80,000 in the pot. I think I have to bet something. If I check, then Barny is bound to bet, and he may bet the pot or more. The moment feels right for a stopper bet – enough to stop him raising with a stronger king, two pair or a straight, because he fears what is in my hand. It needs to be a half-pot bet. I make it 42,000.

And Barny moves all-in.

What? All-in? I was not expecting that. What can it mean? He can only move in with a hand that he knows for certain is winning, or knows for certain is losing. But which? What does he have? Why is a raven like a writing desk? There is a riddle here to be solved.

♠

I wonder what happened to Barny's lucky shirt. He always used to wear it for big tournaments, a short-sleeved blue cotton shirt covered in multi-coloured anchors and boats. Then, one day, he lost it. I wonder if it's been lucky for the finder?

I like it that he used to wear a shirt covered in boats. That was in the really early days of *Late Night Poker*. It feels so long ago. Mad Marty Wilson planted a lucky sapling in a flower bed outside the studio in Cardiff, and now it's a big cherry tree.

♠

Barny cannot make this move with a big king, two pair or even a straight. He just can't. He doesn't need to. With those hands, he should be happy to call my bet and hope he is winning. They have call value, they do not have all-in value.

He could move in with a flush. But what are his cards, if he has a flush? If he has the nut flush, that means he called me before the flop with a suited ace. Surely, with a suited ace, he would re-raise from the button? He would. He does not have that hand. He could have called from the button with small suited hearts. But if he made a flush on the turn with small cards, why check? Too dangerous. Another heart might have come on the river to give me a bigger flush. He surely would not take that risk.

Barny is a tricksy player. He may have completely wrong-footed me with counter-intuitive play from start to finish. Besides, he is an old friend and I do not want to knock him out. I like us being here together. The old stupid emotional stuff coming in again. For heaven's sake, Barny is capable of knocking out his own brother if he has to. I force my mind out of that space and back into the zone and I know, suddenly, that my pair is good. Barny must have a smaller pair and a missed flush draw, that is the only hand which makes sense for the bets. My king is good, and Barny knows what I have, and he thinks I cannot call his all-in with this hand.

Well, I bloody can. I call, suddenly, and Barny taps the table, rolling over A♥ 10♦. He is out of the tournament in 22nd place. And I wish he weren't. I am glad to have the chips, but I wish they could have been someone else's.

♠

Isabelle Mercier, a fully-fledged Team PokerStars Pro, is out in
16th place. Tom Parker Bowles, after a heroic performance, finishes
15th and collects £10,000. His exit is preceded by some unwise
table talk; did he crumble after two long days of poker? At 2.15
in the morning, Tom tried to order a beer but was told the casino
bar shuts at 2 a.m. Tom really wants a beer. He wonders aloud
about nipping to an off-licence, but Neil Channing points out
that these would be shut, too.

'I know where I can get a beer,' says Tom. 'At home.'

If he hadn't said this, Neil might not have called with AJ
when Tom moved all-in a few minutes later. But Tim Flanders
would still have called with QQ. As it turns out, Neil hits an ace
and knocks them both out.

But then Neil gets unlucky in a pot with Emad, and another
pot with Michael Muldoon, and he goes out in 13th place. With
twelve players left, at 3 a.m. we stop for the night.

♠

I can't sleep. I think back to Ram on the Isle of Man, six years
ago, 'Can't stop thinking about them moves . . .'

I try reading, but the words turn into clubs and diamonds on
the page. I try watching TV but it feels like a distraction. I wish
we didn't have an overnight break. I could have kept playing for
another ten hours. Now I don't know what to do with myself,
waiting to go back and see if I make the final.

At 4 a.m., I find myself standing in the back garden, watering
the roses. I'm prepared to bet that the other eleven remaining
players are not doing this right now.

Still, it's good to water plants at night.

But I hope the neighbours aren't watching. They think I'm
quite peculiar already.

♠

At last, the clock crawls round to midday on Sunday and I set off back to the Vic, taking my seat, ordering tea, shaking my chips out of their zipped-up polythene bag and counting them through. *Shuffle up and deal.*

I have a medium stack. Jonas Molander has the same chips as me and is knocked out almost immediately. Then Emad knocks out Ashley Hayles and earns a high-five from Joe Hachem, the world champ, who is supporting Emad from the rail. Then I find AK and knock out Michel Abécassis, the Frenchman who got the *gâteau total* in that magical dice game of 2003.

At 5 p.m., Oscar Schweinberg is knocked out in 9th place and we have a final.

I am in the final of the London EPT, the European Championship! In my own home casino, wearing the professional PokerStars logo for the first time, I have made the final!

I don't care what happens after this, it is my greatest result ever. I go for a cup of tea and phone my parents. And then I go back to play.

♠

I find a pair of jacks and knock out lovely Sid Harris in 8th place.

Peter Hedlund finds KQ against AK and goes out in 7th place.

Joe sends a text from Spain to tell the Vic players they should take away my glass of wine and give me a cup of tea. I hear the Mad Monk being called for a cash game downstairs.

Jules Kuusik makes a move with A5 and goes out in 6th place.

Chad Brown makes a move with Q8 and goes out in 5th place.

I can see them all on the rail: The Sweep and J.Q. and Neil, Rory Liffey and Michael Arnold and Jeff Duvall. In the madness and magic of what's happening at this table, they are solid, they are real, they are life.

Michael Muldoon races against me with 77 against AT and is out in 4th place.

Jan Sjavic makes a good call with 33 but I am in form and he is out in 3rd place.

They put the money and the trophy on the table. A thimble and comfits.

I make a good call against Emad to pick up a lot of chips. I pass 97 from the button to give myself a breathing space. I fold 73 offsuit because I'm out of position and it is no hand.

And then, at three minutes before 11 p.m., I look down and find . . .

. . . 6♣ 7♦.

I feel like playing this hand. Heads-up, you are supposed to raise often from the button, but I am in no hurry. My strategy remains to let Emad make the action. His sense of security may have been rattled by my big call and new chip lead, but I bet he thinks I just got lucky in one pot, or made one accidentally good decision, and can still be pushed around. I have enough chips to be patient, wait for another hand and another opportunity to let him hang himself. But I feel like playing this hand, so I call and Emad doesn't raise.

The flop comes 5♣ 3♣ 4♦.

Oh my God. Oh my God. I think I am about to win this tournament. I have flopped a straight. I just have to play it right.

Emad checks. I must have a stab, make it look like I'm trying to nick it with nothing. I bet 100,000.

Emad raises to 450,000. Oh my God. I have got him. He has something. He is on the hook and I must not let him off it. I ask him how much he has behind. He says he has another 422,000. Whatever his cards are, I know that if I flat call here, he must bet this 422,000 on the turn. So I call.

The turn is 10♦.

Emad says 'all in' and I say 'call' and turn my cards over and stand up so fast I almost knock my chair over and Emad puts his head in his hands and he rolls over 6♥ 8♣.

He can still hit a seven to win the pot. But I know that is not going to happen.

The crowd on the rail is already cheering, making so much noise. Normally, I would hate the early cheer but I know the seven is not coming, like it did not come on the dice table that Vegas night. Emad stands up and I give him a hug.

Then Deano, who is dealing, slides the next burn card off the top of the deck and he reaches for the river card and everything goes very, very quiet . . . No seven . . .

. . . And the river is J♠.

The crowd goes wild like the last scene in a baseball movie. I hug Deano, which is probably breaking about ten rules at once. I kiss Thomas, the tournament director. Then I stagger over to the rail and stare at Hugo, at J.Q., at Neil.

I have won the London EPT. I am the European Champion. The prize is £500,000. Just under a million dollars. Natalie Pinkham tries to interview me but I can't speak. Brian the manager comes over with one of those giant comedy cheques. Cameras flash. Then I am handed the trophy, the huge heavy glass trophy that I can hardly hold.

And it feels like the moment when Alice has worked out how to get her hands on the little golden key, she has bitten into the magic mushroom and grown larger and smaller and larger and smaller but finally found her balance and taken the key and unlocked the door and she finds herself at last in the beautiful garden, among the bright flower beds and the cool fountains.

———

They are pulling at my sleeve for interviews. But I break away and go into the ladies' room, which is completely empty because Vicky Lincoln doesn't play here any more, and I phone my parents and I speak to my dad and he says, '*How* much?' and I can hear my mother in the background, all proud and tearful.

Up in Kentish Town, my brother is getting out of bed and

pulling on whatever he remembers is supposed to comply with
the Vic's dress code and he is driving to the Vic.

I can't take £500,000 away tonight, it is crazy, so I sign a slip
to leave it on deposit, but I take about £80,000 and I pay out
the shares to The Sweep and to Neil and Rory, and give some
extra money to old friends in the cash games who look like they
might need it, and I throw some more at the waitresses and ask
them to bring drinks for everyone in the card room.

And I am here with my Tuesday players and the Vic players
and my brother is talking to Michael Arnold and it is madness,
for once in this room nobody is angry or moaning, they are
clinking glasses and hugging me, I get kisses from Lawrence
Windish and Iraqi Norman – and then Mason, the tribal chief
who stood up to Saddam, then had to flee here but I think his
cousin is now president, he tries to congratulate me but doesn't
speak enough English so he ends up just waving his arms and
smiling – and I love them all so much, it's so right to see my
brother among them, and eventually the casino closes and we
move on to the Gutshot, a strange bunch, me and Neil and Mr
Big and little Pedro and Deano the dealer and some others, a Vic
blur, and we drink till late and go home when it is light and I
sit in my study staring out of the window and waiting for people
to wake up.

It is in the newspapers and it is on the news, my phone rings
all day, and I get hundreds of emails and one of them is from Al
Alvarez. I think back to those days when I knew only his name,
playing in my brother's cash game with my brother's friends who
long since gave up poker, and Al Alvarez was a god and still is. I
reach back and tap my little self on the shoulder, tell her that
she has won a million dollars and Al Alvarez has written to
congratulate her.

She looks satisfied enough, asks a few questions about leaving
school, then shrugs me off and goes back to folding a pair of
tens. Can't be too careful.

At 5 p.m., I go to the special wine shop in St John's Wood and buy a bottle of champagne for £500, even though every glass of fizzy wine tastes exactly the same as every other, and I take it to my parents' house and pour it into glasses and I still can't speak for joy and pride, and 3% of that is because I won a poker tournament and 97% is because my father is here to drink this champagne with me.

25

LET THE RIVER RUN

It is not about the money.

'Congratulations, sah!' shouts Davood, the Mad Hatter of Tehran and Berlin, as he concedes a pot to Maltese Joe. 'You played vell! You gat minimum!'

He swivels back to me and continues his lecture on healthy living. 'Vun year, I drink only green tea. I never gat sick.'

I nod politely, trying to remember the details of the hand as I search through my bag for a pen. It might make a poker column.

'She's not listening,' says Paul Parker. 'She's looking for something.'

'Ear plugs, probably,' says Peter Singleton.

These are the early levels of the £300 tournament, so nobody is taking the game too seriously yet. It will quiet down later. Well, Davood won't. But the competition will start to feel real as we reach the stage when players are getting knocked out. For now, half of them are still looking for their seats, confused by the eclectic numbering system in the Vic card room. The rest are ordering sandwiches, arguing, borrowing money, playing a few early pots and calling for Jeff to change the TV channel from football to racing.

Paul Parker asks if I am on Facebook.

'Vot facebook? Vot facebook?' shouts Davood. 'I vant be on Facebook!'

'To be on Facebook, you need friends,' says Peter Singleton. There is a pause. Peter adds, quietly, 'I'm not on Facebook.'

A few people have asked why I am bothering to play a £300

tournament when I won a million dollars a few months ago. Why? Because this is a Vic festival. I like the tournaments. I play them. It is what I do.

Unearthing the pen, I start noting down the bets from Davood's hand with Maltese Joe. I hunch over my notebook as Davood leans towards me, loudly explaining the differences between British and German culture. I have clearly been chosen as tonight's target for Davood's machine-gun smalltalk.

'What's that you're writing?' asks Peter Singleton. 'A suicide note?'

♠

In the £100 game, Freddie is getting the lot as usual. I'm winning about £400 and Dave Binstock is ordering a steak.

'How do you like it?' asks the waitress, a new one.

'Not the way they serve it here,' says Binstock.

She'll get used to him. Guida would have known better than to ask the question.

They ask me why I still want to play in the £100 game. They say it is too small. Kenny Wong shouts 'European lady champion!' whenever he sees me. Alan Vinson and Mickey Wernick keep telling me how attractive I have become.

They ask why I am not in Vegas playing the Big Game. They ask why I would put the hours in to grind it out for £300 or £500 or £700 playing £3-£3 Holdem. Why I would play $50 Sit & Goes on PokerStars or heads-up for $100. When the Vic cash games get bigger, affected at last by the poker revolution in the outside world, they ask why I sit with £2,000 when others are sitting with £20,000.

Why? Because it is not about the money.

♠

I am now a proper, signed-up member of Team PokerStars Pro. I spend several hours a week on the site, I wear the logo in every tournament I play, I pose for promotional pictures with the Team Pro world champions Chris Moneymaker, Greg Raymer and Joe Hachem.

I took a long time to sign this deal. Even after becoming the European Champion, the first woman to win an EPT, finally confident of my tournament strategy as well as my cash game, I worried that I was some sort of fraud. A gambler with a day job. I worried about calling myself 'pro', about whether I should be making such a big commitment when I was only looking for a small one. I worried about the business side and losing my freedom.

Then my father said, 'Have you lost your mind? If A.A. Baines, turf accountants, had offered Uncle Sid a year's worth of free bets in exchange for wearing a T-shirt, he'd have bitten their arm off.'

♠

And so I wear the PokerStars logo with pride. And if online carpers take the mickey and say I am just a recreational player, or just a woman, I laugh and say yes I am those things, and I am proud of that, too. I will never play poker exclusively, and if my message is that you can work for a safe income and win titles on the weekend, that is fine with me.

Besides, I am the English Pro. It is our job to blush and run ourselves down. I am as likely to correct someone who calls me an idiot as I am to drive a Cadillac or eat a gumbo.

Since I have been on Team Pro I have cashed in another London EPT, finishing 38th for £11,420, and I cashed at the PCA in the Bahamas for $40,000, won a little tournament in the Fifty Spring Festival for £12,000, and I had my first World Series cash in the short-handed Holdem for $6,000 (not a huge finish, but I was out straight after Tobey Maguire and enjoyed queuing behind him).

I made the final of *Premier League Poker*, ahead of some of the world's greatest and most famous players, finishing 5th for £18,000. The following year I finished 9th in the same tournament, a worse result but another £18,000 because the buy-in went up. We will never know what the result might have been if Riverboat Ray had been playing the tournament and I had been driving the cab.

I could give up the day job if I wanted to. But I don't want to. Because it is not about the money.

♠

Even the language is different now, the codes and the jargon. It is fast, efficient, technical, Germanic. It is influenced by European computer slang, not outlaws in the southern states. When little girls sit down in their brothers' home games today, they won't hear about cowboys and bullets and trappers in fur hats, they will learn to say, 'I insta-3-jammed pre, and he snapped me. Lol donkaments.'

But it probably sounds just as bewitching, to them.

♠

'I think it's time we put the blinds up,' says The Sweep.

Val and James look nervous. Ashley says, 'We don't want to make the game too big. Warren makes it big enough already.'

'We could put the rake up,' offers Conrad, generously. 'I'm sure dinner is worth more than we pay.'

I wave the suggestion away. 'To be honest, if I factor in the cost of replacing the carpet because of all the spilt wine, or repairing the broken shutters, or replastering the kitchen wall every time it cracks because someone pointed the spout of the kettle at it, the true rake would be so high that only M.D. could afford to keep coming.'

'If we put the blinds up, we can increase the value of the

green chips,' insists The Sweep, 'and it would be a lot easier to make change. Much less faffing about.'

This argument swings the vote. And so, on a historic night in 2007, the blinds in the Tuesday game finally go up: from 20p to 25p.

It is not about the money.

♠

I am at the cash desk of the swish, art-deco Palm Beach Casino in Mayfair. The £250 freezeout ended nastily so I need money for the cash game and, because I want a large amount and I am not a regular here, the cashier gives me a form to sign asserting that I take responsibility for my own actions. I am supposed to sign my name under the words 'Gambling does not cause problems or obstacles in my life.'

I can't help laughing. How do I know? I have completely failed to get married or have children. I never get enough sleep. When I travel, I see only the inside of a casino. I have never written a novel. I spend my nights playing cards instead of catching up with old friends. I spend my lunchbreaks and free afternoons on PokerStars when I could be jogging healthily in the park or learning Japanese.

But I have won a million dollars. I have paid off my mortgage and saved the rest for rainy days. I have made treasured friends I would never otherwise have met. I have found a sort of life and a sort of love that surround me with a true instinctive logic. I am never lonely. I am never bored. I am often laughing.

I sign the form and take the cash.

♠

It is about a magical world. Down the rabbit hole, through the looking glass, under the sea, over the rainbow, behind the wardrobe door, there is a place where time stops. A place of Mad Hatters and March Hares, Cheshire Cats and caterpillars on mushrooms, tiny keys and treacle wells.

Like every good fairy tale, there is dark magic as well as light. There are mournful Mock Turtles and evil winged monkeys, there are White Witches and West Witches, screaming pig-babies, poisoned Turkish Delight and pools of tears big enough for a mouse to swim in.

But it is all a children's story. Jump up and follow the White Rabbit, push through the fur coats and the mothballs to reach for the woodwork against the tips of your fingers . . . and you are through, free, wandering in a universe of the imagination.

Maybe you will be crowned queen in that land. But whenever you slip back into the other world, no time has passed and nothing has changed.

It is about not wanting to die.

♠

I am standing in my room at the Wynn, Las Vegas, during the World Series of 2007. I am looking through the window at the surreal lines of the landscape, the only one in the world with a pyramid *and* an Eiffel Tower, the rollercoasters and the castles and towers and water-slides like mirages in the July heat with the desert stretching weirdly behind. And my mobile rings and it is my brother's name on the screen and I wasn't going to use my mobile this year because the costs are so crazy, but once again I know that I must take this call so I click the green button and it is time, now. Time to go home.

♠

Autumn frosts have slain July, but it is a bright, sunny October afternoon. The funeral was two days ago. Michael Arnold calls to ask how we are.

Michael is having his own problems. He and his wife have been agents, over many years, for the Master of the Queen's Music, Sir Peter Maxwell Davies. Unfortunately, it seems that £450,000 of Sir Peter's money has not managed to find its way into the composer's bank account. Michael, the grand duke of the card room, has talked to friends in the Vic about the situation. It is all a terrible misunderstanding, expenses were kept back to cover Sir Peter's overheads, vengeful people have put a negative spin on things, Michael was never going to keep that money, it's a stitch-up. He is borrowing chips to pay lawyers. He is quiet, depressed, playing badly. A year from now, Mr and Mrs Arnold will be formally charged with theft. Wags in the card room will shout, 'One jail cell here!' There will be issues with the borrowed money. Players will no longer line up to pay court to Michael. Many will avoid him completely. I wonder if he remembers what he warned, that time, on *Bar Beat*: 'As long as money and power exist, there will be dirty things going on.'

And now, rightly or wrongly, people are making these assumptions about Michael.

But this is what I know. When he calls, on this bleak and bright October afternoon, I cannot tell him how I am. I can't talk about it. It is too big and too frightening. So I tell Michael, instead, about my mother deciding we should have a *shiva*, a traditional Jewish wake, for two nights at the house. This is what my father's ancestors would have done.

I am years away from talking about how I feel, or talking about my father, and it was madness to think that I could make him live again, here or anywhere else, so I push it all away, the first push of many, and chuckle with Michael about how we ran out of Jews on the first night. It is all very well reconnecting, sentimentally around a death, with a distant past, but its distance is also the problem. The family is far away. My parents chose a different life. Giles and I have no idea about any of these customs. And now we are short of Jewish men to perform the prayers, prayers in a language

that we never knew and don't speak, but we will muddle through
and this is one of those things they talk about as 'black humour'.

And on the other side of London, Michael heaves himself up
from the poker table at the Vic, grabs his walking stick, mutters
a few words to Tall Alan on an adjoining table, and half an hour
later they are standing on the doorstep of my parents' house.

When the doorbell rings I expect a drinks delivery or a neigh-
bour, but instead there are two gamblers, ready to lend their souls.
They are not here to win. They are just here.

And as I look across the room, during the prayers, at Michael
wobbling slightly on his infirm old legs and Alan muttering
'Amen' sporadically among words which I would bet he has long
forgotten, each of them looking exactly as I imagine Uncle Sid
or Great-Grandpa Dave must have looked, I know that I lost one
family but gained another.

♠

Devilfish phones. He has heard about my father. He is gentle and
consoling.

A year later, Dave's own father dies. I see him the very next
morning at a poker tournament. As I walk towards him, he holds
his hands up nervously and says, 'Don't say owt soppy.'

But I wasn't going to. In this world, nobody dies. I know that
he is here to play poker, and to forget.

♠

Sometimes you cannot think about the whole game. It is too big,
too difficult. So you have to play it hand by hand. You make the
decisions you are capable of making. You play as well as you are
capable of playing. You are as good as you are capable of being.
You make the mistakes you cannot avoid making. That is fine.
The game has its own momentum. Sometimes, it is enough just

to hang on. Sometimes, hanging on is the toughest challenge and the greatest triumph.

It is all about survival. All you need is a chip and a chair.

♠

Looking around the table, I am the only player who has won less than $2 million. I am flanked by the biggest names in world poker. There is Gus Hansen, the bullet-headed Danish-American playboy ($5 million), Jennifer Harman, the miniature blonde leading lady of international poker ($2 million), Britain's own poker wunderkind, my old Hendon friend, the former snooker hustler Ram Vaswani ($3 million, and a 2007 bracelet), Swedish veteran Chris Björin ($3.2 million) and the former world champion of poker himself, Greg 'Fossilman' Raymer ($5.9 million).

This is Day Three of the World Series of Poker Europe. Yesterday, I sat between Ted Forrest ($5.1 million) and Erick Lindgren ($5.6 million). Gazing shrewdly at a 19-year-old boy in the five seat, Lindgren said to Forrest, 'I've never seen this kid before in my life, but I'll bet you £1,000 he's won more than a million playing online.' Forrest took the bet. The kid nodded silently and performed a hand mime, as an angler would indicate the size of a giant catch. Yeah, he's won a lot more. Forrest removed a fresh, sealed packet of £50 notes from his pocket and tossed it across the baize to Lindgren.

I wonder if they feel rich. I don't. Having never had serious money in the bank before, its arrival has created a sudden nervousness about not having it again. I worry about how long it will last and what I will do when it is gone. I never wanted or needed half a million pounds; now I've got it, I wish it were a million. Or five million. Suddenly I understand how footballers and pop stars, as soon as they can afford to fly everywhere first class, start worrying that they can't afford a private jet.

♠

I remember that night in flashes – hugging Deano, phoning my parents, Giles in the card room, glasses of champagne, leaving the money on deposit at the Vic. I didn't collect it for a long time.

I always suspected that poker was not about money for me. But now it has been tested, I know. I won a £25,000 tournament when that was a life-changing fortune, but it did not make me happy because my heart was broken and money is no cure. I won a £500,000 tournament, but it did not make me happy because my father had come back and I was so happy already that there was not room for any more.

This game with Harman and Hansen and Forrest and Lindgren is the same game that I played nervously for £20 with Giles and Matt and Kris and Adrian around the kitchen table, the same that I play with Freddie and Bambos and Dave Binstock at the Vic, the same that I play on PokerStars for $5 or $50 with cartoon faces and made-up names, the same that I play for 25p blinds with James, Val, Hugo and Ashley every Tuesday. Just one long river, flowing into the distance. All of us drifting down the stream, lingering in the golden gleam.

That's the funny thing about being a poker millionaire, even if only a dollar one. Cash is nothing more than chips, just the tools of the trade, like a fishing rod to an angler. The game is all about money and nothing to do with money.

All you need is a bankroll. You can always find a game to fit. And whoever you are, you will always fit in. In a bubble with the stars, on a Tuesday with the boys, I just want to keep playing, keep playing, keep playing.

5♥ 6♥

The Sweep makes it £1 to go.
I call.

THE RULES OF POKER GAMES IN THIS BOOK

The Button: This indicates the dealer (or nominal dealer if there is a croupier) who will be last to act in the hand. Being 'on the button' is the strongest position at the table. The button moves round clockwise with every new deal.

The Blinds: The two players to the left of the button who must put in compulsory bets before the deal, known respectively as the small blind and the big blind.

Check: To let the action pass on to the next player, without betting. This is only allowed if nobody has bet before you.

Call: To match the previous bet.

Raise: To increase the sum of the previous bet.

Fold: To throw your hand away.

TEXAS HOLDEM

Each player receives two private *hole cards* that nobody else sees. There is then a round of betting.

VICTORIA COREN

When the round is complete, the dealer will deal *the flop*: three communal cards face-up in the middle of the table. Players mentally combine these with their hole cards to make a complete five-card hand.

There is then a betting round, after which the dealer will deal another communal card face-up, called *the turn* or *fourth street*.

There is another betting round, then the dealer deals the final face-up card, called *the river* or *fifth street*.

There is a final round of betting, and if more than one player remains at the end of the action, the pot is won by whoever has the best five cards from the seven available to him.

RANKING OF HANDS

Straight Flush (a hand which is both a straight and a flush; see below)

Four Of A Kind

Full House (three of a kind, plus a pair)

Flush (five cards in the same suit)

Straight (five running cards, e.g. 4-5-6-7-8)

Three Of A Kind (also called *trips* or *a set*)

Two Pair

One Pair

High Card

If two players have the same pair, two pair or set, the winner will be decided by *the kicker*: the highest card you can play alongside your pair, two pair or set.

OMAHA

Just like Holdem, except each player receives four, five or six private cards (instead of two) and they must use two of these with three from the table to make their final five-card hand.

SEVEN CARD STUD

In this variant, there are no communal cards. Each player receives seven cards of his own (two face-down, then four face-up, then one face-down) and makes the best five-card hand out of his own seven cards.

HI–LO

Omaha and Stud can be played *hi-lo*, which means the final pot is split between the highest hand and the lowest hand. (The lowest possible hand is A-2-3-4-5, which is both a small straight and '5 high'.)

SHIFTING SANDS

Each player receives five cards, throws two away, turns one face-up and plays out the game like Seven Card Stud Hi-Lo, except your lowest hole card and any like it is wild for the high, your highest hole card and any like it is wild for the low – except aces, which don't go – and five of a kind becomes the best high, with the sands shifting on seventh street when your last dark card might be higher or lower than one of the cards you were previously using as wild. If you can make sense of that, we'll see you on Tuesday.

PERMISSIONS ACKNOWLEDGEMENTS

The author would like to thank and acknowledge the following sources:

Attanasio, Paul. Screenplay for *Quiz Show*, adapted from the novel by Richard Goodwin. Hollywood Pictures: 1994.

Bradshaw, Jon and Nik Cohn. *Fast Company: How Six Master Gamblers Constantly Defy the Odds – And Always Win*. London: High Stakes Publishing, 2005.

Camus, Albert. *The Myth of Sisyphus*. Translated by Justin O'Brien. London: Penguin and USA: Knopf, 1955.

Craig, Michael. The Professor, *The Banker and The Suicide King: Inside the Richest Poker Game of All Time*. USA: Grand Central Publishing, 2006.

Dunnery, Francis. Lyrics to 'Only New York Going On' from the album *Tall Blonde Helicopter*. Aquarian Nation: 1995.

Eliot, TS and Faber and Faber Ltd for quotation from *The Waste Land*.

Falkener, Edward. *Games Ancient and Oriental and How to Play Them*. London: Dover Publications, 1961.

Frey, Glen and Don Henley. Lyrics to 'Desperado' from the album *Desperado*. Warner/Chappell: 1973. Reproduced with the kind permission of Warner/Chappell Music Ltd Permissions.

Harrold, Glenn. *Create Unlimited Financial Abundance for Yourself*. London: Diviniti Publishing, 1999.

Jessup, Richard. *The Cincinnati Kid*. USA: No Exit Press, 1964.

Lynch, Thomas. *The Undertaking: Life Studies from the Dismal Trade*. London: Jonathan Cape and USA: WW Norton, 1997. Reprinted by permission of The Random House Group Ltd.

(with thanks to Katharine Banner for the thoughtful gift of that wonderful book)

May, Jesse. *Shut Up and Deal*. USA: Doubleday, a division of Random House, 1998.

The McLuhan Estate

Sherman, Richard M and Robert B Sherman. Lyrics to 'Chim Chim Cheree' from the film *Mary Poppins*. Reproduced with the kind permission of Warner/Chappell Music Ltd.

Sturges, Preston. Screenplay for *The Lady Eve*, adapted from a story by Monckton Hoffe. Paramount Pictures: 1941. Reprinted courtesy of Universal Studios Licensing LLLP.

The Times

Wilson, Des. *Swimming with the Devil Fish*. London: Macmillan, 2006.